Lessons in LEADERSHIP®

from
YOUR
Neighborhood:

Making
Connections ...

Building
Relationships ...

Energizing
Communities ...

Where You
Work and Live

by
Bunny and Larry Holman

LESSONS IN LEADERSHIP FROM YOUR NEIGHBORHOOD.
First Edition. Copyright © 1998 by Bunny and
Larry Holman. Printed in the United States.

Portions of this book appeared in the
monthly "Lessons in Leadership" newsletter.

Acknowledgments

From THE DEATH AND LIFE OF GREAT AMERICAN
CITIES by Jane Jacobs
Copyright © 1961 by Jane Jacobs. Reprinted
by permission of Random House, Inc.

From SMOKE by Paul Auster
Copyright © 1995 by Paul Auster. Reprinted
by permission of Hyperion.

From ALL I REALLY NEED TO KNOW I LEARNED
IN KINDERGARTEN
by Robert L. Fulghum
Copyright © 1986, 1988 by Robert L. Fulghum. Reprinted by
permission of Villard Books,
a division of Random House, Inc.

Most photographs in this book are copyright
by one of the following: Harold Roth, Adobe,
DigitalVision, IMSI, PhotoDisc or Stockbyte.
The Amish photo on page 422 is copyright by
Doyle Yoder.

Printing by V.G. Reed & Sons, Inc.,
Louisville, KY.

Holman, Bunny and Larry.
       Lessons in leadership from your
 neighborhood: making connections ...
building relationships ... energizing
communities where you work and live /
by Bunny and Larry Holman —1st ed.
       "A Lessons in Leadership Book."
       ISBN: 0-9648829-1-4
1. Leadership. 2. Relationships.
3. Neighborhoods.

10 9 8 7 6 5 4 3 2 1

*Dedicated to all our neighbors,
past, present and future,
especially those
who believe in thinking*
BIG.

Acknowledgments

A book of this nature and scope does not happen without the involvement of numerous talented people working together toward a shared goal. We are pleased that the very process of putting this one together has served as an exemplar for our theme of can-do, "neighborhood" leadership.

We'd especially like to thank our college and university partners who provided us with examples of exceptional leadership in their neighborhoods. So, in no particular order, we extend our deeply felt gratitude to:

Carol Steadman at the University of Nevada-Las Vegas; Ann VanderMeer-Robinson and Faye Tippee at Indiana University Northwest; Sharon Scott and Rich Sorensen at Virginia Tech; Dr. Ronald Eaves at California State University, Bakersfield; Jim Tarter at the University of Texas at Tyler; Dr. Henry Moon at the University of Toledo; Reba Harrington at Louisiana State University at Alexandria;

Lisa Nordick at North Dakota State University; Christine Gibbons at John Carroll University; Linda Bowman and Carla Hansen at Western New

England College; Susan Cherches at Wichita State University; Larry Bohleber at the University of Southern Indiana; Alan McConnell at Pueblo Community College;

Irene Hurst at the University of South Florida; Dr. Alexander Hill and Ruth Myers at Seattle Pacific University; Doug Gardner, Michelle Maakfried and Cathy Wogen at Rasmussen College; Kim Moncla at Lamar University; Gerry Baertsch at the University of Montana; Andrea Hough at Drexel University;

Nancy Kinsey at the University of Texas at Arlington; Pat Miles at the University of South Alabama; Tamara McLeod at San Diego State University; Dale Bunch and Rhonda Ervin at Midstate College; and Trisha Mosher and Michelle Whittingham at Eastern Washington University.

Of course, this book would not be what it is without all the exceptional leaders who so graciously shared their time, experiences and insights with us — and whose stories make up a substantial portion of this book. We are indebted to each of these people, whom we are happy to call our neighbors.

In addition, we'd like to thank Adam Bruns, Vickie Mitchell and Jeff Walter for their skillful assimilation of a wealth of information and concepts; Maria Pinczewski-Lee for her expertise in making the inside of this book look so wonderful; and Harold Roth for his design of the cover and his neighborhood photographs. Melissa Fightmaster worked closely with our school partners, gathering preliminary information about the leaders we've profiled. Tony Condi helped coordinate the printing of the book and the overall financing of the project. Keith Elkins, Carro Ford, John McGill, Robin Roth and Tim Smith were valued editors and proofreaders. Robin also gave valued creative input on the cover design. We'd like to thank Alexis Roth for assisting with photography, Danielle Roth for making the lemonade stand shoot a success and Jeri Self for assisting with the mechanics of the cover design. Elaine Rutherford went above and beyond the call of duty as an all-around facilitator.

Perhaps, as you read *Lessons in Leadership from YOUR Neighborhood*, stories from your own experience will come to mind. If so, we'd love for you to share them with us — who knows, there might be a sequel! Please write to:

Lessons in Leadership Publications
380 South Mill Street
Lexington, KY 40508

Contents

Introduction 1

1. The Sidewalk 9

2. The Garden 47

3. The Deli 77

4. There's No Place Like Home 107

5. If You're Living, You're Learning ... 133

6. Continuing Education...Continued.... 149

7. The Playground 179

8. There Goes the Neighborhood 195

9. The "Cyberhood" 221

10. The "Cyberbiz" 247

11. The "Mix" 267

12. Citizens of the Globe 295

13. Paying the Utility Bill 327

14. The Garage Band 347

15. The Neighborhood Association 369

16. The Limits of Design 401

17. The Frontier Town 419

18. Growth and Preservation 447

19. Finding a Role 483

20. Epilogue: See Ya 'Round 509

About the Authors 515

"Seems like there is some kind of cosmic Krazy glue connecting everything to everything."
— Jane Wagner,
"The Search for Signs of Intelligent Life in the Universe"

Introduction:

A Walk Through the Neighborhood

"Make no little plans ... they have no magic to stir people's blood."
— architect Daniel Burnham
(attributed and slightly paraphrased)

Let's go for a walk through the neighborhood. We'll be gone for a while, so wear comfortable shoes, and bring an open mind and a taste for the unknown. You never know whom you're going to meet, or what you're going to encounter, when you walk in this neighborhood. Hey, there's the paper girl, Suzy, making her morning deliveries. There's Mr. Jones, out for his daily constitutional with his dog, Sparky. There are the Patels, the couple from Bombay who opened that popular Indian restaurant a few years back. Hear the music coming from the garage across the street? That's the neighborhood garage band, working on yet another "original" song that sounds strangely like the last one. They'll be getting thirsty soon — prime customers for the corner lemonade stand.

It's funny how this neighborhood has grown in recent years. At the same time, it seems smaller, more interconnected, than ever before. We don't know everybody who lives here, but it seems we all know somebody who does know the people we don't. Small world, indeed! The relationships being made here every day are helping each of us to do things we'd only dreamed about in the past.

Let's not get the wrong impression here, though. Everything is not "warm and fuzzy." This is not Mr. Rogers' neighborhood, appealing as that idea might be to some people. There are, unfortunately, parts of this neighborhood where you'd best not walk alone at night. We have our share of problems such as crime, drugs, poverty, homelessness and a variety of -isms. "Not in my neighborhood," you say? Well, think again! Whatever part of the neighborhood you might live in, these problems affect us all, and it is our responsibility to find workable solutions.

As you might have guessed by now, the neighborhood we're walking through is not just a few blocks. It's global. Our neighbors are in other cities, other states, other countries. The more time we spend here, the more we come to the realization that it's all related. You can observe a lot just by watching, as Yogi Berra once said, but you'll learn and accomplish much more by interacting, becoming an active part of the surroundings, and doing what you can to make the neighborhood a better place. And that, more or less, is what this book is all about.

What this book is ... and isn't

It can be easy to get carried away by a good metaphor, and we hope we haven't done that here. On some levels this is a simple book, but we do not intend to be simplistic. The fact is, the neighborhood endures as a microcosm of the world at large. Today, the metaphor is more relevant than ever, with technology serving to break down geographical barriers and increase our ability to reach out and touch our global neighbors.

So what kind of book is this, exactly? Well, the answer to that question is not so simple. It is, to its authors, many things intertwined and rolled up into one big, vast, extremely diversified thing that is somehow all related yet not related at the same time. Like the world itself, like this global neighborhood in which we're walking.

This is a business book, because at its core are principles that have served businesses well and will continue to do so. Yet it is not a business book in the sense that it consists of endless case studies or a blow-by-blow account of one company's rise (or rise and fall).

This is a love story, as it's about loving what you do, doing what you love, working with the people you love and trust and respect.

This is an adventure, as it's about throwing out that outdated "rule book" and genuinely taking some risks. And it's a comedy, because we think it clearly demonstrates the necessity of having a sense of humor and refusing to take life or work too seriously.

This is a book from a man's point of view, and also from a woman's. In some parts, it is indeed warm and fuzzy (Mr. Rogers would be very happy), while in others it is hard edged, street smart and savvy.

This is a work of journalism, a worldwide report from the front lines of today's leaders, large and small, famous and anonymous, both here in the United States and around the world, including many leaders who do not hold "conventional" leadership positions. It's a travelogue across not only distance but also time, which means that in addition to studying our neighborhood in its present state, we'll also make some visits to its past circumstances and take a glimpse into its future.

This is an extended (and, you might say, at times rambling) essay on what is important from the points of views of two people who have formed a rewarding, longtime relationship (both marital and business) with each other. It's also a collection of thoughts from the people who have influenced this partnership, which means that in at least some ways it must be considered an inspirational work.

This book is all these things, yet really none of them. It is all these things and more, largely because we, the authors, had a most difficult time in setting limits for it. For better or worse, we have followed our modus operandi of making no small plans. This is a big book filled with some big ideas. These ideas are not all original, but they are personal, filled with intense personal meaning for us and, we hope, for you.

One thing this book is NOT is a comprehensive or authoritative ANYTHING. It is a collection — of thoughts, experiences, ideas, stories. We have covered a lot of ground, but we've also left much territory unexplored. Many neighborhood elements have been discussed in some depth, while others have been merely touched upon or ignored altogether. Some of that is by design, some by oversight, some by the sheer natural laws of space (we couldn't fit it all in).

We are fortunate to have friends and associates throughout America and the world. Many of them provided us with the "inside scoop" on exceptional leaders in their backyards. These leaders, in turn, shared their own personal lessons in leadership with us. We are confident that you will find their stories to be of value.

The truths remain

When we began writing this book, our goal was to make it an "evergreen" — that is, a book that would remain relevant over time, without a lot of examples that were likely to become obsolete. At the same time, we wanted real "meat," or substance, rather than a bunch of lofty concepts that sound good on paper but do not translate into real-world practicalities.

In considering these seemingly contradictory goals, we couldn't help ponder the landmark work *In Search of Excellence* by our good friend and colleague Tom Peters with co-author Robert H. Waterman Jr. That book, first published in 1982, highlighted companies that were, at that time, embodiments of excellence according to the principles espoused by Peters and Waterman. Things change, of course. Many of those companies have long since fallen on hard times. Some have recovered, while others have fallen by the wayside. Yet their stories continue to offer valuable lessons to those who will heed them. And, indeed, *In Search of Excellence* continues to be one of the best-selling business books of all time. The facts may change, but the truths remain.

It is worth noting here our opinion that, despite what some historians say, we humans do learn from our mistakes. In the world of business especially, while fads and trends come and go, those organizations that find the greatest sustained success will be those who recognize and honor such basic concepts as human dignity and the capacity of each individual to make a valuable contribution. Those who ignore these concepts will be rewarded with, at best, short-term profits. Consider, for example, the Frederick Taylor/Henry Ford school of scientific management and mass production. Taylor and Ford made definite progress with their attempts to reduce management to a science, but their lack of attention to the human side of the equation doomed them to ultimate failure — and they died of broken hearts.

As we walk through this global neighborhood, traversing distance and time, let's be sure to keep our eyes and ears open, as well as our minds and our hearts. We'll look for the order that is present where, at first glance, there appears to be only chaos. We'll find opportunities hidden amid what some people might view only as problems or crises. We'll meet people whom we'll be happy to call our neighbors.

Wouldn't it be great to work with people like the ones profiled in this book? These are dedicated employees and leaders with positive, "can do" attitudes who have come to a realization of their potential for making a difference in a world of nonstop change, breakneck paces and brutal competition. Our goal should be to create and foster environments in which *everybody* feels included, connected and empowered to do whatever they can for their organization, their neighborhood, their world.

There are so many people who can teach us, many of whom might appear at first glance to be unlikely teachers. We would be wise to heed their words, for, whatever their job position or geographic location, they are our neighbors and our partners. Throughout this book, our neighborhood theme will be ever present, sometimes in the background but always there, reminding us how, indeed, "it's all related."

We did a lot of walking through the neighborhood before deciding to write this book, and we'd like to share some of our experiences (and a bunch of vicarious ones) with you. Writing this book meant visiting and revisiting the people, places, events and ideas that have influenced us, and we've had a blast doing just that. We hope you enjoy the journey as well.

— Bunny and Larry Holman
Lexington, Kentucky
July 1998

1

The Sidewalk

When you drive through some of the newer developments that sprout on the edges of towns, one of the first things you notice is that everybody else is driving, too. Where are all the people? Where are the kids playing outside, the neighbors walking around?

Happily, both well-established and some more recent neighborhoods recognize the need to make the basic human feel welcome in the landscape. On our street you do. People are out doing their yardwork, walking the dog, waving hello. It's a blend of design, habit and the natural goodwill of our fellow residents. But there's one absolutely concrete element that binds every neighborhood — the sidewalk.

The sidewalk is a thread, a slender patch of common ground that everyone treads. It's the familiar path whose every inch you know by heart as you make your way to the bus stop, or walk the dog, or stop in at the newsstand for a morning paper and a coffee. You've been leaping over that same buckle in the concrete for years now, just like you avoided the cracks as a kid. This way leads to your mailbox or favorite restaurant or workplace.

It's interesting to observe what people look at as they walk. In New York or any other bustling city, you half expect to be run over as hundreds of co-walkers proceed down their tunneled and efficient paths. It's laughable to imagine any actual greeting occurring, but it does occasionally happen.

Yet even in more quiet neighborhoods, there are still a good many people who won't look your way as you pass down the other side, or who don't necessarily return your salutations. They've brought their domestic cocoons with them into the great outdoors.

You might have encountered a similar dynamic in any number of service establishments. You need some help and have to search far and wide for a sign of life. Then when you finally find someone, he's so consumed with his assigned tasks that he just points in a general direction, or perhaps she is busy catching up on the interoffice e-mail. Oh, one more thing ... you weren't expecting eye contact, were you?

Back to the basics

Yes, like the silent, fenced-in neighbor, some folks in the service industry occasionally forget that their number one product is that very service. Just like the main part of being a neighbor is being neighborly. But there are exceptions:

The genuine article

66 Recently, I was going down to breakfast, and this young lady took me to a beautiful table by the window. I remembered this — **99** it just started my day off in a major way better than what I was used to, which was usually right next to the kitchen with the door banging back and forth. I felt so special — it just set the tone for my whole day, even though the meal itself was nothing spectacular. I went up to this little girl — her boss was very nearby, and I knew he was — and I said, "Whoever hired you should be very proud of you because you made me feel very good about eating here. You treated me like a real person. Whoever your boss is better appreciate you because you have what it takes to make customers feel the best they can feel." And I meant it.

It's hard to get that point across. Even people you think would care sometimes don't give a hoot. The challenge is to bring a fresh face to each customer, to not do everything by rote. You want systems, but you don't want your expressions and the way you communicate to be systematized. And the key here is a winning combination of hiring the right people and then setting them loose to do their best.

This young man was working over at our favorite deli, Cosmo's, in the bread area. He made eye contact; he didn't have any stock phrases; we had an intelligent little conversation. Then we started talking about the bread, and he was knowledgeable without being weird about it — much more knowledgeable than I thought he was going to be just by looking at him (he looked like he was 12 to me). It was a fun experience. He was slicing my bread with his back to me, but he was still talking to me, maintaining that connection.

He was a cool kid, another one who made my day — and he'll do well in the world. He didn't tell me to have a nice day. He had nothing programmed into him. You could just tell he was one of those people — he genuinely liked people; he made that connection with his eyes right away as soon as I came up to the counter. Those are things you can't really teach.

Or perhaps those are things we need to merely allow to happen, to make way for genuine interaction through unteaching.

— *Bunny Holman*

It's all about paying attention

Do you know what modernist poet Wallace Stevens did for a living? He was an insurance attorney. Every day he walked to work, composing and editing lines and developing images that would one day coalesce into poems. These poems in turn have come to be recognized as some of the most extraordinary work of the century, receiving the Pulitzer Prize and becoming part of the literary canon. Now that's a way to use the sidewalk!

How did he operate during these strolls? Was his attention directed inward to language exclusively, or was the opposite the case? Perhaps his attention was so great that the journey became a liberating meditation.

There's probably a walk you take all the time — same route, same time of day. The barking dog, the honking horns, the puddle you almost always leap over with success ... all the familiar comforts. Perhaps the deli owner is opening up his shop; the florist is setting out her fresh

blossoms. You're counting the steps, checking your watch to keep pace.

Or maybe it's the same old cubicle shuffle, making your way from another endless meeting back to your professional nest. Hey, they route those things like mouse mazes anyway, right? Might as well oblige by putting your head down and scurrying from point A to point B.

It can be easy to fall into a rut on these apparently innocuous little journeys. What was once charming has turned into an annoyance. The obligatory exchange of niceties has become a mere obstacle in your efficient and streamlined day. Some folks have found that these walks need to be filled with cellular conversations — all the better to cut down on frivolity and get things done, by golly!

But these jaunts can also hold the key to your day. If truth is indeed in the details, then there must be some value to slowing down enough to take in the ever-changing scenery, and by observation of small things arrive at the proverbial Big Picture.

It seemed to work for Wallace Stevens:

OF THE SURFACE OF THINGS

I

In my room, the world is beyond my
understanding;
But when I walk I see that it consists
of three or four
hills and a cloud.

II

From my balcony, I survey the yellow
air,
Reading where I have written,
"The spring is like a belle
undressing."

III

The gold tree is blue.
The singer has pulled his cloak over
his head.
The moon is in the folds of the cloak.

— Wallace Stevens

Steppin' out

That's a quick journey, isn't it? From the confines of the poet's room to the moon. Such is the power of language, and of perception.

So how do you translate "making the rounds" into a more holistic exercise that can connect disparate parts of a team? First it's time to see those other worlds, those beyond your room that surpass understanding ... until you take the trouble to look. The distances and chasms between people, departments and specializations are often more imagined than real. And even if these other perceptions do vary widely from your own, you might just learn something from the view — especially the view that looks back at that tiny figure in the landscape: you.

Tom Peters called it "Management by Wandering Around" in his seminal book *In Search of Excellence: Lessons From America's Best-Run Companies* (1982: Warner Books, New York), written in 1982 but still ripe with evergreen lessons. In studying excellent companies, he and co-author Robert H. Waterman Jr. suggest that this method is the only way to really know what's going on, relate to your colleagues and customers, and see what's working and what's not. You're out there in the arena: behind the cash register, sweeping out a corner, helping unload a truck shipment. Only here do you catch the important details of the work your organization does. Perhaps casual banter yields an insight into employee attitudes, or you realize that a certain work process that's been done the same way for years is in serious need of an overhaul.

Investing this level of attention in everyday things can be one of the most worthwhile ventures you'll ever undertake. It's an exercise in using your basic five senses, plus that all-important supplement, common sense. Listen to those two customers, dreaming of how great it would be if a store would do this ... look at that neglected, wasted corner of the building, gathering dust when it could be storing tools or products within easy reach ... and what about that scent? Oh, that's the rose garden behind the picket fence you've been drumming your fingers along for months.

This kind of consciousness has made its way from individual behavior to revolutionary community and workspace design. Peters and Waterman caught this trend too:

Another vital spur to informal communication is the deployment of simple physical configurations.

Corning Glass installed escalators (rather than elevators) in its new engineering building to increase the chance of face-to-face contact.

3M sponsors clubs for any groups of a dozen or so employees for the sole purpose of stray problem-solving sessions at lunchtime and in general.

A Citibank officer noted that in one department the age-old operations-versus-lending officer split was solved when all members of the group moved to the same floor with their desks intermingled.

These excellent companies, with their excellent management teams, are seeking out "a high volume of opportunities for good news swapping," say the authors.

Sounds like something we say a lot at WYNCOM. There's so much bad news out there that people feel obliged to share with us or cover in every detail on the television. But do they give the same enthusiasm to the good stuff? That's why we ask people all the time, "Do you want to hear some good news?" Whether we're telling customers about an upcoming conference or kicking off an early morning company meeting, the old song still rings true: "Ac-centuate the positive, e-liminate the negative."

Stairs:Pathways for communication

The ways to do that are as numerous as the routes you take on your wanderings. One day may reveal a new angle on an old issue, the next might bring an employee's promptness and neatness to your attention. So what do you do — go write it down as something to bring up in a management meeting for a possible reward recommendation? Heck no, you go up to the person and tell him or her about it! Tell people how much you appreciate their sharp, attentive professionalism, share your observations on that thorny technical problem. As Bob Nelson tells people every day, the ways to reward employees are more than a thousandfold — according to his book *1,001 Ways to Reward Employees* (1994: Workman Publishing, New York) — but it's really just the public recognition that counts in the long run. Sort of like complimenting somebody on her lawn or that new bed of perennials.

Ken Blanchard calls it "catching people doing things right." It's one of the pillars supporting his hugely successful One Minute Manager method and philosophy. Organizations worldwide have prospered because of introducing his management and leadership ideas to the workplace.

According to Blanchard, catching people doing things right is what managers need to be doing after setting goals with their team members. The key follow-up is the One Minute Praising, which lets people know how good you feel about what they're doing. During that exchange, you specify precisely what they are doing right — greatly increasing the chances that they'll keep doing it.

Even when things may not be going your way overall, Blanchard counsels, it's important to be consistent in this one-on-one activity. People like to know that what they're doing matters, and the reinforcement will usually inspire them to observe their own actions in a new light — an important step in this era of self-managing teams.

At WestAmerica Graphics in Santa Ana, California, they call it C.O.P.S. — Catching Other People Succeeding. It's part of their Teamwork for Total Quality Program, and it's helping their small company of 60 employees reach new heights in morale and team productivity.

One C.O.P.S. point is worth one dollar. You can get a point by receiving or writing a ticket, or for making a suggested improvement in procedures or service. Employees accumulate and cash their points in during the course of the year. Other arms of the quality-improvement program include

Whatever It Takes awards for superior departmental work and the *Great Game of Business*, a bonus game whose goal is to exceed company profit targets each quarter.

Of course, incentive programs have always been a double-edged sword, balanced between expected performance and a high expectation of reward. But what small programs like this do better than dole out money is to build a sense of common purpose that unites the specialists, crosses functional boundaries, and delivers momentum to both the bottom line and the staff's sense of job satisfaction.

And to think it all comes from just paying attention.

An open environment

Back to design. To further what Peters calls the "adhocracy," organizations have taken to opening up their office spaces and even manufacturing environments for more productive communication and teamwork. While privacy and confidentiality are necessary in certain instances, tearing down unnecessary privacy fences brings neighbors and neighboring departments face to face. There's nowhere to hide!

While some might say this points to Big Brother paternalism, the positive outlook sees that all the good work people are doing is no longer concealed behind closed doors and cubicle walls. Common areas, break rooms, reception and meeting spaces — they all contribute to a sense of unity and common purpose. Not to mention a light and airy atmosphere, in stark contrast to the dungeon effect of so many fluorescent mazes stacked high with file cabinets and sleepy office chairs.

Well-known workplace architects Franklin Becker and Fritz Steele talk about the "total workplace" and "organizational ecology" in putting forth their arguments for a saner, more holistic approach to workplace design. They discuss concepts like status, identity, integration and culture. They could just as well be talking about your street, your particular block.

What connects the parts? How do you accomplish movement — whether it's ideas, products, your body or projects being moved? The sidewalk or corridor is one way to achieve this linkage. The wider and better maintained it is, the more use it will see. The more natural the locomotion, the more natural the communication.

It could even be virtual, extending the metaphor to the kind of ambling public forums you encounter on both internets and intranets. People can swap recipes or work shifts, check off on a completed task or ask for more to do. As companies grow more tentacles and extend their reaches well beyond headquarters, this kind of path grows ever more feasible and productive, with neighbors waving to each other from the four corners of the globe or from opposite ends of the factory.

Neighbors and strangers

There's nothing like a real sidewalk, though. Especially in a big city. One of the most lucid accounts of the universe of activity that a good urban sidewalk encompasses comes from Jane Jacobs' monumental book *The Death and Life of Great American Cities* (1961: Random House, New York), which is still revolutionary to this day.

In her perceptive and open-minded style, Jacobs tackles the "Peculiar Nature of Cities" by first addressing the three main uses of sidewalks aside from pedestrian circulation: safety, contact and assimilating children. The full section runs to more than 100 pages and is as pure a delight to read as the rest of her marvelous book. Jacobs sees the disappearance of the sidewalk as a direct measure of an equally disappearing community vitality. Think about how these lessons translate to organizational neighborhoods as well:

> A city sidewalk by itself is nothing. It is an abstraction. It means something only in conjunction with the buildings and other uses that border it, or border other sidewalks very  near it. ... Streets and their sidewalks, the main public places of a city, are its most vital organs. Think of a city and what comes to mind? Its streets. If a city's streets look interesting, the city looks interesting; if they look dull, the city looks dull.
>
> Sidewalks, their bordering uses, and their users, are active participants in the drama of civilization versus barbarism in cities.

Jacobs goes on to describe how good city neighborhoods make an asset out of the presence of strangers: clearly demarcating private from public space, orienting buildings — and therefore pairs of eyes — toward the street, and constantly using the sidewalk, thereby providing both walking and homebound pairs of eyes with something to do. She is at her most striking when describing her home block, Hudson Street in New York City:

> Under the seeming disorder of the old city, wherever the old city is working successfully, is a marvelous order for maintaining the safety of the streets and the freedom of the city. It is a complex order. Its essence is intricacy of sidewalk use, bringing with it a constant succession of eyes. This order is all composed of movement and change, and although it is life, not art, we may fancifully call it the art form of the city and liken it to the dance — not to a simple-minded precision dance with everyone kicking up at the same time, twirling in unison and bowing off en masse, but to an intricate ballet in which the individual dancers and ensembles all have distinctive parts which miraculously reinforce each other and compose an orderly whole. The ballet of the good city sidewalk never repeats itself from place to place, and in any one place is always replete with new improvisations.

As Jacobs repeatedly notes, what distinguishes a city from other types of community is the relatively large number of strangers always present. She also cautions against attempting to transfer any of her observations and conclusions to other models: the town, the village, the suburb. But she proceeds to create such a thorough and insightful study that the temptation to make that leap is overwhelming.

Take the presence of strangers, for instance. If there is one business practice that's dominant at the century's close, it's outsourcing. More and more companies are shifting particular burdens of their workload to outside vendors. Consequently, the old model of the behemoth organization encompassing every process within its long reach is giving way to a new paradigm — one that employs independent, outside firms to deliver certain services, thereby relieving the organization of human resources costs while extending its reach through a new, less structured network of relationships.

In other words, there are a lot of strangers walking through your neck of the woods. They might be consultants, they might be technicians, trainers or maintenance personnel. Part of their value may lie not only in their specific contracted duties, but in their very presence — as outside pairs of eyes, linking processes, sharing ideas and vision from outside the organizational framework. They just might hold an interesting view of your way of doing business.

At the same time, strangers aren't the only ones doing some walking. Flexible working arrangements are just as dramatically catapulting company resources and people out into the field. The organization's eyes are going places they've never gone before, getting closer to the customer, bringing in new business and fresh approaches, even helping to redefine a company's direction.

It all comes from walking around, checking things out, drawing connections that continue to open eyes and revolutionize the way we work and live. It's only through this kind of activity that strangers become familiar ... yes, that word that's based on family.

Jacobs thus ends her sidewalk discussion:

> We are the lucky possessors of a city order
> that makes it relatively simple to keep the
> peace because there are plenty of eyes on the
> street. But there is nothing simple about
> that order itself, or the bewildering number
> of components that go into it. Most of those
> components are specialized in one way or
> another. They unite in their joint effect
> upon the sidewalk, which is not specialized
> in the least. That is its strength.

Finding trust in a loose-knit world

You may have heard the expression "social capital"
being batted around in the media the past few
years. Jane Jacobs invented that term back in
1961. (As Montesquieu so rightly observed, "There
is nothing new under the sun" . . . was he the first
to say that?) Here Jacobs describes some of its
essential ingredients, the results of happenstance
that are so fundamental to connecting:

> In speaking about city sidewalk safety, I
> mentioned how necessary it is that there
> should be ... an almost unconscious assumption
> of general street support when the chips are
> down. ... There is a short word for this
> assumption of support: trust. The trust of
> a city street is formed over time from many,
> many little public sidewalk contacts. It
> grows out of people stopping by at the bar
> for a beer, getting advice from the grocer
> and giving advice to the newsstand man,
> comparing opinions. ...

The sum of such casual public contact at a
local level — most of it fortuitous, most of
it associated with errands, all of it metered
by the person concerned and not thrust upon
him by anyone — is a feeling for the public
identity of people, a web of public respect
and trust, and a resource in time of personal
or neighborhood need. The absence of this
trust is a disaster to a city street. Its
cultivation cannot be institutionalized. And
above all, it implies no private commitments.

It's not far-fetched to say that the "web of
public respect and trust" that Jacobs lauds has
eroded somewhat in our communities, our workplaces.
The sense of identity that casual public contact
ought to engender often never comes to fruition.
The major obstacle is speed.

We're not just talking about the efficiency of
getting things done, or the pace at which we move
from errand to errand. We're talking about the
furious rate at which total experiences occur:
employment at one company, living in one apartment
or house, regularly attending a particular church
or working out at a certain YMCA. The transience
and mobility of the people in a given neighborhood
can make the daily journey through it an odyssey of
discovery as much as a reinforcement of stability.

The pace of change in an organization can be
equally intimidating: departments materializing
and disappearing, teams forming and then dissolving
into other teams. But it is this very act of
making your way around, taking the time to check
things out and check in with your colleagues,
that establishes the kind of "workplace capital"

that can strengthen an enterprise. It doesn't matter how fast things happen if we don't know their details or the people who make them happen.

One more important point from Jacobs: "Its cultivation cannot be institutionalized." The whole point of "casualness" is its very lack of planning and systems. The closest you can come is to create spaces and thoroughfares where such contact between individuals can blossom. How this contact materializes and multiplies depends on the attention and imagination of those individuals.

Stephen Covey calls it the "inside-out approach" to organizational effectiveness. Covey's entire message, developed in one bestseller after another, is built on the foundation of personal qualities, individual attitudes and actions that spring not from a systematized mode of behavior but from a person's character, personality and beliefs. In his phenomenal *The 7 Habits of Highly Effective People* (1989: Simon & Schuster, New York), Covey tells us about one manifestation of trust — the Emotional Bank Account:

> An Emotional Bank Account is a metaphor that describes the amount of trust that's been built up in a relationship. It's the feeling of safeness you have with another human being.
>
> If I make deposits into an Emotional Bank Account with you through courtesy, kindness, honesty, and keeping my commitments to you, I build up a reserve. Your trust toward me becomes higher, and I can call upon that trust many times if I need to. I can even make mistakes and that trust level, that emotional reserve, will compensate for it. My communication may not be clear, but you'll get my meaning anyway ... When the trust account is high, communication is easy, instant, and effective.

What better way to keep a healthy balance in that account than with a simple hearty greeting, a brief exchange sparked by our casual meandering? Covey goes on to describe what happens when that account is not maintained:

> I'm walking on mine fields. I have to be very careful of everything I say. I measure every word. It's tension city, memo haven. It's protecting my backside, politicking. And many organizations are filled with it. Many families are filled with it. Many marriages are filled with it.

Have you ever encountered such a place? If you have, you know it could rightly be called a "bad neighborhood." Nobody talking, everybody holed up in their cubicle turf, conversation turning into a formal exercise in caution. And nobody making the rounds — the tumbleweeds are blowing down the main thoroughfare, the wind is whistling past our carefully closed doors.

The only way out of an abysmal situation like this is "inside-out." Open that door and keep it open — maybe even take it right off the hinges. Shock your unhappy co-worker with a positive, upbeat visit, for no particular reason. Conversation can be the root for conversion, for change into the vibrant neighborhood you seek. Then move on to the next "block" and the next, and watch the process of connection unfolding in your wake. This magic may also strike your own vision as you look ahead, the input from so many sources coalescing into new ideas and methods, a string of relations taut with potential.

Setting the pace

"On my first day of work at a new university job, the man who hired me did an unusual thing for orientation: We walked the campus. I'd been a teacher and I had also worked at State Farm Insurance when I was in college, so I mean, that's my big work experience. I couldn't believe that he was taking that much time with me. He said, "What I want you to do is to walk; we'll walk around."

He introduced me to everybody on campus whom I would ever, ever have any dealings with so I could see them eyeball to eyeball: the printing people and the mailing people, the President's office, everybody. It was a beautiful day. I was new to Kentucky so I hadn't been on this campus at all — I didn't know anything about it. It was a real fun thing to do. I thought that was a very unique way of orienting somebody to a new job instead of showing her a desk and saying "Here's your key."

— Bunny Holman

Maybe we can plan this kind of activity to a certain extent. But, as Jacobs states in her primary thesis, efforts at large-scale planning and urban renewal have largely failed precisely because they haven't recognized the intrinsic merits of a neighborhood's layered, patchwork growth over time.

Again, Peters and Waterman, in observing the "bias for action" that excellent companies exhibit, note in *In Search of Excellence* the benefits of non-planning:

> The name of the successful game is rich, informal communication. The astonishing by-product is the ability to have your cake and eat it too; that is, rich informal communication leads to more action, more experiments, more learning, and simultaneously to the ability to stay better in touch and on top of things.

Successful neighborhoods know exactly what the authors are talking about. In the middle of all the rules and architecture and projects are real human beings, making it all happen.

Look at how your organization is "zoned." Check out the carefully planned, perfectly ordered layout of your office, your classroom. Are great things happening there? Has a preponderance of rules and regulations hindered the creative paths people might choose to take? Maybe it's time to remove the tunnels and their tunnel-visioned tenants and let in a little light. Get the blood flowing with a quick — or not so quick — lap around the whole compound.

All your systems will feel better.

Walking in the suburbs

Cities don't have a monopoly on sidewalks — at least they're not supposed to. Over the past 50 years, suburban growth has acquired its own models, good and bad, for community development. In *A Better Place to Live: Reshaping the American Suburb* (1994: University of Massachusetts, Amherst, MA), author Philip Langdon takes his cues from Jacobs and his own far-ranging research to look at some options for improving the vitality of these places that so often call themselves "communities" but fail to truly act as such. As you might surmise, Langdon finds that "comprehensive networks of sidewalks are essential."

He believes modern thinkers are a little too quick in dismissing the lessons of the past. He suggests that the attention we pay to historical preservation, and appreciation of buildings be extended to the life of the neighborhood those buildings occupy. For instance, the idea of segregating land use — putting the factories all over here, the cozy homes all over there, etc. — has played a key role in the phenomenon of sprawl. It separates people geographically and affects all the patterns of our daily lives: transportation, employment, stores, parks, street configurations. The purported "safety" of the suburbs can sometimes translate into loneliness, isolation, a stunted vision of the world from the children who grow up there.

> When I bike past the area ... it occurs to me that this is not a neighborhood; it is only a collection of unconnected individuals. Unfortunately, America has devoted most of the past fifty years to building neighborhoods that foster just such individualistic impotence.

Langdon suggests that traditionalism is all about connection, and that local informal gathering places are the knots that tie a community together. Such places are not about lifestyle or consumption (like the mall), but operate in a lower key, where we feel free to speak of things and learn about each other as human beings.

Langdon illustrates this point by alternately looking at mall wanderers vs. dog walkers. While both have their advantages and disadvantages (like what might fall from the sky, canned music or what you might step in!), the sense of community and conversation relevant to the actual neighborhood was much stronger among the dog group. Langdon calls on sociologist Dr. Judith Coady's study of a peculiar style of locomotion she calls the "mall walk":

> It's primarily a slower walk to the rhythm of music in the mall. The eyes are unfocused. Generally speaking, there's a kind of glaze on the eyes and a benign stare on the face. The mall brings it on.

As "green" architect William McDonough reminds us, we are "people with lives, not consumers with lifestyles." And the stress of those lives has increased for a number of reasons.

One major factor that we can all appreciate is the problem of time. We work longer, more intense hours, we commute longer distances, and, for good and ill, the rising employment of women has increased the stress on the family. Commuting especially has reached its furthest limits, with people traveling many hours each day, sometimes even staying at the office overnight to avoid the numbing, exhausting travel to home and back again. Why not just move, then? Well, there may not be a place to move to, for one thing. Whereas traditional communities used to have industrial, residential, and commercial uses patchworked together, today's factory may be out in its own zone in the hinterlands, drawing people from many miles away to its well-paying jobs, and being able to pay those wages because of its low overhead and liability in such a location. Keep your distance and you keep your incentive. But at what price?

Langdon also notes that communities should be places of learning for the children growing up there, where they can acquire street smarts as well as classroom education:

> People gather much of their knowledge not in a formal, planned way but as a spin-off of some other activity. Youngsters riding their bikes through town see how a variety of people conduct themselves, mull their observations over, and form insights, all because of exposure to surrounding areas. The traditional street system draws youngsters out, pretty much at their own pace. The world beckons as an interesting place.

Imagine finding the world outside your door more interesting than a video simulation. For all the benefits of modeling and theory, nothing quite compares to covering that mileage with your own two very real feet. Kids and adults alike can thus acquire basic knowledge like their neighbors' names, a recurring litter problem, or what's going on down at the park. Common interests like these can dissolve the cocoons, bringing creatures called neighbors into the light.

'Smoke' lights up connections

Proximity to a variety of places and people will naturally draw people out and encourage relationships that may go beyond a shared personal background or work life. We turn back to the streets of New York for a cinematic example — where, as in other fictions, truth often resides and reverberates.

Paul Auster's screenplay for the celebrated film *Smoke* consists of many beautifully constructed vignettes, all poised to show us how three individuals can cross paths and change one another's lives by discovering their common humanity. A pivotal scene features Harvey Keitel as Auggie, the owner of Brooklyn Cigar Company, and William Hurt as Paul, a reclusive widower novelist hooked on Schimmelpenninck cigars:

8.EXT: EVENING. FAÇADE OF THE BROOKLYN CIGAR CO.

A shot of the darkening sky. A shot of the cigar store. We see the lights go out. Auggie comes outside, locks the door, and begins pulling down the metal gate in front of the windows. Cut to:

A shot of Paul running down the street toward Auggie.

PAUL:
(Out of breath) Are you closed?

AUGGIE:
You run out of Schimmelpennincks?

PAUL:
(Nods) Do you think I could buy some before you leave?

AUGGIE:
No problem. It's not as though I'm rushing off to the opera or anything.

Auggie lifts the gate and the two of them go into the store.

9.INT: EVENING. THE BROOKLYN CIGAR CO.

Paul and Auggie enter the darkened store, Auggie turns on the lights and then goes behind the counter to fetch Paul's cigars. Paul, on the other side, notices a 35-millimeter camera near the cash register.

PAUL:
Looks like someone forgot a camera.

AUGGIE:
(Turning around) Yeah, I did.

PAUL:
It's yours?

AUGGIE:
It's mine all right. I've owned that little sucker for a long time.

PAUL:
I didn't know you took pictures.

AUGGIE:
(Handing Paul his cigars) I guess you could call it a hobby. It doesn't take me more than about five minutes a day to do it, but I do it every day. Rain or shine, sleet or snow. Sort of like the postman. (Pause) Sometimes it feels like my hobby is my real job, and my job is just a way to support my hobby.

PAUL:
So you're not just some guy who pushes coins across a counter.

AUGGIE:
That's what people see, but that ain't necessarily what I am.

PAUL:
(Looking at Auggie with new eyes) How'd you get started?

AUGGIE:
Taking pictures? (Smiles) It's a long story. I'd need two or three drinks to get through that one.

PAUL:
(Nodding) A photographer ...

AUGGIE:
Well, let's not exaggerate. I take pictures. You line up what you want in the viewfinder and click the shutter. No need to mess around with all that *artisto* crap.

PAUL:
I'd like to see your pictures some day.

AUGGIE:
It can be arranged. Seeing as how I've read your books, I don't see why I shouldn't share my pictures with you. (Pause. Suddenly embarrassed) It would be an honor.

The next scene takes us to Auggie's apartment, where Paul is leafing through the cigar store owner's large photo albums, all fourteen of them, each labeled with a year. Each picture in each album is of the same city corner, at Third Street and Seventh Avenue:

10. INT: NIGHT. AUGGIE'S APARTMENT

PAUL:
(Astonished) They're all the same.

AUGGIE:
(Smiling proudly) That's right. More than four thousand pictures of the same place. The corner of Third Street and Seventh Avenue at eight o'clock in the morning. Four thousand straight days in all kinds of weather. (Pause) That's why I can never take a vacation. I've got to be in my spot every morning. Every morning in the same spot at the same time.

PAUL:
(At a loss. Turns a page, then another page) I've never seen anything like it.

AUGGIE:
It's my project. What you'd call my life's work.

PAUL:
(Puts down the album and picks up another. Flips through the pages and finds more of the same. Shakes his head in bafflement) Amazing. (Trying to be polite) I'm not sure I get it, though. I mean, how did you ever come up with the idea to do this ... this project?

AUGGIE:
I don't know, it just came to me. It's my corner, after all. It's just one little part of the world, but things happen there, too, just like everywhere else. It's a record of my little spot.

PAUL:
(Flipping through the album, still shaking his head) It's kind of overwhelming.

AUGGIE:
(Still smiling) You'll never get it if you don't slow down, my friend.

PAUL:
What do you mean?

AUGGIE:
I mean, you're going too fast. You're hardly even looking at the pictures.

PAUL:
But they're all the same.

AUGGIE:
They're all the same, but each one is different from every other one. You've got your bright mornings and your dark mornings. You've got your summer light and your autumn light. You've

got your weekdays and your weekends. You've got
your people in overcoats and galoshes, and you've
got your people in shorts and T-shirts. Sometimes
the same people, sometimes different ones. And
sometimes the different ones become the same,
and the same ones disappear. The earth revolves
around the sun, and every day the light from the
sun hits the earth at a different angle.

PAUL:
(Looking up from the album at Auggie) Slow down,
huh?

AUGGIE:
Yeah, that's what I'd recommend. You know how it
is. Tomorrow and tomorrow and tomorrow, time
creeps on its petty pace.

This moving scene expresses the heart of the film, and the heartbeat of any good neighborhood. Slow down, look around, check out that person on the other side of the counter — he might be a Shakespeare-quoting cigar store owner whose vocation is photography.

Many of us only display a single dimension most of the time, but it only takes a casual conversation, one question or shared observation, to bring out our fuller selves. Of course there's risk involved: We might accidentally establish a relationship, or at least end up talking to that same person again with some familiarity. Who knows where such a perilous path might lead!

In a conversation with Columbia University Chair of Film Annette Insdorf published with the screenplay, Auster probes the underlying qualities of his film and his vibrant characters. Speaking of their universal propensity for smoking, he points out that "maybe all this is connected to the way the characters act in the film ... to what you might call an undogmatic view of human behavior. ... I mean, no one is simply one thing or the other. They're filled with contradictions, and they don't live in a world that breaks down neatly into good guys and bad guys."

That's a good lesson: *an undogmatic view of human behavior*. A familiar saying around our workplace is that those people you're having a hard time dealing with didn't get up this morning intent on ruining your day. Often, just when you think there's no way to conquer an impasse, another route presents itself. There are a lot of ways to know a person that don't necessarily fit into our prescribed notions about them. They say first impressions count most, but cumulative impressions count longest.

Auster situated his story in his beloved Park Slope neighborhood in Brooklyn, which he says "has to be one of the most democratic and tolerant places on the planet. Everyone lives there, every race and religion and economic class, and everyone pretty much gets along. Given the climate in the country today, I would say that qualifies as a miracle. I also know that terrible things go on in Brooklyn, not to speak of New York as a whole. Wrenching things, unbearable things — but by and large the city works. In spite of everything, in spite of all the potential for hatred and violence, most people make an effort to get along with each other most of the time."

Yes, something happens as you make your way around day after day — you begin to care about the things and people you notice along the route. Miracles like Auster describes are probably happening in your organization or community. The only way to find them is to get out there and pay attention.

Even the mere act of walking around, as several authors have noted already in this book, unites the neighborhood. It's another pair of eyes passing through — and another activity for other pairs of neighborhood

eyes to watch. While the path is the vessel, the locomoter is the actor, the human circulatory element that pumps some life into the landscape.

Of course, the porch sitters count in this model too — they're the way stations of the system, the monitoring organs. Give those quality control people some rocking chairs and a pitcher of iced tea! They deserve it for the work they do keeping their eyes and ears open to the goings-on, the flux, the standards and anomalies of the community.

Stepping on the cracks

Of course, not everything emanating from the sidewalks is sweetness and light. Take panhandling, for instance. There seem to be more sidewalk beggars now than ever before, a result of a combination of several factors: homelessness, lack of proper care for some of the mentally ill, even downright homespun American laziness. We won't endeavor to do a sociological analysis of this complex problem, but in our walk along the sidewalk, what do we do when we encounter these human mascots for blight? How do we rekindle hope, positive thoughts, and industriousness in the hearts and minds of the alienated, the perennial outsiders?

One short answer is that some people just revel in that role, no matter the price. And just like people inside an organization, there are some who excel in a certain framework and some who don't. Period. *Wall Street Journal* writer Rita Kramer found that out when she tried to give the panhandlers on her walk some cards good for three nights' lodging at a shelter and some counseling: "With one exception, none of the 20-some men to whom I offered the card seemed particularly interested in the offer of an opportunity to change their circumstances," she wrote. "I was reminded of Alfred Doolittle, the philosopher dustman in George Bernard Shaw's *Pygmalion*, who says: 'I ain't pretending to be deserving. I'm undeserving; and I mean to go on being undeserving. I like it; and that's the truth. ... Undeserving poverty is my line.'"

But if such a person were looking for a way to extract himself from such a downtrodden situation, he might need only look down the block ... at the street vendor.

Sidewalk vending is serious business, as anybody who treads the streets of New York knows well. First come the proper permits, then the literal struggle for turf, for that primo spot that will draw the customers like flies (well, the hot dog vendors might use another expression). The sidewalk vendor may be part of a network maintained by one supplier, or a completely independent operator who procures the supplies and goes on his merry self-directed way.

They might be selling coffee, pretzels, goofy hats or t-shirts, but one thing they hold in common is the supreme challenge of the straight sell to total strangers — talk about your cold calls! The patter may be high-pitched or low-key, but it's the positive mental attitude of the most successful that draws the customers. The movers and shakers

Street Vendor

Sales team inspiration

demonstrate their enjoyment of what they do, and their smiles and cajoling conversation carry an infectious spirit. The same holds true among the vendors at the ballpark, always endeavoring to deliver those peanuts into your strike zone.

Sales like these are not so simple. Ask any vendor in any business, whether he's traveling or stationary. (Actually, most salespeople worth their salt don't stand still for very long — given today's mobile office tools, many firms have taken the step of eliminating desks for sales staff.) The goal is to establish a relationship, from the stage of face and name recognition (which suffices for many transactions) to playing a full role in a customer's planning and strategic processes.

But how many suppliers, having built up or inherited longstanding accounts, carve themselves into a rut of dependence and expectation? They do what it takes to maintain the status quo, but nothing else. Or they begin to expect the big cheese to come through for them in times of need, with only a modicum of expended effort on their part. It's handout time, and they're lining the curb waiting for their fair share.

Those folks could learn a lot from a decent sidewalk vendor, starting with a good swift kick of gusto. They'd see the value in direct conversation, in engaging that customer in an environment free of expectation. They'd learn not to play the savior or oversell what is essentially a well-defined product or service. They'd see how to make their cart as enticing as possible, while learning not to waste time selling bagels to the people looking for cotton candy.

Most of all, they'd absorb the life of the bustling thoroughfare (read "today's workplace") and reflect its energy back to their customers. They'd be hustling, perspiring, laboring to earn their spot in the neighborhood, keeping alive the patter of commerce ... and the pitter patter of their customers' satisfied feet.

Well, enough talking. It's time to walk that talk. Lace 'em up and stride into the day. Your pace is your own, not some mindless lockstep. What your senses and perceptions tell you will change things, in ways both big and small, instant and gradual. It's such a simple notion, to use the path laid out before us, to seek connection and transition, to engage our surroundings by first and foremost being physically there. But it's a notion, a potential, that's widely ignored and untapped.

> *There is a place where the sidewalk ends*
> *And before the street begins ...*

writes Shel Silverstein in his wonderful and typically imaginative poem *Where the Sidewalk Ends*. In that place he found wonders, a sense of slow delight that escapes the denizens of the dark, smoke-churning streets. And how did he find such a kingdom? By following the children, of course:

> *Yes we'll walk with a walk that is measured*
> *and slow,*
> *And we'll go where the chalk-white arrows*
> *go,*
> *For the children, they mark, and the*
> *children, they know*
> *The place where the sidewalk ends.*

Shel Silverstein, © 1974

We would do well to heed his and the children's example. First one foot, then the other. Stop and listen. Go ahead, play the hopscotch someone left in your path. Look and learn. There's no telling what you may discover today.

2

The Garden

Spring is a lovely time to stroll through the neighborhood. The dogwoods and redbuds are starting to bloom, as are many other varieties of flowers, shrubs, trees and plants. Look at Mr. and Mrs. Green, working together in their yard. She's planting tulips and jonquils and hyacinths and hostas, while he's tending to his vegetable garden; you just _know_ that, come July, he's going to show up at your door with a sack of tomatoes, peppers, zucchini and onions. It brings to mind a classic song by Guy Clark: "There's only two things that money can't buy, and that's true love and homegrown tomatoes."

There's something special about a neighborhood where people still know one another well enough to share their homegrown tomatoes. Perhaps they will share other aspects of their lives as well. Of course, when it comes to produce, it's not always necessary to be close friends. (A friend of ours has a neighbor who's always been something of a loner. At least that's the view that many in the neighborhood have had of him. You rarely find him out having conversations with others. However, when his vegetables begin to ripen, paper grocery bags of fresh produce mysteriously appear on people's front porches, each bag bearing the

mysterious signature "from the Jolly Green Giant."
Someone caught him in the act, and it didn't take
long for word to get out, which kind of lends a
new perspective to Ken Blanchard's exhortation
to "catch people doing things right!" These days,
as you might expect, one can't help but look at
the "Giant" a little differently.)

It has been said that our lives, in essence, are
all about the seeds we sow. "Whatsoever a man
sowest, that shall he also reap," says the Bible.
A modern equivalent of that saying, for today's
computer generation, is "Garbage in, garbage out."
In other words, what you get out of life — whether
in business, social circles, your family — has a
lot to do with what you put into it.

Most of us would like, in our own way, to do
something for the good of the whole world, to
somehow make that world a better place. To do so
requires our active involvement — planting seeds,
as it were. A successful life demands interaction
with other people, taking the time to look at and
listen to the world around us in an attempt to
understand what it's trying to tell us.

Botanical metaphors abound. We want to grow our
companies. We want to cultivate fruitful relationships.
We'd like to use our failures as fertilizer. And, in
the end, we hope we're able to find time to stop and
smell the roses — the roses that we have helped plant
over the years.

And what better place to sow what Denis Waitley called
"the seeds of greatness" than in our own backyards,
our own neighborhoods — both literally and
metaphorically.

Is <u>your</u> neighborhood a community?

But how are we to successfully carry out new initiatives, formal or informal, to build a thriving neighborhood or workplace, unless we have a sense of shared purpose and community?

Unless we develop a real connection with our neighbors, we are less likely to see them as complete people with their own lives, their own troubles and hobbies and hopes and dreams. Do we get together with them over a backyard burger and a cold drink, talking about shared goals and what we'd like to see the neighborhood become? Have we come to an understanding of how much we have in common? Are our neighborhoods defined merely by proximity, or is there something deeper at play here? Do we dare to speak of our own neighborhood as a *community*?

Wendell Berry offers a definition of "community" in his insightful and often troubling essay "Sex, Economy, Freedom, and Community," which is contained in his book of the same name (1992, 1993: Pantheon Books, New York):

> By community, I mean the commonwealth and common interests, commonly understood, of people living together in a place and wishing to continue to do so. To put it another way, community is a locally understood interdependence of local people, local culture, local economy, and local nature. (Community, of course, is an idea that can extend itself beyond the local, but it only does so metaphorically. The idea of a national or global community is meaningless apart

from the realization of local communities.) Lacking the interest of or in such a community, private life becomes merely a sort of reserve in which individuals defend their "right" to act as they please and attempt to limit or destroy the "rights" of other individuals to act as they please.

A community identifies itself by an understood mutuality of interests. But it lives and acts by the common virtues of trust, goodwill, forbearance, self-restraint, compassion, and forgiveness.

M. Scott Peck, in his audiocassette program *The Different Drum* (1987: Simon & Schuster AudioWorks, New York), puts forth a similar definition when he says that "the vital first step to community (is) two people, side by side, with a shared understanding of their own need for each other."

Ah, yes: *a shared understanding of their own need for each other.* America may be known as the land of rugged individualism, but we're not really so individualistic as the myth would make us appear.

After all, our own capitalist economic system — which, despite its flaws, has sustained the nation for well over 200 years — is a system based on the need for cooperation.

Is the 'invisible hand' still at work?

Adam Smith, the native Scotsman who is generally regarded as the founder of modern economics, viewed cooperation in the marketplace not so much as a matter of choice or even necessity, but as something that just happens, seemingly taking on a life of its own. Smith believed that people who pursued their own economic interests would automatically act in a way favorable to society's economic interest. By acting in their own self-interests in order to make money, he said, people produce things that other people will buy. Buyers spend money for the things they most want and need. When buyers and sellers meet in the marketplace, they create a production pattern that results in social harmony. According to Smith, this happens as if guided "by an invisible hand."

In order to achieve our personal best, we must help other people. A company that produces more cars will help its workers by providing more opportunities for work. If it produces a better car, consumers will want to buy it, and that will help the company, its workers and its consumers. So, Adam Smith's argument goes, it is simply not possible to make yourself better off without, in some way, also helping the rest of the world. One cannot succeed in a vacuum.

Even self-employed people rely on partnerships. Entrepreneurs have long been aware of the need to network with others who have similar and complementary skills, goals and needs. In recent years, networking has spread to relationships between organizations, in some cases even organizations that were once competitors. In this Information Age, networks of special interest groups are linking up with one another electronically and spontaneously.

It is important for each of us, while concentrating on our strengths, to recognize our limitations and then find people who can provide assistance in those areas. Allies, role models and mentors can help everyone from entrepreneurs to large corporations.

Adam Smith's best-known work, *The Wealth of Nations*, is one of the foundations of American capitalism. Perhaps fittingly, it was published in 1776, the year of this great nation's birth. Under Smith's theory, teamwork is more a law than a principle. Because of the "invisible hand," we simply *must* work with other people in order to improve our own situation.

It is important not to put too much emphasis on what might be interpreted as the "greed" aspects of Adam Smith's capitalistic theories. Equally important is the "invisible hand" that makes capitalism work for the good of society. The strength of capitalism is that, by helping ourselves, we are automatically helping others. Competition is the "watchdog" that makes the system work, for those who are hurting others through unfair practices will ultimately hurt themselves.

To do the best job of producing and maximizing profits, a business must cooperate with consumers. Thus a partnership exists between producers and consumers. Within the organization, management and labor also have a partnership. In addition, partnerships exist between producers and suppliers. Once a business has decided what product it is going to produce, or what service it is going to offer, then the various internal and external partnerships can get the job done most efficiently — using the fewest resources — to maximize profits.

Any true partnership, of course, must be built on a win-win relationship; both parties should feel that they have gained in the transaction, that they are better off than when they started.

But does Adam Smith's ideal still exist? Noted organizational theorist Henry Mintzberg claims that, in today's world, it does not. In his lecture-turned-essay "Society Has Become Unmanageable as a Result of Management" — contained in his book *Mintzberg on Management: Inside Our Strange World of Organizations* (1989: The Free Press, a division of Macmillan, Inc., New York) — he writes:

> In a world of large organizations, the competition of Adam Smith's brewer, baker, and butcher becomes the oligarchy of giant corporations, massive governments, and huge trade unions making deals with one another for their mutual convenience.

Perhaps. But we keep looking for successful neighborhood brewers, bakers and butchers — the "mom and pop" establishments that hearken back to the days of yesteryear. They may be getting fewer and farther between, but we believe they're still out there.

Bank's community focus pays dividends

Bob McNeely
SAN DIEGO, California

Union Bank of California prides itself on being a community bank.

That statement might come as a surprise to the casual observer who would make assumptions about an institution based on such factors as its size. Union Bank of California is a large bank, with $31 billion in assets and 241 branches, including three in Washington state and two in Oregon. Its major shareholder, with 80 percent ownership, just happens to be the largest bank in the world, the Bank of Tokyo/Mitsubishi Bank.

Community bank, you say?

Yes. Positive evidence is growing throughout California, Washington and Oregon, in the form of numerous community development projects made possible through the bank's corporate community development department. This department's mission is to reach the under-served, low- to moderate-income and minority markets and let them know how the bank, either alone or in community partnerships, can help give them access to the services they need to improve their quality of life. Among the initiatives being tested are the relatively new "welfare to workfare" programs, which seek to find suitable work for those previously unemployed.

Meanwhile, Union Bank of California (UBOC) is gaining high marks in customer service, with a philosophy that plays a major role in its community development efforts. Through it all, that ubiquitous bumper-sticker phrase, "Think Globally, Act Locally," seems increasingly appropriate.

The simple reasoning behind the bank's community development efforts is that once people are able to improve their own situation, they can become productive members of society. They will make their own contributions to the local tax base and the general economy. They will be in a position to purchase more goods and services, supporting local businesses, potentially spurring the creation of new businesses, maybe even opening their own. In addition, society will no longer bear the cost of supporting or training them. The potential ripple effect is significant.

"It all comes back to how we utilize the resources that are available, whether those resources are financial or human," says Robert A. McNeely, senior vice president and manager of corporate community development for UBOC.

From his position, McNeely is able to access a variety of types of dollars that are available: charitable dollars, investment dollars, lending dollars. Each has its purpose, its short-term and long-term cost, its anticipated return. But McNeely sees them all as part of a continuum. "All capital that is at our disposal," he says, "almost needs to be viewed as having the same value. It's just as difficult to come by, however it's used." He looks for synergy between charitable contributions, investments and lending.

"From a synergistic standpoint, if you provide some kind of training or technical assistance to equip an individual mentally, that individual theoretically could be positioned to start a business. If so, he or she will need a source of funding to start that business. It could come in different forms: seed capital, training, lending to take that business to the next level. Our philosophy is to move raw material in a continuum from start-up to sustainability."

Whatever the type of investment, McNeely points out, it *is* an investment, with an expected return. "The return may be mid-term to long-term in some cases. But any time you use capital, there needs to be an eventual return. There is no such thing as giveaways."

Differentiating through customer service

Through all these efforts, the bank's emphasis on customer service must remain at the forefront. McNeely is well aware of the phenomenon of commoditization: In banking, as in many businesses, everyone is selling essentially the same thing. "The bank has for some time been sensitive to what it is that differentiates one financial institution from another," he says. "There really isn't a patent on products or services in this field. It's how those products are delivered that makes the difference from a customer perspective."

While working to maintain an excellent service quality ethic, the bank has decided to apply for the state Malcolm Baldrige quality award, with the ultimate goal of winning the national one. Such awards cut two ways, of course. While making a business look good, they also bring higher expectations and increased pressure to do the right thing. McNeely has a clear picture of what entails a "positive customer service environment" in his business — a picture that ultimately results in a win-win situation for everyone involved. His philosophy:

"You raise your customers' level of expectation to where they always expect to come in and be called by name, be waited on in a reasonable amount of time, and so forth. If customers see service levels dropping, they will leave. Then there is a negative gap between expectation and what they get. We want to create a positive gap, where people get more than what they expect.

"At the end of the day, good service is making sure that every time you touch a customer, that customer goes away with a good feeling about you. The better you are, and the higher the expectation of you, the more difficult it can be to satisfy that expectation. But people are willing to pay a premium for good service. As a consumer, I pay more for quality, whether it be in a restaurant or at the dry cleaner. I usually reach for the best in an attempt to have consistency in satisfying my expectations."

UBOC's quest to satisfy and surpass customer expectations extends to its community development efforts. Says McNeely: "Whether an individual is low-to-moderate-income or upper-income, they are people, and people have expectations. In the low-to-moderate category, you have everything from students in grad school to individuals who are struggling and under-employed, people in environments that make it hard to be successful. They are all part of the community, and we need to draw on that resource to help us.

"It all comes back to how we utilize those resources that are available to us, whether financial or human. We need to find a way to transition our human resource potential. In the past, maybe it was a burden on the federal, state and local budgets. But if you can reverse the situation to where these people become employed, not only do you benefit from the absence of those expenses — aside from any training expense — but you also have an opportunity for the individuals to start paying some kind of income tax, plus sales tax, and that can benefit the community.

"Again, from a community development perspective, you also end up with the opportunity for these individuals to be in a position to purchase goods and services, which can stimulate business creation. The result is a circular flow of funds."

In his more than two decades with Union Bank of California, Bob McNeely has formed some solid ideas on how to bring out the best in one's organization, its employees and its community:

Share expectations ... provide training ... inspect. "We let the employees know what we expect of them. We share the vision, and we share our level of expectation with them," McNeely says. It's a process that starts with hiring employees whose personal skills align well with UBOC's customer service ethic. "Once we identify these people, we let them know what we expect. We let them know we always put the employee first."

Training ensures that employees get the picture —
and keep it. Beginning with orientation and continuing
through an ongoing series of training sessions,
employees are acquainted and reacquainted with their
charge to continuously surpass customer expectations.

Finally, "We inspect what we expect." The bank's
quality assurance department constantly tests
UBOC branches and their employees, rating each
branch as well as each employee who has contact
with customers in person or by phone. Those who
exhibit excellent customer service are identified
and rewarded; those who need improvement are
targeted for appropriate training.

"Run fat" with employees. Part of UBOC's growth
has come through the inevitable mergers, the most
recent in April 1996. But, McNeely says, the bank
has maintained its community and customer focus
by not losing sight of the fact that it's the
employees who make it happen:

"As we have merged with another institution,
there has been a fundamental belief that you
don't jettison all the employees and try to run
with a minimal staff, which has been a driving
force with many mergers. Everything needs to be
tailored against the absence of any kind of negative
perception or impact on the customers. The merger
needs to be absolutely transparent to the customers.
We will run fat with employees to make sure the
customer service ethic is maintained.

"We are not interested in customer churn — losing
them out the back door, bringing them in the
front door — but in customer retention. Labor is
always going to be your major expense. As you
jettison labor, you dilute customer service. So

we carry excess staff in anticipation of maintaining good, strong customer service levels."

Maintain a view toward the long term. McNeely credits the Japanese ownership at least in part for UBOC's willingness and ability to take a more long-term view. Bank of Tokyo/Mitsubishi "understands that good customer service is a long-term prospect," he says. "Nordstrom didn't develop its reputation in a year or two."

He suggests that publicly held companies, beholden to a broad base of shareholders, are likely to take a more short-term approach to satisfying that public. But "our primary stockholder has been patient, allowing us the dichotomy of carrying out good customer service while growing large. We keep staffing levels to where we can provide service, while cultures of new employees come in and blend in a positive fashion. All that takes time."

Keep an open mind. That has "positioned us well to be aware of what's going on," McNeely says, and it has also increased the bank's visibility and influence in the community. UBOC's open mind has allowed it to think of each challenge as a business challenge, with an eye toward creative thinking and innovative solutions. As a result, bank officials are often called to participate in community forums and task forces.

"We are pushing the envelope with others," McNeely says. "That calls for new thinking and testing of ideas. We're sharing with a lot of people, and we can also learn from them."

McNeely feels strongly about the need for affluent communities to form partnerships with disadvantaged communities, much as large trading blocs draw from the strength of their partners.

"Part of our responsibility is to find a way to make a distribution of dollars from those who have, and are looking for a return, to those who have not, and are looking for a way to give a return, to make a contribution. We do need to reinvest," he says.

"At the end of the day, I really do believe that banks play a significant role in the development of communities. They are a major means of distributing capital from one sector to another, causing the whole to be better as a result. When you overlay that on the global economy, it becomes clear we all have to be involved to make the entire effort a stronger one. Otherwise, we end up cutting off part of our valuable human resources."

Mature trees and permanence

It can be comforting to visit an older, established neighborhood. With its tree-lined streets and houses that really look "lived in," there is a sense of permanence and stability, a sense of history. About such neighborhoods, it is often said that "people don't move, so if you're looking for a house here, you'll have to wait for someone to die." We're talking about the types of neighborhoods where children grow up, move away and then eventually return to raise their own families. What was once an area full of young families slowly transforms into a neighborhood of largely retired people, then becomes a neighborhood of young families and children again. The cycle of life continues, with strong values that remain intact throughout the generations.

Today's newer subdivisions too often lack that sense of permanence. There are either no trees or only recently planted ones that have yet to mature. Maybe someday these neighborhoods, too, will develop some longevity and character — or maybe not. After all, these days we tend to buy our homes in stages: the "starter" home for a young couple, the "room to grow" house for the developing family, the executive showplace, the retirement home.

Perhaps that is a result of these chaotic times, when it can be frightfully easy to lose our grounding or our direction. Are we drifting away from the things that are truly important to us? Have we forgotten the passion that got us into this business in the first place? Are we pursuing goals with which we have no real emotional connection?

And how about our neighbors? In a world of seemingly non-stop mobility, our neighbors sometimes tend to be casual acquaintances whom we acknowledge with a wave of the hand as we pull into the driveway and, flipping the remote-control garage door opener, into the safety and anonymity of our house. Human contact is reduced to a minimum. No matter. We don't plan to stay in this location for very long anyway.

In many ways, the current attitude toward homes mirrors today's workplace. No longer is a job seen as a lifetime situation, a long-term contract between employer and employee built on loyalty and security. Instead, a career now typically consists of a series of jobs with different organizations, quite likely with one or more periods of self-employment. High turnover rates mean a frequent influx of new "neighbors" in the workplace. Don't get too attached to your co-workers, for by tomorrow they might have moved on to a better-paying position in another city. On the other hand, why not make a little human contact with your neighbors? Your time together may be brief, but that doesn't mean it can't be a positive experience!

The good news about all the moving we do is that human beings are resilient creatures who adapt well to new circumstances. Leaving the old neighborhood behind can be difficult, but we soon settle into a new one, making new acquaintances and friends, forging new adventures with new partners and co-workers. With a minimum of effort, we can keep in touch with those we've left behind. Even better, if we've truly been a good neighbor, we have left a little something of ourselves behind. It could be a smile that, like that of the fabled Cheshire Cat, lingers long after we're gone, bringing cheer to our old friends. It could be a tree that we planted, a mere sapling that will one day bear fruit or provide shade for people we might not even know. It could be an idea that we implemented in our workplace, in the process bringing about improvements that continue to be felt even after our departure.

Apples, bamboo, a long-term view

Think of John Chapman, the American pioneer who has been immortalized in legend as Johnny Appleseed. As is common in myth-making, many of the stories about Chapman are exaggerations of fact or outright flights of fancy. But it is known that, in his own way, Chapman was indeed an American hero who unselfishly helped others both directly and indirectly.

After Chapman planted his first apple seeds, he began selling seedlings to settlers who would then plant them on their own land, cultivating them for up to seven years before the trees began bearing fruit.

He soon began describing himself as "by occupation a gatherer and planter of apple seeds," according to several written accounts. Each spring and summer, he traveled throughout Pennsylvania, and later Ohio and Indiana, planting new seedlings and tending to the existing orchards he had previously begun on frontier land. The spread of apple trees was important, for the fruit was a year-round staple of the pioneer diet. The easygoing, storytelling Chapman became a popular visitor among both white settlers and Native Americans.

In his later years, Chapman was actually known as John Appleseed, and soon after his death, the legend began spreading, his name and deeds kept alive through poems, stories, books and songs. Next time you take a bite of homemade apple pie, rich with cinnamon and sugar and perhaps topped with hand-cranked vanilla ice cream, be thankful that Mr. Appleseed did his part to promote the growth of this all-American fruit.

Of course, it helps to be patient when cultivating — whether you're cultivating orchards, gardens, friendships, families or business relationships. In *First Things First: To Live, To Love, To Learn, To Leave a Legacy* (1994: Simon & Schuster, New York), Stephen Covey uses the metaphor of the Chinese bamboo tree to talk about the importance of looking past the immediate and not always focusing on short-term results:

The Chinese bamboo tree is planted after the earth is prepared, and for the first four years, all of the growth is underground. The only thing visible above the ground is a little bulb and a small shoot coming out of it.

Then, in the fifth year, the bamboo tree grows up to eighty feet.

Principle-centered leaders understand the metaphor of the bamboo tree. ... They know what it means to pay the price to prepare the ground, to plant the seed, and to fertilize and cultivate and water and weed, even when they can't see immediate results, because they have faith that ultimately they will reap the fruits in the harvest.

And what wonderful fruits they are!

Your organization's culture is the one competitive advantage that cannot be duplicated. Technology can be copied. Information can be acquired. Capital can be bought. But the ability of your organization to collaborate effectively ... to put first things first, cannot be bought, transferred, or installed. A high-trust, empowered culture is *always* home-grown.

Speaking of home-grown ...

In his book *Main Street, Not Wall Street: Investing Close to Home — The Smart Way to Make More Money* (1998: William Morrow and Company, Inc., New York), veteran investor John Rubino tells why it makes perfect sense to take a serious look at hometown stocks:

Main Street, in just the past few years, has become an extraordinarily good source of market-beating investments. In most metropolitan areas, a boom in initial public offerings is creating a whole new generation of emerging growth stocks, and it's doing it far too quickly for out-of-town money managers to keep up. Meanwhile, coalescing around these swarms of newborn companies are local investment communities, made up of the following:

- Local business journals, which serve as mini-*Wall Street Journals* with a focus on one metropolitan area;
- Regional brokerage and investment banks, which specialize in the stocks of a single city or region;
- Venture capital clubs, which bring together people interested in investing and working with emerging local companies;
- Investment clubs made up of people who pool their connections and knowledge of the local business scene to find promising companies nearby;
- Individual investors who have realized that their fortunes are best sought close to home.

Together, they form a kind of Wall Street in microcosm, with two big differences: The ideas they're generating really can help you beat the market, and their ideas are readily available — if you know where to look and who to ask.

When a company in your hometown makes an initial public stock offering, chances are that you'll be a few steps ahead of potential investors elsewhere. After all, in all likelihood, you're already at least a little familiar with the company, its products or services, its reputation. Perhaps the local newspaper has run a profile on the business, and brokers in the area might be recommending the stock. You may even know some of the principals in the organization — the vice president might be your neighbor. So you'll have the opportunity to get in on the ground floor as a charter investor, before the stock price goes up.

There's a sense of pride, of course, in sowing seeds of support for a local business, especially when that business becomes successful. There's also a sense of belonging, and helping contribute, to something worthwhile. You'll be helping a company that is contributing to the local economy through the creation of jobs and also to the local tax base. If the business is a responsible one, part of its profits will go back into making the community a better place to live.

Simple actions, complex results

In his influential book *Chaos* (1987: Viking, New York), James Gleick tells about the discovery of the Butterfly Effect by research meteorologist Edward Lorenz:

> Traditionally, when physicists saw complex results, they looked for complex causes. When they saw a complex relationship between what goes into a system and what comes out, they assumed that they would have to build randomness into any realistic theory, by artificially adding noise or error. The modern study of chaos began with the creepy realization in the 1960s that quite simple mathematical equations could model systems every bit as violent as a waterfall.

Tiny differences in input could quickly become overwhelming differences in output — a phenomenon given the name "sensitive dependence on initial conditions." In weather, for example, this translates into what is only half-jokingly known as the Butterfly Effect — the notion that a butterfly stirring the air today in Peking can transform storm systems next month in New York.

While the discovery of the phenomenon was relatively new, the Butterfly Effect actually "had a place in folklore," Gleick writes, quoting the 17th century British poet George Herbert (in the process describing the phenomenon in more human terms):

For want of a nail, the shoe was lost;
For want of a shoe, the horse was lost;
For want of a horse, the rider was lost;
For want of a rider, the battle was lost;
For want of a battle, the kingdom was lost!

Scientists continue to grapple with ways to discover and understand what Gleick calls "order *masquerading* as randomness" (the emphasis is his). Meanwhile, can most of us, in strictly human terms, ever come close to comprehending the full effects of our actions on other people? Do we have any real idea what has grown from the seeds we have sown? In a word, no. We perhaps see the immediate effects, but our actions reverberate into the world in ways we will never be able to measure.

The idea of a "ripple effect" suggests a certain predictability, as in the circles that spread out on the surface of a pond when we toss a stone into the water. But life is much messier than that! When we add the unpredictability of human idiosyncrasies and personality quirks into a mix that is already growing by exponents — not only the people whom we personally influence, but also the people whom they influence and then the people whom those people influence, ad infinitum — we begin to realize a type of human Butterfly Effect.

Cinematically, something akin to this is at work in Frank Capra's beloved classic *It's a Wonderful Life*. George Bailey, played by Jimmy Stewart, is given a unique opportunity: to see what the world would have been like had he never lived. As the suicidal Bailey discovers, his own life had affected the world in ways he could never have imagined. His own brother, whose life George had saved during a childhood sledding accident, went on to save an entire platoon of men during the war. Yet another life was saved when young George realized a potentially fatal error made by the grief-stricken druggist, Mr. Gower, in filling a child's prescription. In far too many other ways to count, George Bailey's life had had a positive effect on untold people, whose own lives subsequently affected others — and so on and so on and so on.

And so do our own lives influence the lives of others in ways that we could never imagine or predict, in ways that we will never know. Now, imagine how this same phenomenon translates into our workplace relationships and our dealings with our partners, suppliers, customers and clients. What kind of communication is in place, for example, between various internal departments such as orders and shipping and invoicing?

In his modern classic *The Fifth Discipline: The Art & Practice of The Learning Organization* (1990: Doubleday Currency, New York), Peter Senge relates his experiences with the "beer game" developed in the

1960s at the Massachusetts Institute of Technology's Sloan School of Management. We won't get into many details here — you should read the book for that, plus a wealth of insights. But suffice it to say that the beer game is "a laboratory experiment — a microcosm of how real organizations function, where you can see the consequences of your decisions play out more clearly than is possible in real organizations."

The beer game involves a production/distribution system with three major players, or groups of players, representing (1) the retailer, (2) the wholesaler and (3) the brewery. Simulating a 24-week period of orders and deliveries, the experiment shows what happens when a system causes its own crisis, through no fault of the players themselves. Typically, what happens in the beer game is that the players individually and collectively worsen the crisis through their misguided attempts to correct it. For many business types who play the game in Senge's workshops, the experience is a humbling eye-opener.

"To improve performance in the beer game," Senge writes, "players must redefine their scope of influence. As a player in any position, your influence is broader than simply the limits of your own position" because the behavior of each player directly influences the behavior of everyone else. "Either the larger system works, or your position will not work. Interestingly, in the beer game and in many other systems, in order for you to succeed, others must succeed as well."

Legacies and modern-day heroes

What will be our legacy after we leave the neighborhood for good? Will it be one of having succeeded by helping others succeed? Will we have fulfilled the responsibilities that have been given us? These are questions we all must face at some time in our lives.

In his book *First Things First: To Live, To Love, To Learn, To Leave a Legacy*, Stephen Covey writes:

> There's no way we can escape accountability. We do make a difference — one way or another. We are responsible for the impact of our lives. Whatever we do with whatever we have — money, possessions, talents, even time — we leave behind us as a legacy for those who follow. And regardless of our own scripting, we can exercise our unique human endowments and choose the kind of stewards we want to be. We don't have to pass on abuse, debt, depleted natural resources, self-focus, or illusion to future generations. We can pass on a healthy environment, well-cared-for possessions, a sense of responsibility, a heritage of principle-based values, and the vision of contribution. By doing so, we improve quality of life both now and in the future.

In the long run, it is perhaps those people who make a lasting contribution to life, who help bring out the best in other people, who will be seen as heroes. These days, we might well wonder:

Are there any heroes in the world today?

Judging from most of the news we get daily, it would be easy to come to the conclusion that the hero is, at best, a dying breed. In the corporate world, we are flooded with stories of corruption, greed, selfishness and irresponsibility. It's almost enough to make you think that "business ethics" is an oxymoron. We could use some business heroes!

In a *Parade* magazine article a few years ago, Daniel Boorstin, noted historian and former U.S. Librarian of Congress, made some interesting comments about the difference between heroes and celebrities. "The hero is known for achievements, the celebrity for well-knownness," Boorstin said. "The hero reveals the possibilities of human nature; the celebrity reveals the possibilities of the press and the media. Celebrities are people who make news, but heroes are people who make history. Time makes heroes but dissolves celebrities."

According to one dictionary definition, the attributes of a hero include courage, strength and nobility, as well as a willingness to sacrifice for the good of others. These are all traits that each of us, as leaders in our organizations, communities and families, should exhibit.

People who have been placed in positions of authority have great responsibilities to the people they lead. And the people they lead also have great responsibilities to the rest of their organization. In today's world, everyone must be a leader. During these times of often mind-numbing change, we need all the strong, committed, passionate leadership we can get.

Wouldn't it be great to build an organization of heroes — employees who serve as an example and an inspiration to others? One such employee at WYNCOM was Dennis Deppisch, who remains a shining model of self-leadership for our employees to follow. His "whatever it takes" philosophy, unfailing integrity and passion for the job were unmatched. His commitment to always giving his personal best made him an inspiration to everyone. Dennis, who died of cancer at the age of 46 in June 1995, would probably be embarrassed to be called a hero — but he definitely is one in our book.

During the final months of his life, Dennis maintained a positive attitude and eagerly shared his personal convictions with anyone who would listen. During one of his last talks, he posed a provocative question:

What would you do if you found out you had only a few months to live?

Think about it!

Dennis understood the importance of leaving a legacy for those he loved — and that group included those in his workplace as well as friends and family. Among his other contributions, he left us with the following message, which he recorded on video; we think it's an excellent way to end this chapter:

Dennis Deppisch

The concept of planting a shade tree is that it is an investment in the future. However, the sapling we plant today will not reach maturity in our lifetime. So why make the effort?

Future generations will reap the benefits of the trees that grow from the saplings we plant and cultivate today. The ideals by which we live our lives will live on well beyond our lifetime. The planting of shade trees is about stewardship, about nurturing. Ultimately, it is about leaving a legacy.

Good leaders leave a positive legacy. They pass on their ideals by example. A strong work ethic, spirit, strength, courage and integrity — these are qualities that often inspire and motivate others. People appreciate these qualities and, when motivated by a positive example, will naturally gravitate toward living and implementing these ideals. When we are placed in a position of authority, our stewardship — of our co-workers, employees, family, friends — must be uncompromised.

Our nurturing abilities are vital to the positive growth of those who are influenced by our example. These people, in turn, grow and bear fruit that will help to nurture others. As leaders, we have been endowed and entrusted with the stewardship of these qualities. It is our responsibility to pass these gifts and ideals on, so that future generations can recognize and nurture these qualities in themselves and others, and thus grow into the strong leaders of tomorrow.

We must plant and nurture those shade trees today, in order to leave the legacy of our ideals as our gift to future generations.

"Give the lady what she wants!"

—*Marshall Field*

3

The Deli

Beginning a chapter called "The Deli" with a quote from a man who made his name in the department store business might seem a bit odd, but let us assure you there is a good reason. It's just another example of how everything in life — and in this book — is connected.

Do you ever get an ache for a healthy helping of real life, an escape from predictability and routine? We do, fairly often. When that urge for realism strikes, we take ourselves to a small, locally owned business like a deli, where you can bet the flavor of business is anything but vanilla.

A real, honest-to-goodness deli — not those meat and cheese counters at your local supermarket, mind you — is a mixed bag. It's part grocery store, part restaurant and part live theater. If you haven't had the experience, perhaps you need to take a trip to a metropolitan area like New York City, where decades-old delis do a bristling business beneath World War II era signs that exhort you to "Send a salami to your boy in the Army."

We like Jane and Michael Stern's reminiscence of a visit they made to Katz's deli on East Houston

Street in New York City. It's in their book *GoodFood* (1983: Alfred A. Knopf, Inc., New York).

"We stepped up to the counter and ordered a couple of sandwiches from a man who looks like he was born when Katz's opened, in the late 1800s," they write. "Just to get him going, we asked for pastrami on white with mayonnaise. He looked at us as though we had said wallpaper paste on a Brillo pad; he shrugged wearily; and in a heavy New York accent, he called out to the sandwich-maker next to him, "Sold American!"

The Sterns redeemed themselves minutes later by telling the old fellow they were kidding, that they actually wanted pastrami with hot mustard on rye. The grizzled counterman softened just a tad. He forked a piece of pastrami over the glass case. "Here," he said. "I'll give you a sample." As they devoured the meat, he held out another slice. "So you shouldn't starve."

Ah, what an eating adventure — the polar opposite of the quick and predictable fast-food counter or the squawking speaker box of the drive-through lane. The fast-food experience is mostly just that — fast. At fast-food restaurants, there are few surprises, fewer thrills. This batch of fries perfectly matches the last batch. In their quest for consistency, it sometimes seems chain restaurants have cut the heart right out of their business.

Stepping up to the deli counter — or in the door of any business that sells itself in creative ways — can be just the jump start our desensitized minds need. Just think of what a group of business school students could learn from a field trip to a deli. What, you ask? How to slice meat so thin you can see through it? The proper mayo-to-mozzarella ratio?

Actually, the lessons are much more bountiful and broad. The deli is a bastion for full-flavored eating, where many of the principles of good business are put into practice daily. Here are a few of the lessons we think you can learn at your local deli.

Give the lady (or the gentleman or child or the grandpa) what she/he wants. See, we told you everything was connected. The same command that Field gave to his store's manager is the dictum of the deli. You can't get much more customized than a deli sandwich. If the Sterns had really wanted pastrami on white, well, that's what they would have gotten. Delis were doing "have it your way" long before Burger King ever did.

What delis have been doing for years is the future of business, according to Stan Davis and Christopher Meyer, the authors of *BLUR: The Speed of Change in a Connected Economy* (1998: Addison-Wesley, Reading, MA). Their advice: Customize Every Offer. "It used to be one size fits all," they write. "Now, Porsche says it never makes the same car twice. Whatever your offer, you must tailor it each and every time, with the needs of the individual buyer or user in mind. Customize, customize, customize. It is the great differentiator of the 21st century."

Look 'em in the eye; tell 'em what you are all about. What we're talking about here is customer service with flavor and flair, not the kind that's gleaned from some ring-bound training manual or hospitality video. There shouldn't have to be signs reminding us to smile and be nice to our customers, although often there are. The insincerity of it disgusted supermarket box boy Brett Hauser, one of the people Studs Terkel interviewed in *Working.* Hauser grimly reflected on life at the end of the supermarket line: "There's a sign on the cash register that says: Smile at the customer. Say hello to the customer."

There are times when the genuineness that comes from being proud of your product and of your company comes through. And, according to Tom Peters in *The Pursuit of WOW! Every Person's Guide to Topsy-Turvy Times* (1994: Vintage Books, a division of Random House, New York), we usually notice when it happens:

> Overwhelmed by new technologies, new competitors, new everything, we hold the gift of human attention — from the sales clerk or nurse who looks you directly in the eye rather than conversing while staring blankly at the computer screen or medication tray in front of her or him — to be the most munificent of blessings.

In *The Pursuit of WOW!,* Peters recounts his memorable visit to Khuri's Deli Café in San Francisco. He went into the deli in search of a simple tabbouleh and left with a deep appreciation for the way Khuri runs his business.

Khuri told Peters about his deli from top to bottom — the history of the dishes (complete with samples), the differences in his mother's cooking style and his own, his catering service and even the nutritional value of various items.

And Khuri's enthusiasm wasn't fueled by the fact that he knew Peters was one of the world's leading commentators on what makes successful businesses tick. Peters' wife got a similar introduction to the wonders of Khuri's when she stopped in days later — except that Khuri's mom was doing the talking this time.

"If you're ever in San Francisco," Peters writes, "don't fail to stop by Khuri's for lesson No. 1 in how the potentially mundane need not be so. ... The Khuri's of the world probably have more to teach us about winning business performance at home and abroad than the Generals Electric, Mills and Motors."

As Ken Blanchard says in *Raving Fans: A Revolutionary Approach to Customer Service* (1993: William Morrow and Company, New York), to give our customers what they want, we have to have a vision of what we want their experience to be, sort of a home movie of the mind. He writes:

> You need a vision of perfection about everything you do. In terms of your customer, that means if you had anything to do with it, how would customers be treated? If a television show was coming in to do a story about how you're wowing customers, what would they see? What would people be saying? What would they be doing? And how can you create

that vision of perfection? And it doesn't mean you're going to do it perfectly every time. But if you don't have a sense of how customers should be greeted, how the phone is answered, what you should do when you make a mistake, and all the different things that go into dealing with customers, then you never have a chance of getting near perfection.

The best things in life are free (to your customer) and they really don't cost you a dime. The wizened counterman at Katz's did more than give Jane and Michael Stern a free piece of pastrami. He created a bond, a relationship. The Sterns will always remember that gesture of generosity.

If your product is good (and it better be if you're going to make it in business) give people a sample of it — a taste, a test drive, a send-it-back-if-you-hate-it-and-we-won't-ask-a-single-question guarantee. One of our favorite bakeries has at its counter loaves of bread on a wooden cutting board. There's also a crock of real butter. Whether you buy anything or not, the cashier offers you a thick slice of bread. It's the way the famous Mrs. Fields of Mrs. Fields Cookies got her start — she gave her cookies away on the sidewalk, and you see where it got her. If you demonstrate that you believe in your product, others will believe in it as well.

You can bottle a tomato, but you can't bottle atmosphere. Jane and Michael Stern have an enviable occupation. They travel the U.S., eating at the establishments that define America's heart and soul — independent diners, delis, doughnut shops, dinner houses. After their meal, they recount these eating expeditions in books, in a *Gourmet* magazine column and on National Public Radio. The Sterns like their food with peppery personality, with spice. And they like a little atmosphere on the side.

"We have friends — serious eaters — who say they don't give a hang for atmosphere and ambience; that food is the only criterion," they write in *GoodFood*. "We put food atop the list, too, but relish the fringe benefits of good food in a good place. For us, it's bogus atmosphere that is a bore; you can't buy character from a restaurant design firm."

It takes a good product to attract customers. But atmosphere is often the glue. Take Reisner's Deli, a 53-year-old institution in Norfolk, Virginia, that closed a couple of years ago. The place had a loyal following. As one regular lamented: "With the business closing, it's really going to put a hole in the area. You can always buy meat and make a sandwich, but the atmosphere of the place just feels like home."

And atmosphere goes well beyond the pictures on the wall and the color of the Formica on the floor. Personalities like Khuri and Katz's counterman provide a lot of the ambience at small businesses. Like one business executive says in Peters' *The Pursuit of WOW!*, "You get no character without characters."

Customer service companies

 " Whether you are a check-out clerk or a corporate lawyer, you are in customer service.

" That's right. No matter what business we work for or what job title is on our office door, we all influence how potential customers and the public perceive our organization. We're all "goodwill ambassadors" or, as Denis Waitley says, "maitre d's" for our companies, and we'd be wise not to forget it.

As Jan Carlzon, who became president of struggling Scandinavian Airlines, told Karl Albrecht and Ron Zemke in their *Service America* (1985: Dow Jones-Irwin, Homewood, IL), "We have 50,000 moments of truth every day." Each of those moments is "an episode in which a customer comes into contact with any aspect of the company, however remote, and thereby has an opportunity to form an impression."

Just imagine the difference it would make if we all abandoned our customer service departments and instead became "customer service companies."

—Larry Holman

Breaking the mold

There are plenty of small businesses and companies out there that are emulating the more notorious rulebreakers like the rebel of the skies, Southwest Airlines. Until Southwest came along and shook up a staid industry, we assumed we were forever doomed to hear the dull drone of the FAA safety spiel. But Southwest surprised and delighted us by turning routine into standup comedy with lines like "There are 50 ways to leave your lover, but only six exits from this airplane."

There are companies like University Bank & Trust in Palo Alto, California, which, according to Tom Peters, has free shoe shines, balloons for kids, and sends customers a huge bag of Walla Walla onions every August.

Or the Golden Gate hotel and casino in Las Vegas, the oldest in the gambling town. Amidst gargantuan hotels where volcanoes erupt and Atlantis sinks, the tiny Golden Gate thrives by filling a niche that others forgot — the real Vegas.

"We're minuscule," owner Mark Brandenberg told the *Wall Street Journal*, "but we're authentic."

Look around you. Isn't there a business in your town — maybe not a deli, or even a restaurant of any sort, for that matter — but a small business that is breaking out of the mold and doing a bang-up job?

He aims to please

Steve Lambert
PLANT CITY, Florida

When you hear the term "neighborhood business," what images pop into your head? The deli around the corner, where you stop in for a salami on rye and some small talk? The bank branch, where the tellers know not only your

The Aim crew

(Steve Lambert, back right)

name but also the name of your Springer spaniel? Or, perhaps it's the drugstore down the street, where the pharmacist is happy to lean over the counter and recommend a plan of attack for that patch of poison ivy on your forearm.

But when you think of a neighborhood business, you rarely, if ever, think about a wholesale supplier — that mysterious business typically tucked away on some seldom traveled road or among a maze of boxy, windowless buildings in an industrial park. A place with a narrow appeal that seems to have little to gain by becoming a bit of a neighborhood hangout.

But drop in on Steve Lambert, owner of Aim Electric Supply in Plant City, Florida (population 25,000), and you'll soon think differently. Lambert's business could easily be a show-and-tell story for a Tom Peters presentation. Lambert has practiced what Peters preaches. He's built a business with soul, with heart, with charisma. And it's paying off.

1,200 accounts in 24 months

Plant City is one of those towns where people know one another. But no one knew Steve Lambert when he opened his business two years ago. As he recalls, "I knew one or two people, tops."

Now he knows at least 1,200 other companies and businesses in town — the number that have opened accounts with his business. It's four times as many as he hoped to have after a mere 24 months. It's such an incredible start that you wonder what fueled it. The promise of some fantastic giveaway or prize? Prices so low that Aim is nearly giving electrical supplies away?

Actually, the key to Lambert's success is much, much simpler — and ultimately cheaper. It's figuring out what the customer wants, needs and likes, and then delivering it. It's living by the company's motto: "We aim to please," which hangs prominently above the service counter. It's becoming a valued and giving member of the neighborhood. And it's creating an atmosphere that feels as if you stepped into your best friend's kitchen.

"We want to welcome you as a friend," says Lambert, who hails from Alabama. "Make you feel at home. We've got free coffee, free water, free doughnuts, free candy and, listen, we've got an old Coke machine and for a quarter, you get an ice cold Coca-Cola in a bottle — one of those little bottles."

You don't have to be an economist to figure out that Lambert is pouring some cash into those freebies and quarter Cokes.

"Those Cokes cost me 47 cents; I sell them for a quarter. Am I losing money?" Lambert asks. "Do you know how many times I've been told by a customer, 'You know, I was going to stop and spend 89 cents at the 7-Eleven but you've got those Coca-Colas in a bottle for a quarter, and I need some supplies anyway.' Those Cokes aren't costing me."

The Cokes are a small, but magic, touch. They are six ounces of Southern culture, a reminder of youth to many of Lambert's customers; an inexpensive, atypical refreshment to others. They evoke just the kind of down-home, hound-on-the-porch feeling that Lambert wants his company to convey.

It's apparent that Aim is a different kind of place from the minute you walk in the door. That's because there is no door — at least not a traditional glass or wooden one. Aim's front door is an opening, covered by a sheet of plastic strips that separates the indoors from outdoors.

Maybe the door got blown away in the last hurricane or tropical storm? Well, no, Lambert will tell you, the plastic is actually there on purpose, a very practical approach to a common problem: how to open a door when your hands are full of fixtures, wiring, switches and the other electrical needs.

"If you are bringing something in, or you are leaving with an armload of supplies, you don't have to mess with any doors," Lambert says.

The focus on the customer doesn't stop at the unusual doorway. Customer service is Aim's reason for being. Call the company and the voice on the other line, no matter which of the six employees you talk to, is chipper and upbeat.

Aim is not in danger of becoming one of the "gutless, soulless" kinds of companies that Tom Peters warns about. The little company has pizzazz and personality.

But why go to such lengths, when you have not a scrap of local competition?

Lambert knew better than to think that no local competition meant no problem. He realized that though a community will welcome a stranger, it won't go out of its way to support a newcomer who doesn't bring a benefit. His potential customers were traveling to Lakeland and Tampa to get supplies before he opened his business, and if they didn't like him or his company, they'd just get back in their car or truck and drive on down the road.

A lifetime of ideas

Ask Lambert where he gets his ideas, and he will chuckle. It's easy, he explains, when you begin planning your company in the sixth grade.

That's when he decided that one day he would open his own business. By the time he was finally ready to do so, he had a head full of ideas.

Like many future entrepreneurs, Lambert first served his time working for others. And he graciously credits his more than two decades in the electrical supply industry as a linchpin to his current success. Lambert started out as a truck driver. He went to night school while he worked full time, earning his degree in management. It took him six years. Then he worked his way up to top management for one of the nation's largest electrical wholesale suppliers, in charge of the company's operations in the state of Florida.

Through the years, Lambert was taking mental notes. What did the companies he worked with and for do right? What did they do wrong?

One of the main problems Lambert saw in his work for a large company was the loss of local control. His company would come up with marketing plans and business approaches that didn't fit his territory. Sometimes, he was given the authority to go a different route. But often he wasn't.

He also began to feel out of touch with his market because he was being called away constantly to meetings. "I was responsible for what went on in Florida for the company, yet I was out of the state in meetings 100 business days a year. Now, there are only 260 business days in a year. That's an awful lot of meetings."

Having his own business gives Lambert the satisfaction of tailoring his business to his market and the chance to use his sizable skills as a strategist to the full extent. He's a plainspoken guy, proactive, with a plan of attack that shouts of common sense. If Norman Schwarzkopf was looking for a right-hand man, Lambert would be a good one.

For example, when Lambert began to seek a site for his business, he didn't turn the task over to a real estate agent. He scouted locations himself. A reasonable price was just one consideration.

Lambert wanted a place that would put him directly in his customers' path.

"I knew if they were currently buying electrical supplies, they had to be driving one way to Lakeland or the other way to Tampa," he says. "So I did both drives myself and determined that most of the time, it was quicker to go to Lakeland. So then I thought, 'I'm in Plant City, I need electrical supplies, I'm going to go to Lakeland. But how am I going to get there?' So, I took a look at the roads and I made sure my business was on the Lakeland side of Plant City on the road they would most likely drive to get there."

"Bright" ideas really pay off!

By being on the way, Lambert knew there was a good chance contractors and others would stop by to check out his business.

"I thought they'd say, 'We'll head for Lakeland, but we'll stop in and see if he's got what we want, see if we like doing business there. If he doesn't, no time is lost hardly and we'll just drive on to Lakeland,'" Lambert explains.

He doesn't see anything brilliant about his tactic. "I'm just trying to put myself in their shoes. If I want some electrical supplies, what do I do, how do I go get them. It's just ... thinking."

(Ah, just thinking, the task that Roger Fritz, the founder and president of Organization Development Consultants, calls "the hardest work there is.")

And, even though Lambert's calculations showed that Plant City had a sufficient number of electrical contractors and electricians to support his business, he decided to do some dinner table research.

A Rotarian, Lambert attended several of the Plant City club's meetings. "I knew the people at those meetings were going to be the leaders of the community. I would go and sit down at the table. Most weeks, someone would be friendly enough to say, 'What's up? What are you doing here?' And I would say, 'I'm considering opening an electrical distributorship here. Do you think I ought to do it?'" The positive response he got was the kind of personal encouragement that an entrepreneur craves.

Exploding business myths and mysteries

Many an owner of a start-up business would be compelled to do nothing but work, but Lambert takes time each week to go to Plant City High School, where he is a Junior Achievement instructor for a ninth-grade economics class. The students have a lot of misconceptions about business, gleaned from movies and television, Lambert thinks. He's doing his best to dispel them.

"They'll ask me, 'Who did you cheat this week?' They think if you sold something for $1, you probably made 70 cents profit. I really explode a lot of misconceptions in those eight weeks," he says. "I walk them through what actually happens in business. It's made me realize we need to work as businesspeople to educate the general public about business."

Lambert admits that he has had a blast in class. Inattentive students begin to sit up and listen after Lambert plops down on their desk and jokingly threatens to stay there until they answer a question or participate in a discussion. When the semester ends, he gets the most heartfelt thank-you notes from the students whom he good-naturedly harassed.

Recruiting 'round the clock

Whether Lambert is visiting the local high school, picking up lunch at a fast food restaurant, buying groceries at the local market or talking to friends at a Rotary Club meeting, he's always on the lookout for potential employees.

"I don't use employment agencies. I don't pay fees. I'm constantly recruiting for people — 52 weeks a year," he says. "That doesn't mean that I hire them. But I just try to keep them on the list and touch base with them every so often, and when that right opportunity comes along, hopefully it's the right time for them. If not, I've got someone else, but the first person stays on the list."

The list? Yes, Lambert says, he's got a list and it's not just a mental one. He has a piece of paper with the names of people he wants to hire — never more than a single page, but from 10 to 30 people nonetheless.

Is Lambert being overly optimistic? After all, how many new employees can a small company like his need?

"Once we get past the early years and the financial hurdles to the point where money is not a problem, when we reach that point — and we *will* reach that point — I know what the problem is going to be: finding enough good people," he says.

Employers who complain about not being able to find good workers get no sympathy from Lambert: "They don't look until they need someone. You've got to look all year round."

What does he look for? How do you make Lambert's "list"?

"I look for communication skills, a smile. I'm looking for a thread of success," he says. "People who have been successful will probably continue to be; people who have not will find ways not to be. You know what I'm looking for. You occasionally bump into somebody and you say, 'Oh, that was a pleasant experience, they've got their act together.' You see it, you just don't see it very often."

A contribution to the community

In such a short time, Aim Electric has made a contribution to its community. It's become an upstanding citizen, a valued contributor.

"Number one is the convenience we provide," Lambert says. "The community has opened their arms to us. People have said, 'We are going to try and give you all the business we can. We don't want you to close. We want somebody here. We don't like making those hourlong trips to get supplies.'

"But number two is for the first time they have someone who is going to stay open who knows what they are doing in business. With our knowledge, we can help them have much better lighting layouts and more efficient lighting. We've got expertise that Plant City didn't have."

The corner store

A story in *Newsweek* a few years ago delved into ways we could restore the feeling of neighborhood to our communities. One idea was to bring back the corner store. Writer Jerry Adler said:

> Obviously, malls and supermarkets, with their vast selections and economies of scale, will never be supplanted by neighborhood shopping streets and corner groceries. But it still should be possible to provide some of the necessities of life within walking distance of many people. Then you could send your kid out for that bread — and a newspaper while he's at it.

When we were growing up, it seemed markets were on every corner. We popped in to these stores on lazy summer afternoons and bought an ice cold Coca-Cola, a Hershey bar and some bubble gum. And the folks who ran the store, well, they knew us. Maybe not by name, but they knew our family tree. They'd say, "Oh, you're so-and-so's son, daughter, brother, sister. ..." At an age when anonymity is considered an asset, we had none. We were known.

Although we sure didn't think so at the time, that familiarity was to our benefit. It kept us from getting in trouble (well, not completely; we still managed a few scrapes) and deep down somewhere in our not-too-intellectually fulfilled adolescent minds, we knew there were a lot of people around who cared about us.

The books we read tell us we are not alone in those memories. In her powerful book *The Measure of Our Success*, Marian Wright Edelman remembers her hometown of Bennettsville, South Carolina, in much the same way: "I went everywhere with my parents and was under the watchful eye of members of the congregation and community, who were my extended family. They kept me when my parents went out of town, they reported on me and chided me when I strayed from the straight and narrow of community expectations, and they basked in and supported my achievements when I did well."

Gil Walker grew up that way, too. Lisbeth Schorr talks about Walker in her book *Common Purpose: Strengthening Families and Neighborhoods to Rebuild America* (1997: Anchor Books, Doubleday, New York). He grew up in Gary, Indiana, and now runs a midnight basketball program for inner-city kids in Chicago. "I can remember, when I was coming up, walking home from school with my report card in my hand," Walker said. "Before I got home, five or six people wanted to see it. If it was a good report card, I got hugs, I got kisses. ... If it was a bad report card, every one of those individuals said, 'Gil Walker, you know you could do better.'"

Is it possible that through his basketball program, Walker is restoring that watched-over feeling that a close-knit neighborhood gave its kids?

Memories of the caring attitude of the corner market are what first drew us to Cosmo's, a deli/grocery/bakery/café combination that officially calls itself a fine foods specialty store. We watched with interest as it was being built on a busy corner in our neighborhood.

On looks alone, Cosmo's has little in common with those clapboard convenience stores of our youth. Cosmo's is more cosmopolitan. Out front there are patio tables with umbrellas, providing cool circles of shade.

When you walk in the door your nose goes on alert. Something smells good, very good. Could it be the big loaves of bread baking in the back? Or is it the garlic that's just erupted in the sauté pan in the open kitchen? Perhaps it's the smell of fresh Romano cheese. In the store's middle are all shapes and sizes of tables — some small, some communal.

There are newspapers and magazines — even a few cookbooks. In the winter, a real fire burns in the fireplace, and customers are welcome to throw another log on the fire.

There is nothing canned or preconceived about this place. It's not manufactured by some "hip" design firm in New York City. This is a place with an appeal like the old corner grocery store. It is alive. It's got a heartbeat.

We've discovered that Cosmo's is fulfilling a feeling of neighborhood that many who live in the area sensed was missing.

Bill Farmer's family has run a jewelry store around the corner for decades. He's convinced Cosmo's is bringing back a sense of community that was slowly ebbing from the neighborhood business district. "Cosmo's re-creates that sense of neighborhood that we all have in our mind. It combines the best attributes of an Italian market, the family grocery and your favorite deli."

Krisia Rosa comes to Cosmo's to see people she never sees when she's at home — those who live around her. "Everyone has garage-door openers and they drive into their garage and walk into the house and you just don't see them. I see my neighbors here."

Like us, Jessica Morris, an artist and teacher, believes Cosmo's has energy. She stops in when she needs a bit of inspiration. "A lot of times if I'm in a slump and need to get going again, I come in and get a cup of coffee and say 'hi' to some people and maybe get a hug from a friend," she says. "Cosmo's doesn't just nourish your body; it nourishes your spirit as well. It touches all your senses."

Spoken like an artist — or maybe a poet. Golden words, nonetheless.

In its effort to become an anchor in the neighborhood, Cosmo's has gone a step beyond the typical market by leasing space a few doors down for a community center. It's a well-equipped meeting place that neighborhood associations, civic groups and nonprofits are welcome to use, free of charge.

Will places like Cosmo's become a trend (not trendy as in here today, gone tomorrow, but a revival of those places in our communities that brought us together: the diner, the corner market, the deli, the coffee shop)? Places that wake up our senses and remind us of life's many overlapping layers? Places where we see people we know and care about? We hope so.

Cash register resumés?

If you've read Dick Schaaf's *Keeping the Edge: Giving Customers the Service They Demand* (1995: Dutton, New York), you'll remember Stew Leonard's dairy store in Norwalk, Connecticut. Stew's has become a tourist attraction, what *New York* magazine calls "the Disney World of Supermarkets."

At Stew's, you'll find friendly, helpful employees everywhere, always ready to answer questions and give directions. And when you walk up to one of the many checkout lines, each has a color picture and a short resumé of the person running the register. What a great icebreaker, a way to make a connection with someone to whom we otherwise might say only "Please," "Thank you" and "Paper."

Maybe more places should be like Stew's. The emphasis on the individuality of the employee says a lot about the company's philosophy. It's a very tangible way of demonstrating that Stew's really does believe that worn-out corporate phrase, "People are our margin of difference."

But that cash register resumé becomes needless if your business has the right atmosphere — the kind that makes customers open up rather than shut down. It starts with genuinely friendly people, whose conversation with customers goes beyond "Have a nice day."

It comes down to looking for attitudes instead of aptitude. Herb Kelleher, the mastermind of Southwest Airlines, told *Fortune* magazine: "What we are looking for first and foremost is a sense of humor. We don't care that much about education and experience, because we can train people to do whatever they have to do. We hire attitudes."

Changes in latitude, changes in attitude

Bill Phifer
LEXINGTON, Kentucky

"We don't know who we are until we are in relationship with someone else or some idea, or some event. ... We're waves of potential, moving through space in our organizations. And where we meet up with another person or an event, or a thought, it evokes something, it brings forth some potential in us."

—Margaret Wheatley,
Leadership and the New Science

Bill Phifer's search for who he could be began with his abandonment of who he was.

Looking in from the outside, the New Rochelle, New York, native had the kind of career that sounds impressive. He traveled a seven-state territory in the Northeast for Gourmet Award, a division of Tree of Life, one of the nation's largest specialty foods companies. Being a director of sales put him in charge of 200 people and 1,500 retail accounts.

And no one could dispute that he had worked hard to get where he was. His 23-year career in distribution and merchandising had begun at the bottom, stocking shelves by day as he attended college at night.

Phifer had all the perks that we have come to associate with success, from a healthy paycheck to a well-worn set of luggage. But time spent on the job left little time for much of anything else, and Phifer's spirit and his attitude were flagging. He knew that within him was untapped potential just waiting for the right catalyst.

He'd always been in control of his life, driving it in a direction in which he felt confident. Suddenly, he felt the need to veer, to turn the wheel over to some other force, to fate perhaps.

"There came a point where I said, 'I need to make a change,'" says Phifer. "I decided I'm going to let my creative juices flow and take a different road."

Road leads to Lexington

That road led to Lexington and wound its way into two local small businesses, one a longstanding stalwart and the other a young upstart.

Lexington seemed a logical place to move, since other family members had relocated there. His sister, Virginia, had left a successful law practice in New York City to start an herb business in Lexington. "I could go over to her house at all hours and she would be in her greenhouse working. She thoroughly enjoys it," Phifer says.

One day, not long after his move, Phifer was out running errands. He stopped off to pick up some items at the Good Foods Co-op, the city's first health foods store, and struck up a conversation with an employee.

He mentioned that he had worked for Tree of Life. "The next thing I know, they had asked me if I was interested in helping them implement some operations systems and working with their purchasing department," Phifer says.

Through his work at the food co-op, he became friends with the store's manager, Anne Hopkins. Working together, they were able to increase business at the co-op by 40 percent in just two years.

"We make a very good team," says Phifer. "We don't necessarily agree on a lot of things, which makes us more effective because when we come to a final conclusion about something, we have really exercised that thought."

Seeing opportunity

There was one point the pair agreed upon. They had gone on a mission to check out some possible new competition: Cosmo's, a fine foods specialty store near the co-op. They immediately realized the two businesses targeted different audiences. But they also saw that the market had incredible potential.

"I looked at her, and she looked at me and I just said 'Wow! What an opportunity!'" Phifer says.

Cosmo's was definitely not a thriving operation at the time. Changes in management and ownership had left employees — and customers — feeling disoriented and disconnected. The store seemed to lack direction. It didn't know what it should be.

Phifer and Hopkins decided that what Cosmo's needed was their combined skills — Phifer's knowledge of purchasing, merchandising and management and Hopkins' strength in financial analysis and management. They made a proposal to the store's new owners to serve as management consultants. Their proposal was accepted.

"With our combined background, we certainly felt we could bring a lot to this party," he says.

When they came to Cosmo's in early 1998, the atmosphere was anything but a party. The store's first year in business hadn't been a good one, and employees were tired of frequent changes in direction and multiple management overhauls. They viewed their new managers as just part of the revolving door syndrome.

Phifer and Hopkins wisely chose to tread lightly. "We did not want to shock the system. We wanted to get a feel for the store and understand its culture before we started to move it in certain directions. We were background music for quite a while," Phifer says.

Opening the book

Little by little, they instituted changes. One of the most dramatic, and most beneficial, was the shift to open-book management, a concept that Phifer had seen work successfully at Tree of Life.

Companies that practice open-book management share with all employees the real numbers that determine the success or failure of the company's objectives and hold individuals responsible for their part in the company's performance. Employees, in turn, are given a financial stake in the success of the company.

With open-book management, Phifer says, "suddenly people take a real interest in how the store itself operates. The more that employees take ownership of this store, the more they get enthusiastic about what's taking place here.

"I really feel strongly that we should empower our staff and be able to educate them in how the business works. They are educating us with the expertise they have. This is a melting pot of talent."

Through open book, employees have begun to take charge of their jobs. "These people really take pride in what they do," Phifer says. "They have a passion for it. I wish customers could see the effort that goes into what comes out of our kitchen.

"We have a new pastry chef and she is so excited about it, she says, 'I'm going to bake cakes, I'm going to make muffins, I'm going to do this and that.' I say to her, 'Go crazy with it. Just have fun with this whole thing.' There are no restrictions when it comes to creative thinking."

Adding years to life

Although he is by no means taking it easy, his job shift has made Phifer a more relaxed and contented person. He has time to spend with his family, particularly his niece Justine, an aspiring ballerina and a basketball player.

"I have certainly added a few years on to my life," Phifer says. "People have noticed. I still talk to many of my friends in the Northeast and they say, 'My gosh, Bill! You're so calm!'

"The criterion I had for what I was going to do, career-wise, was that I have to have fun. I want to have fun at what I do."

By the same token, he wants those around him to enjoy their work, too. Judging from the feedback he's getting, many of them do. "I was very thrilled to hear an employee come back from vacation and say that for the first time they enjoyed coming back from vacation," he says. "When I get that kind of feedback, I realize things must be going in the right direction."

In the end, success in business, and in life, is not so much tied to what you do, but how you do it. Says Phifer:

"When I'm hiring people, I look for attitude. You could have the best qualifications in the world, but if you've got a lousy attitude, what's it worth? You can take someone who has no experience but who does have the right attitude, and big things can happen."

*"Be it ever so humble,
there's no place like home."*

— John Howard Payne

4

There's No Place Like Home

Ah, home. There's no place like it (click your heels together three times and repeat that, Dorothy). It's where the heart is, or so they say. We're inclined to believe them. For the two of us, "home" is a word that resonates with images: family ... friends ... satisfying home-cooked meals prepared with that special (non-caloric) ingredient called love ... memories of childhood and growing up and lessons learned, some of them painfully ... homecomings and holidays and hugs and kisses and laughter and tears. "Home" is such a wonderful word for poets and songwriters because its mere intonation can evoke vast worlds of emotion in those who hear it.

Home can mean many different things, depending on whom you ask. To some people it's a physical structure, whether that be a Philadelphia brownstone or a little cottage in the woods or a loft apartment or a sprawling old farmhouse or a high-rise penthouse or a doublewide trailer or an executive mansion or a suburban ranch or a tenement or a tent or a geodesic dome. To others it's a little larger: a street or a neighborhood or a town. Yet others view home as a state of mind: It could be wherever you are, or wherever you find yourself dreaming about when you dream, or wherever you feel most comfortable, most alive, most ... well, at home.

Home isn't a perfect place, but it's *your* place. Chances are that, spread across the time line of your life, you have had more than one home. There's the place where you grew up — where you formed your first impressions about life and people, about good and bad and indifferent. Where you took your first steps, both literally and in the more figurative sense of stepping out into the world with both eyes open and mind intent on discovering what makes it all tick. Where you formed your first impressions of who you are, where you came from, where you are going and what you are all about.

In *Wait Till Next Year: A Memoir* (1997: Simon & Schuster, New York), Doris Kearns Goodwin writes beautifully of her remembrances of her childhood home in Brooklyn:

> Unlike more affluent modern suburbs, whose fenced homes are encircled by large ornamental lawns, the houses on my block were clustered so close to one another that they functioned almost as a single home. We felt free to dash in to any house for a snack from the mother-in-residence, race through the side door in search of playmates except for my own house, where my mother's need for tranquillity was respected, making it not only the quietest but sometimes the loneliest house on the block. Since all the families were bringing up children at the same time, babysitters were rarely necessary, for we could usually stay at each other's houses. If one of the mothers was sick, there was always a neighbor or older sister to take her child to school or to the beach. Clothes, bikes, and roller skates were routinely handed down from the older children in one family

to the younger ones in another. For me, there was a special benefit in the clustered structure of our block. For the lives within these homes, the stories of each family, formed a body of common lore through which I could expand the compass of my own life.

Alice Taylor's recollection of her own childhood in rural Ireland differs significantly, but the picture she paints in *Quench The Lamp* (1991: St. Martin) is no less inviting:

> The entire household revolved around the fire which provided warmth, cooking facilities, and a social center ... the heart of every home and its warm glow was never extinguished while people still lived in the house.

In addition to the home where you grew up, there, too, have been your homes away from home. Workplaces where, as an adult, you spend approximately one-third (or more) of your life — and where, over time, people sometimes tend to become like family or neighbors. Taverns or parks or wherever you find yourself when you've got time to enjoy yourself and the people you enjoy being with.

There's the home you moved to when you left home for the first time, determined to make your mark on the world. And then, perhaps, there is the home that you made when you started your own new family.

The last of Thomas Wolfe's novels was titled *You Can't Go Home Again.* Maybe you can, maybe you can't. Perhaps, for whatever reason, you choose not to even try. Those of us who do try to go home again generally find that it has changed, sometimes significantly. Still, the connection remains. As Robert Fulghum writes in *All I Really Need To Know I Learned In Kindergarten* (1986, 1988: Ballantine Books, a division of Random House, Inc., New York):

> (T)here are places we all come from — deep-rooty — common places — that make us who we are. And we disdain them or treat them lightly at our peril. We turn our backs on them at the risk of self-contempt. There is a sense in which we need to go home again — and can go home again. Not to recover home, no. But to sanctify memory.

In today's frenetic world, maintaining connections with whatever it is that says "home" to us is quite possibly more important than it's ever been. However we define it, home is what keeps us grounded, what keeps us in touch with those aspects of life that are most important to us. In a very real sense, home IS who we are.

Home is also where, often, the important decisions are made. You might say the family that plans together stands together, as the following story illustrates:

It's never too late to learn

The Lombardi family
MILWAUKEE, Wisconsin

Jeff Lombardi is going to be a schoolteacher.

That in itself might not seem all that remarkable (though many people will gladly tell you that today's kids are disrespectful and difficult to teach, and that it's remarkable that *anyone* would want to be a teacher in these troubled times). But Jeff Lombardi is not your typical teacher-to-be. He's a 40-year-old father of four daughters — two sets of twins — who has spent the last 18 years as a machine tool technician. Now, at a point in his life where many people find themselves growing comfortable with their positions, he's going back to college to get his elementary teaching degree.

As Tom Peters might say of the situation, Lombardi is "reinventing himself." But why such a drastic career change ... why *now*?

It wasn't that he disliked being a technician. He had entered the field as an apprentice and earned an associate degree in engineering technology. His job with MasterLock afforded him the opportunity to solve problems, work with state-of-the-art equipment, and tackle the creative challenge of developing preventative maintenance programs to reduce "down time" for employees and the company. But it seems the thought of teaching had long been a dream for him:

"I have a strong desire to help kids learn, and I truly enjoy being around children. It brings me a great deal of joy when I see children use new skills they've acquired. There's a sense of accomplishment on their part as well as mine.

"Having children of my own helped me to realize how much joy there is in helping a child to learn something new. I believe it's a privilege to have the opportunity to work with children. It's both rewarding and fun."

The decision to change careers was not made hastily; it came only after much thoughtful consideration, research and discussion with the entire Lombardi family. An occupational aptitude test, which Jeff took a few years ago through the educational resource center at his workplace, helped pave the way: Its results indicated a strong aptitude for engineering and teaching.

"Since I had been in the engineering field for almost 20 years, I felt it was time for a change, and teaching was the first thing that came to mind," he says. "Deep down I've always wanted to teach, but my life journey kept leading me into engineering positions.

"I don't believe the two careers are mutually exclusive. The problem solving and team skills I've learned through engineering channels will serve me well in my teaching career."

Once the final decision was made, he quickly began the transition — a process that involved not only his return to school, but also a change of jobs. He's now a junior in Marquette University's four-year elementary education degree program (he was able to transfer many of the liberal-arts credits he had amassed while earning his earlier associate degree). Although he is taking a part-time load, his wife, Lorraine, notes with a laugh that it's "almost a full load." Meanwhile, he is still working full time, now as a manager in preventative maintenance at Pressed Steel Tank in Milwaukee. The leadership position, the Lombardis explain, is a "transitionary" one intended to help Jeff make the gradual change to elementary teaching.

"After discussing the idea with my family, I began the transition to position myself for the changeover," Jeff says. "It did not make sense to delay the process any longer since we agreed as a family to work together toward my goal of becoming a teacher."

The family weighs the issues

As a general rule, people do not enter the teaching profession for the money. In a perfect world, the best teachers would be compensated on a scale much more indicative of their worth, while certain spoiled, egotistical athletes would be struggling to pay the monthly mortgage. But it is, alas, far from a perfect world, and that fact only increases our need for more dedicated teachers.

When Jeff Lombardi becomes a teacher, one of his "rewards" for doing so will be a pay cut. Sacrifices have been and will continue to be made. Yet this is not a major issue with the Lombardi family.

The pay cut was not a high-priority factor in the decision-making process.

"We know that our family will manage," Jeff says. "We've been very blessed in our lives, and we have a strong faith that helps us to know that everything will work out in the end. Don't get me wrong, I know we'll be adjusting our lives, but we've earned a lot less earlier in our careers, and I don't remember those years as being so terribly difficult. It seems the more you make, the more you spend, so I guess the less we make, the less we'll spend.

"Besides, compensation takes on many forms beyond financial value. For me, it means the value placed on doing what I want to do and knowing that I'll have an opportunity to make a difference in a child's life.

"Also, Lorraine has this sixth sense when it comes to our personal finances. She works with our whole family to set value-centered financial goals. She helped us understand financial independence, so we readily accept the idea of cutting back to meet both individual and family goals. No one feels as if they're missing out, because everyone's goals count in our family.

"All right, there is that one issue about being the only family in the third grade without cable television, but we're beginning to accept it — albeit slowly."

The decision-making process was a methodical one that involved input from Lorraine as well as daughters Carolann and Angela, both 13; and Jennifer and Kristen, 9. The family compiled a list of pros and cons, then subdivided those according to priority. To wit:

Pros

Very high priority: Jeff's strong desire to teach.

High priority: (1) The decision fulfills Jeff's desire to once again pursue a formal education. (2) The change is the result of a proactive desire rather than a reactive response, because Jeff was not dissatisfied with his other career. (3) The Lombardis had "worked as a team" to achieve financial independence and stability, which allowed the family to consider the option without feeling financial strain.

Medium priority: The daytime schedule of a teacher will allow Jeff to coach more children's athletic programs.

Cons

High priority: The career change would involve four years of part-time school, which would take Jeff away from family activities.

Medium to low priority: Some friends, colleagues and family members did not support the idea, some voicing their opinion that Jeff was "insane" for even considering a career in teaching.

Low priority: A teaching position at the elementary level would result in reduced family income.

So how do the girls feel, now that the final decision has been made?

"I think it's awesome. My dad has the confidence to be a good teacher. He gives a lot of encouragement, and he likes to help," says Carolann. Then she adds the clincher: "He's an old guy, and he's lived a long time."

Her sisters are no less enthusiastic.

Angela: "I'm glad he's going to be a teacher because it's what he wants to do. He has the experience from having kids of his own. He likes to teach kids new things, and he makes the learning fun."

Jennifer: "I think it's good that my daddy's going to be a teacher because he can help other kids just like he helps me. He will be a good teacher because he'll be doing something that he really wants to do."

Kristen: "I think it's nice that my daddy's going to be a teacher because he'll make the children happy by helping them learn new things. He enjoys teaching and coaching children, and he'll take the time to work with the kids. And sometimes he can be very silly."

It runs in the family

Jeff will not be the only Lombardi with a career in education. Lorraine is assistant director of the Marquette University Division of Continuing Education. In that role, which includes the coordination of the school's live "Lessons in Leadership" programs, she has long espoused the value of lifelong learning.

"It's important to help kids realize that learning goes beyond 12 or 16 years of structured learning," Lorraine says. "The skills required today are changing so rapidly that we must actively pursue the many learning opportunities available. This is not as difficult as it sounds because we've come to recognize that learning takes place through many platforms, including self-taught learning, structured classes, peer training, team development, computerized training on the Internet and so much more.

"I encourage Jeff to have fun, create a nurturing environment for the kids and provide participative learning opportunities as often as possible. Also, I'm encouraging Jeff to keep an open mind because he has an opportunity to learn as much from his students as they learn from him."

Jeff credits his wife for being both informative and supportive during discussions about the career change. "Her insights into the value of lifelong learning helped me to realize that learning should be emphasized and encouraged throughout a person's life. If children learn the value of education, they will come to acknowledge learning as an ongoing process."

About those children
... and other challenges

Jeff, of course, is more than familiar with what seems to be the standard line on today's kids: disrespectful, difficult to teach, far more prone than their predecessors to violence and antisocial behavior. While he recognizes the sad truths behind such broad statements, he doesn't buy into the generalizations.

"Children are not as disrespectful as others would like us to believe," he says. "I've seen many an adult treat another adult rudely, and adults who treat children with no regard for kindness or courtesies. So why is it that we focus so much of our attention on the child-to-adult interaction? Shouldn't we view it as how one person treats another person? If only we, as adults, would examine our own behavior before we judge that of our children. In most cases, children are simply emulating what they see and hear every day.

"I believe that values are breaking down and that kids are getting the bad rap for it. It's a combination of values breaking down at home and in society as a whole. Fortunately for our children, the classroom provides an environment to teach and reinforce values through cooperative learning."

In the face of the increasingly frequent headlines about school shootings, gang violence, drugs and other problems troubling America's educational system, Jeff chooses to focus on the solutions. "The media concentrate too much on the negative and not on the positive," he says. "I'm not denying that there are children out there with serious problems. We need to find a way to help support the children who are eager to learn. We also need to increase the security at schools so children can learn in a safe environment. I believe that fear is one of the major learning deterrents in our school system today."

Plenty of challenges await Jeff in the Milwaukee Public Schools, including a growing number of dropouts. "So many kids today do not place a value on education," he says. "Try as we may, we can't always convince a child that learning opportunities are gifts. We need to establish a way for the kids who have fallen by the wayside to get back on track. The sooner the better because it's never too late to learn.

"We also need to encourage and empower teachers to utilize a multitude of teaching platforms. It's too basic to think one teaching style will work for all children.

"We also need to get the largest demographic — the baby boomers — back into our classrooms to provide the support needed to customize learning to meet the needs of the students."

Those are no small tasks, but Jeff Lombardi, with the support of his family, is up for the challenge. It's sure to be a learning experience for all.

Front-porch communications

"If the world had a front porch like we had back then," goes a recently popular country song, "we'd still have our problems, but we'd all be friends."

The front porch, as suggested earlier in our "Sidewalk" chapter, may serve as the "eyes" of the neighborhood — where people sit and watch out for their neighbors, monitoring people's comings and goings, keeping alert for any sign of suspicious activity or, in some cases, gathering fodder for gossip. But we'd suggest that the front porch might also serve as the neighborhood's "ears," its communication center.

It's an informal communication center, where people go to relax and unwind after a hard day. And it's a place where connections thrive! The front porch is a place where we can have meaningful conversations. Aided by the big swing, the handmade rocking chairs and perhaps a pitcher of lemonade or iced tea, we can let our guards down and be ourselves. We can speak of the things that really matter to us, with the people who really matter.

There's some risk involved, of course, when you're sitting on your front porch. The main risk is that you might have to interact with other people. You may feel snug and secure from the rest of the world when you're sitting in your den with the television on, but on your front porch you're closer to the action. You might make eye contact with a neighbor, who'll feel compelled to walk over and tell you about her family's recent vacation or his surgery. A pair of strangers might walk by and have the audacity to call out a cheerful hello. You're out in the open ... exposed, vulnerable.

Might as well brush up on the fine art of conversation!

The acclaimed interviewer Studs Terkel, author of such classics of oral history as *Working,* thrives on being a great conversationalist. Using only a tape recorder and his considerable listening skills, Terkel has managed to document — by book and radio — decades of *real* American life, as lived in the trenches. In his own words: "I've become celebrated for celebrating the uncelebrated people of the world, built myself a world reputation for giving voice to the voices of those we never hear."

What do these voices talk about? In a word, everything. Work. War. The Great Depression. Race. America. Jazz. Life and death. Hopes and dreams and frustrations. Everything indeed! Terkel's ability to find the extraordinary that lives inside ordinary people has earned him widespread acclaim, including a Pulitzer Prize for *"The Good War": An Oral History of World War II.*

"The way I look at it, it's like being a gold prospector. You find this precious metal in people when you least expect it," he tells Tony Parker, talking about his interview process, in Parker's book *Studs Terkel: A Life In Words* (1996: Henry Holt and Company, New York).

In that book, Parker, a skilled interviewer who might be described as "the British Studs Terkel," provides a revealing glimpse into his subject's mind, heart, soul and processes. He achieves this through Terkel-style conversations not only with the man himself, but also with his friends and colleagues, and through snippets of past Terkel interviews.

The late Mike Royko, a beloved Chicago columnist, praised Terkel's broad range of interests and knowledge, his aptitude for asking "the right questions," his willingness to let people speak, his obvious interest in what they have to say, and his ability to put the interviewee at ease. Terkel describes himself as naturally curious (he says he'd like "Curiosity never killed this cat" inscribed on his tombstone).

How has Terkel, who in *Working* described the majority of workers as "the walking wounded," been so successful in probing the American psyche, in uncovering such a wealth of simple, honest and eloquent truths? In a nutshell, he has succeeded through his skilled application of this bit of advice: "Don't be the examiner, be the interested enquirer."

When he's interviewing a person for his long-running daily radio talk show from Chicago, Terkel prefers the word "conversation" to the word "interview" because he doesn't want his guest to feel as if it is an interrogation. As he tells Parker in *A Life In Words*:

> Questions and answers, questions and answers. Well, I don't want it to be like that. I want it to be like a conversation, and I want it to be entertaining and I want it to be enjoyable. To me, to the guy I'm talking with, and to all that audience of eavesdroppers out there who're overhearing it. That's exactly the atmosphere I want to try and create, that they're eavesdropping. They're excluded from the conversation, but I don't want them to feel that, I want them to feel they could join in if they wanted to.

Unlike many hosts of radio or TV talk shows, Terkel also believes in doing his homework. For example, if he has an author as a guest, he prepares by reading the author's latest work, and at least looking at any others he has written. That's how "I pay him respect," he says. "You'd be surprised how many people don't do that elementary thing."

Terkel's technique for interviewing the "uncelebrated" is altogether different from his style on radio, where he generally talks to people with at least a nominal recognition factor. With the uncelebrated he is more experimental, more flexible, marked by sensitivity to the likelihood that the other person is nervous or scared, having never done this before. In these cases, Terkel says, he takes advantage of his own inability to operate his tape recorder, the main tool of his trade. This "ineptitude," he says, is "one of my biggest assets" because it makes the interview subject see the interviewer as human, and thus not be afraid. And when it comes to the actual interview process, Terkel has no doubts as to the key to success.

> The first thing I'd say to any interviewer is ... "Listen." It's the second thing I'd say too, and the third, and the fourth. "Listen ... listen ... listen ... listen." And if you do, people will talk. They'll *always* talk. Why? Because no one has ever listened to them before in all their lives. Perhaps they've not ever even listened to themselves.

And he tells why the entire process continues to fascinate him.

It's the uncertainty, the not knowing where you're going that's the best part of it. People aren't boring. Interviewing people is discovering people, and one of the biggest thrills you can get is discovering that somebody who sounds boring isn't boring at all.

The highest form of listening

Stephen Covey's approach to conversation might be considered similar to Terkel's. In his own way, he's prospecting for gold: understanding. He calls it "empathic communication," the principles of which make up Habit 5 in *The 7 Habits Of Highly Effective People*.

In our daily conversations with family, co-workers and friends, we often try to offer advice before we truly understand the problem, Covey says. In *7 Habits*, he writes: "If I were to summarize in one sentence the single most important principle I have learned in the field of interpersonal relations, it would be this: *Seek first to understand, then to be understood*. This principle is the key to effective personal communication."

There are actually five kinds of listening, Covey says. At the low end is ignoring, then pretending, selective listening, attentive listening and, finally, "the highest form of listening, *empathic*

listening ... listening with intent to *understand*."
He elaborates:

> Empathic (from *empathy*) listening gets inside
> another person's frame of reference. You
> look out through it, you see the world the
> way they see the world, you understand their
> paradigm, you understand how they feel.
>
> ... In empathic listening, you listen with
> your ears, but you also, and more importantly,
> listen with your eyes and with your heart.
> You listen for feeling, for meaning. You
> listen for behavior. You use your right
> brain as well as your left. You sense, you
> intuit, you feel.
>
> ... You're focused on receiving the deep
> communication of another human soul.

"The deep communication of another human soul" —
coming, quite possibly, from "the voices of those
we never hear." Put those two ideas together, and
you just might get someone like Cabell Brand. His
story follows.

Fighting poverty on the home front

Cabell Brand
SALEM, Virginia

Cabell Brand is living the American dream. And, in doing so, he is also helping give others less fortunate an opportunity to pursue their version of that dream.

Brand, who was born in 1923, has accomplished much in his three-quarters of a century on this earth. But he is far from finished. He is on a mission: a broad-based and ambitious mission of eliminating poverty, first in the Roanoke Valley, then around the world. You see, Cabell Brand detests poverty. He detests it so much that he has, in his career as a highly successful businessman, made so much money that he need never look poverty in the eye, not even from a distance. His business acumen has ensured him and his family all the perks of success: the lavish home, luxury automobiles, exotic vacations, art collections.

Yet he continues to look poverty in the eye, up close and personal, because it is his mission to eliminate it from the lives of other people. Throughout the Roanoke Valley, he has spearheaded efforts to feed the hungry, house the homeless, teach the uneducated, rehabilitate ex-offenders and addicts, protect the elderly, revitalize urban areas, bring cultural opportunities to deprived areas and much more. Total Action Against Poverty (TAP), the nonprofit community action agency that Brand established in 1965, has grown steadily into a powerful force for its region and a model for other such agencies nationwide.

Since starting one of the nation's first Head Start programs for poor children preparing to enter first grade, TAP has started more than 40 organizations that focus on its key demographic segments, all of whom have in some way been lacking in opportunities to better themselves.

Brand is, at this writing, in his 33rd year with TAP. Now chairman emeritus, he was the agency's president and chairman for 30 years — a national record among heads of communication action agencies. (The agency's board of directors, made up of local government representatives, members of other community organizations and agency constituents, elects its officers each year.) As a result of this long-running vote of confidence and his track record, he has gained visibility and credibility as a national anti-poverty spokesman.

"I'm a free-enterprise capitalist," Brand says. "I believe in the democratic system and in the free-enterprise economic system. But we have 14 percent of the people in this country who don't participate, and that's the poor people. The organizations I work with are trying to bring that 14 percent into the mainstream of society."

Brand, whom a 1985 profile in *The Roanoker* magazine described as "business conservative, social liberal," is an outspoken advocate of "Think Globally, Act Locally," which is one of his favorite quotations. He strongly supports federal funding for programs that help give local communities the power to solve their own problems. And, as evidenced by the makeup of the TAP board, he strongly believes in giving the downtrodden, those who are being served, a voice in *how* they will be served.

A mind of his own

Cabell Brand has long distinguished himself as a man who is committed to excellence — and to his own beliefs. Although he grew up in a socially conservative family, at an early age he began developing his own liberal agenda, inspired by such role models as Franklin Delano Roosevelt.

After being voted his high school's Most Outstanding Senior in 1940, he attended Virginia Military Institute. Although his college education was interrupted by World War II — he fought in the Army's 70th Infantry Division as an officer — he nevertheless graduated in 1947, first in his class in electrical engineering. He continued his government service after the war, working as an economic analyst in the U.S. intelligence office in Berlin during the Soviet blockade.

In 1949, however, "I decided I was better suited to business than being a bureaucrat," he says. He decided to take a job as vice president and sales manager of his father's small business, The Ortho-Vent Shoe Company. For nearly four decades, he steadily built the business, becoming president in 1962 and changing the company's name to The

Stuart McGuire Co., Inc. He took the company public in 1970, and in 1986 he sold it to the Home Shopping Network. By that time, The Stuart McGuire Co. was a multimillion-dollar direct-selling organization with 225,000 sales representatives and 12 mail-order companies. "Home Shopping Network primarily wanted our distribution center, which is now shipping 80,000 packages a day," Brand says.

In 1962, the same year Ortho-Vent became Stuart McGuire, Brand started another business venture, an advertising agency now known as The Packett Group. This agency, the largest advertising firm in the area, was for years a subsidiary of Stuart McGuire. But eventually, Brand says, "the employees wanted to branch out and not be limited to a few clients. I figured the price out, financed it and let them go on and do their own thing. It's a very successful agency, and I continue to work with them."

Brand's current company, Recovery Systems Inc., founded in 1986, performs national and international consulting on sustainable development of the environment and the economy.

Seizing the opportunity

The turning point in what would become an increasingly active career as a force for social change came in 1965. Under the new Economic Opportunity Act, federal money was available to local communities to fight the War on Poverty led by Sargent Shriver, director of the Peace Corps and the Office of Economic Opportunity. Brand's eyes were opened, and he decided to take action to get some federal money for his community.

First he took three months off from his business to do some serious research, which culminated in a speech on the War on Poverty before the Roanoke Valley Torch Club, an elite group of area business leaders. His speech was a rousing success, helping to generate interest.

Years later, Brand told interviewer Anne Colby: "Somebody had to do it. And I just happened to be there at the time and so seized the opportunity. That has been the way I have operated all my life. When you have an opportunity, do what you can with it." This conversation became a full chapter in the 1992 book by Colby and William Damon, *Some Do Care: Contemporary Lives Of Moral Commitment* (1992: The Free Press, a Division of Macmillan, Inc., New York).

Since then, Brand's passion for his calling has increased, as he's consistently seized opportunity after opportunity. Education, which Brand sees as the best long-range solution to poverty, is the cornerstone of TAP programs. But healthcare and a wide range of other support for school-age children and their families are also important elements — it's hard to concentrate on homework, after all, when some of the basic necessities of life are missing on the home front. Such initiatives as the Virginia Water Project, which has brought water to tens of thousands of Virginians who had no water on their property, have directly and indirectly helped spur economic development and other positive benefits like more poor children attending school.

Brand has also focused his effort to get young people involved in poverty and environmental issues through The Cabell Brand Center for International Poverty and Resource Studies, a research study and action center on the campus of Roanoke College's Elizabeth Campus.

'If you're a salesman, you're a salesman'

The same skills that Cabell Brand has put to such effective use as a businessman are in abundance in his anti-poverty work.

"I think if you're a salesman, you're a salesman," he says. "I've been fortunate to have developed some skills of salesmanship. You just try to put yourself into the shoes of the other person, think about that person's wants and needs and how you might help."

A willingness to take charge when others are reluctant has also served him well. Brand, whom a longtime colleague describes as "a salesman par excellence," has never hesitated to pick up the phone and call somebody — whether it be a potential customer or someone with money or support to lend to a start-up education program.

"People are generally scared to make appointments," Brand says, with amazement in his voice. "They'll ask me if I can set up a meeting with so-and-so for them. But I'm not afraid to go after somebody myself. I just get the person's phone number and call them. I've had a lot of luck on the phone, just talking to people directly. It's strange to me that so many people, especially in positions of responsibility, don't do that."

As for the passion he so deeply feels for his mission, and his ability to make other people feel that position, he says it's often just a matter of letting the results speak for themselves.

"I don't have any secrets about it," he says. "I wish more people had the passion and would work in the community. It's happening more and more. I give a lot of talks to young people, and I try to tell them what I've done and why. You can't create passion by lecturing to people — but you can show them the results and hope that will get them interested and involved."

Eventually, he hopes, that involvement spreads in ever wider circles. But it all begins at home, he says, offering his interpretation of "Think Globally, Act Locally":

"We do have one world, and it is a finite planet with a finite amount of water and a finite atmosphere. So you need to be aware of that as the population of the world increases, and then you see how those pressures affect you locally.

"The only way that I think you can do anything about those local problems is to start locally. But in doing it locally, if you've got the global perspective of what you're doing and why you're doing it, you'll be more effective locally."

5

If You're Living, You're Learning

If there's one image we love above almost any
other in describing optimum performance and energy,
it's *fluid intelligence*. You know the feeling?

It's not having the same software on every laptop,
or passing on gossip just as soon as you hear it.
What we're talking about is an open learning and
doing environment, where the freedom to produce
ideas is second only to the freedom to put them
into action. Like good neighborhood conversation,
this phenomenon is contagious.

When we're at our best, we're teaching, doing and
learning at the same time. This is at the heart of the
phrase "continuing education." It's not about
taking a course in basket weaving, or keeping up that
accreditation (though those are expressions of this
energy). It's a way of working, playing and being
that's a part of who we are at every age. From
babyhood to seniorhood, in your neighborhood or
Hollywood, we're learning from so many sources:
schools, mentors, parents, media, children, books,
animals, trees ... even direct experience.

When intelligence is fluid, it's first and foremost
non-rigid. There is an openness to possibility, a

willingness to share and to be changed. Think of the other aspects of water: It surrounds, it soothes, it keeps things afloat. Fluid intelligence does these things, too. It also circulates, filling all available space, flowing, ebbing, lapping at the edges of those things we think to be fixed and permanent.

Let's explore some different notions of education, notions that involve communities as tiny as a classroom, as big as the world. We might find that we're part of more learning organizations than we thought.

A concept close in name to fluid intelligence is emotional intelligence, first coined by Daniel Goleman in his book of the same name. The latest manifestation of this stream of thought (sorry, there goes that water imagery again) is Robert Cooper's *Executive EQ: Emotional Intelligence in Leadership & Organizations*, co-authored by Ayman Sawat (1996: Grosset/Putnam, New York).

Essentially, what Cooper and a host of leaders are saying is that you can have the best systems, structure and concepts in place, but if you don't have the heart and sensibility in the right place, the rest is for naught. Like Stephen Covey, Cooper turns to the inner person, the substance and fiber of that person's character, to find the keys to effectiveness in any setting. Some people might call a high EQ by other names: maturity, perspective, a humane brand of knowledge that transcends mere book learning or systematized sets of rules and regulations.

If we were going to express the gap between IQ and EQ in neighborhood terms, it might be the difference between the sterile, manicured lawn that you're not supposed to walk on and the backyard where people gather and say hello over the fence (if there is one). It's the difference between the rote lecture delivered by a graduate assistant with pre-drawn charts and the one-to-one consultation over a manuscript between a young writer and her mentor. Above all, emotional intelligence is about depth of understanding. Blend it with the fluidity we covet, and you have oceans of ideas to discover.

Emotional intelligence helps us discover the oceans of ideas within.

Allowing the day to change you

" I studied in a two-year program at Kellogg Community College in Michigan. It was actually an excellent school, and they were doing really innovative things. I had the best teachers there that I ever had anywhere. "

I started out as a music major but I switched over to English when I found out how many times I was going to have to perform. I didn't like that, so I switched to English and then I minored in French and music and secondary education. I was the "Snow Queen" there as well.

It was sort of like a Miss America thing. Since it was in the snow, we didn't have to do bathing suits! That was my first plane ride. I had to fly from Battle Creek to wherever Northern Michigan University is, in the upper peninsula. I'd never seen that much snow in my life. And we flew in this DC3 and landed four times in five hours, and we were picking up different people and stuff. So that was pretty scary, but even scarier was that I had to do evening gown and play the piano. I didn't win there, but I was Miss KCC Snow Queen.

I taught English, French, Spanish and journalism for nine years in ninth grade. I used to teach in a very rural area in North Carolina, where I was known as "Europe Lady." I would take my students to Europe in the summer. The first year, I had to literally go out and beat the bushes to get people to go because this was a very rural area and the people couldn't believe that anybody

would want to go to a foreign country and be
with all those foreigners.

So, I just had to go out and talk to the library
people and school groups and church groups. I
put in a lot of time and energy, not knowing
whether I would get enough kids to go with me
the first time or not.

When I came to work at the university, it was
like going out into the world. It was like
somebody releasing me from bondage, you know,
whoopee, I could do anything I wanted to do!
I could eat lunch with adults — that alone was
great! I could be outside if I wanted to. I
didn't have to have predictable days. I mean,
everything about it was just so fun.

Your day changes you every day. Every time you
interact with somebody, you either learn
something or you feel something or experience
something that makes you a different person.

I think back on the old days ... all my
classmates when I graduated from college went
into staid old companies because that was the
thing to do. You join a company and stay there
for life. Talk about the most boring thing you
can think of, that would certainly be it! Even
teaching can be a little bit that way, although
when you get a new class the game is different
— you have 30 little rascals who are all
different. But I think that if you get stuck
in a mindset about what you think you are,
then that's exactly what you are — stuck.

— *Bunny Holman*

From microchips to Micronesia

Joanne Everett
MAJURO, Marshall Islands

There's a broad tendency nowadays to speak glibly about the shrinking of the world. The patter goes that communications and transportation technology have brought us so far that distance is no longer an obstacle. Similarly, the spread of English usage and the rapid extinction rate of other languages and their dialects might tempt one to view the achievement of the "global village" as a *fait accompli*.

Not so fast, buckaroo. You might have to go farther than you used to in order to find what might be termed "frontiers," but they're out there on the actual, non-virtual planet, and there's a distinct sense that their very cushion of remoteness and distance is something to be respected. We're not talking about the latest vacation hideaway to be discovered by the masses (much to the chagrin of those first leisurely pioneers), we're talking about real neighborhoods that are just plain hard to reach.

Take the Marshall Islands. See if you can find them on the map.

(Go ahead, we'll wait ...)

Oh, all right. They are an archipelago located in the western Pacific about 2,500 miles southeast of Japan, one of the four main island groups that make up the area known as Micronesia. A former district of the Pacific Islands Trust Territory administered by the United States for the United Nations, the islands became independent and entered into a free association with the United States in 1986, only just recently being recognized as a sovereign nation, in 1991.

There are 33 major island units containing 1,136 individual islands formed exclusively of coral. Their range extends for 800 miles, but the total land area is only 68 square miles — a true water world. The islands are divided into parallel chains: the Ratak (sunrise) to the east and the Ralik (sunset) to the west. They were named for a British captain, John Marshall, who sighted them in 1788.

The Marshalls are a neighborhood of about 50,000 people. The Marshallese are Micronesian, a mixture of peoples who emigrated from southeast Asia long ago. Over the last couple hundred years, they have been variously administered, protected, governed, fortified and aided by the likes of Spain, Germany, Japan and the United States.

After World War I, Japan received a League of Nations mandate to govern German Micronesia. In violation of the mandate, Japan fortified the Marshalls, the Carolina Islands and the Marianas except for Guam. They all fell to U.S. forces during and after World War II. In 1947, the United States was given the authority to administer them as a strategic trust of the United Nations.

As evidence of their extreme remoteness, the most well-known thing about the Marshalls for most Americans is that the U.S. government used two atolls — Bikini and Enewetak — for nuclear explosion testing. The technology of defense made

the world a lot smaller for the Marshallese long
before modems came along. Since that time, we've
been trying to make amends with various educational
and infrastructure programs like the Peace Corps,
setting up what amounts to a welfare state.

As you might expect, it's hot and humid there.
Tropical fruits and vegetables, fish, poultry and
pigs are the staples of the diet. The chief commercial
product is copra (the dried and broken kernel of the
coconut). The capital and largest city is Majuro.

In that city you'll find an American woman named
Joanne Everett, a long-time Chicagoan and actress
turned teacher, born in Florida and raised in
South Carolina. At age 53, though, she embarked
on a completely different adventure, an individual
commitment to literacy education that took her to
the Marshalls on a Peace Corps mission in 1988.
After that initial experience, she taught English
as a Second Language in her native state of
Florida for a few years. Much of that challenge
was in instructing Haitian immigrants, many of
whom were illiterate in their native language. In
1997, she had the opportunity to serve as co-
chair of the English Department at the College of
the Marshall Islands community college in Majuro.
She leapt at the chance.

Many Korean-born and other Asian students come to
Majuro to study as their entryway into the Western
world. Some take courses in nearby Saipan.

Everett has a warm, well-spoken and dignified
presence, blending Southern gentility with big
city street smarts. In a phrase, she knows what's
what. Let her letter from Majuro (written on the

back of our query letter for lack of paper) speak for itself in describing the environment and human spirit of a far-flung place like the Marshall Islands:

How would I describe the spirit of the students I work with?

College is a "pass-time" for students here. They come because it is something to do with their day. If education points their way to the future, first they must have a concept of "future." They don't. They're products of a hunting and gathering society. Get up when the sun rises and pass the time until the sun goes down.

On the outer island, whence they came, they'd go fishing or swimming, build something, mend something, play a game or bwebwe nato — sit around and talk. Here in the capital city, where daily activities of this sort are crowded out by the confusion of the sheer numbers of people, they search for a place or purpose to sit. So, they come sit in the classrooms of the small community college.

Somebody told them going to school was a good thing to do, like the missionaries told them that going to church was a good thing to do. So, why not?

They come on a semi-regular basis, depending on if they get a better offer for the day's time. They may bring their class books, but often don't, finding it difficult to make even that connection between the printed page and why they're here.

The culture allows them to sit patiently for long periods of time. They watch the foreign white man (a teacher) go through a myriad of emotions in front of the class, mostly frustration that borders on anger. The teacher vainly attempts to get a response from them — it's against their culture to be singled out for an answer. They read the foreign words ippendrone (together) as a class, understanding few of the words. Abstract thinking is impossible. Connect the dots in history or experience, or in what they read? Why? To what purpose? "Fill in the blank" is a fun game and they shamelessly check with their neighbors to see if they wrote the same answer.

The Chair of the English department considers it progress if they learn just a little each semester. Remember, the concept that education will further their opportunities in the future is a difficult one for them to connect with.

So education here has no parallel with anything we know in the States. It is incumbent upon the teacher to define a realistic goal. The students are very smart. They just did not have the window of learning at what we consider the normal age of five or six years old. Most of the students are now in their twenties.

As in most Third World countries, they are "see-do" learners: "Let me show you how to mend this fishing net, let me show you how to carve a canoe." Anything on a printed page has little or no meaning. Besides, they are expected to go to college in a foreign language (English) which they do not know very well!

The students are very respectful of the teacher. They are gentle, loving, kind people who show no frustration with the learning process. They will bring in homework weeks late and wonder why it doesn't get counted ... so I count it. Why not?

When I was going to a conference in Seattle and would be off-island for a couple of weeks, they used the opportunity to throw me a party. I got to class and they announced there would be no class, and immediately took charge. They made speeches to me, sang songs, prayed — and then, one by one, brought me a handicraft gift and shook my hand. They had brought a lunch of fish and rice and we all ate together. It was the one day they seemed really comfortable in class — doing what came naturally.

So what is their spirit like? They have the spirit of total acceptance. They accept one another, they accept you, and they accept whatever you think you're doing for them, and whatever the day brings. Is this the mentality of the perfect welfare state (which they are, thanks to our BIG BOMB), or is it cultural?

Will our gift of Pell Grant-driven education bring them into the modern age? Doubtful. Can we learn anything from them? How about the concept of "one day at a time" that our 12-step programs preach so hard? In fact, isn't that realistic?

Though we've only existed for 222 years as a nation, it's hard for many Americans to understand the feeling of being "discovered" and "protected." (Actually, one subgroup of our country, Native Americans, will be glad to fill you in on what this feels like.) But the Marshallese have endured such imperialist assaults (couched in ever more creative terms) for hundreds of years, from Spain, Germany, Japan and the United States.

Imagine how much this contradicts the notion of empowerment, and how the national identity seeps into and out of each individual's behavior, desires and aspirations. Only as recently as the 1980s did the Marshalls sign a Compact of Free Association, whereby the United States provides security and defense while the Marshallese govern themselves in domestic and foreign affairs. Only now are the building blocks of infrastructure and education coming slowly into place, via people like Joanne Everett.

It provokes some questions to ask ourselves about the communities we move around in:

- At your workplace, do you feel like "it's a free country"?

- What are our educational goals? How do we balance instruction on how to live and on the cultures and histories of the world with course work geared toward eventual employability? Is it possible to blend these two strands of thought, so that liberal arts and concentrated talents coexist?

- How good are we at accepting views of life and of the world that are different from our own, and are likely to remain that way?

This last question is intriguing from the point of view of a learning organization. After all, as we interact more every day with folks who come from not just the next county, but perhaps the next continent, how well equipped are we to understand how they view the world?

Differences in priorities

The qualities that Everett observes in the Marshallese students can be found in other cultures too, especially in the Second and Third worlds. Pat and Jean Smith, a Habitat for Humanity volunteer couple from Lexington, found similar conditions, outlooks and frustrations in the elementary schools of Ghana.

"The kids wear school uniforms, but school itself is like a zoo," says Jean Smith. "Children don't necessarily sit in the schoolroom like they do here. If they want to leave, they just get up and walk out. There's children all over the place. How they ever teach them, I don't know."

But the difference in overall priorities isn't necessarily parallel to a different level of economic development. Look at Japan.

In discussing "Japanese Rhythms" in his book *A Lateral View: Essays On Culture and Style in Contemporary Japan* (1992: Stone Bridge Press, Berkeley, CA), longtime arts critic and Japanese resident Donald Richie considers a different notion of time:

> Cultures have their own rhythms: how they divide the days and the nights, when to go fast and when to go slow, in what manner to fragment time.
>
> Some of the differences are familiar. A well-known temporal gulf exists between the global north and south. The latter have, for example, their famous siesta — night again in the middle of the day....

"Another familiar gulf, this time a chasm, exists also between East and West, the Orient and the Occident. We speak of the slower pace, calling it leisurely if we like it, indolent if we do not. ...

"These various temporal differences are well known. Not so familiar are those cultures which blend the differences and bridge the gulfs. Among these, the most spectacular is Japan. Here the rhythms of the West have been rigorously applied and yet, under these, the old pulse of Asia is still strongly felt."

Richie goes on to describe how we in the West view punctuality as a good thing, while in Japan and the rest of Asia, it is not as high a priority. Indeed, the very borders between work and social life are blurred more in Japan than anywhere else in the world (something we're just now undergoing in the States). Social talk and events take place throughout the work day, and work teams go out together almost every night to dine and imbibe and bond as whole people, not just specialized workers. Richie writes:

> Time is not moral in Asia; it cannot be used as a weapon. (Do you realize that you have kept me waiting for 15 minutes?) And it cannot really be used to indicate virtue (hard-working, efficient) or vice (lax, late for appointments).

> It is rather a seamless entity, an element like the air in which we live. To live naturally with time, says Asia, is to pay no attention to it. And Japan, despite its modernization, still subscribes to this ancient tradition. Dig down through company minutes and office hours and there, firm, eternal, is time itself.

The endless graduation

It is gaps, chasms and gulfs like these that lifelong learning is constantly bridging. If such differences, however slight or seemingly inconsequential, exist between such similarly modern countries as the United States and Japan, what then can we know of the rhythms of China? As American companies rush to locate there and establish a presence in what so many promise is an unprecedented economic boom, how much attention are they paying to the human potential there? What kind of respect are we giving to traditions that existed long before some of our traditions ever got started?

One thing we need to do is learn history. Often this step is avoided, as the arrogance of our fast-paced life insists that it's creating its own history anyway, blitzing the past with an array of technology and genuine know-how that's beyond compare. History stands up. It needn't limit us, but, like any background or foundation, we'd better have it in place before proceeding.

Another way we can learn is to actually go there. Go to the rain forests of Ecuador; visit the seething metropolis of Hong Kong; experience an African safari; see the actual lives of rural Appalachia, the former Soviet republics or Mexico. Then report back. It's entirely possible that what we see, hear, taste, touch and ponder will be a bit different from all the data-rich Internet pages put together.

If we can't afford all that globetrotting, maybe we can afford to visit the next town or state. Maybe we can even go over to that industrial park or neighboring office building, just to see what's going on over there. Untold worlds are transpiring right under our noses.

What all this learning can do for us is open up vistas, create opportunities for connecting. In the case of classroom education in the Marshall Islands, what may appear to be laziness is really a different way of being in the world, an almost existential world view that is hard for us to grasp. But we can try, and in doing so, become a little more well-rounded and understanding, while at the same time growing and benefiting from another's justifiable point of view. It is evident that this has happened with Joanne Everett. As the cigar store owner in *Smoke* reminded us, "The earth revolves around the sun, and every day the light from the sun hits the earth at a different angle."

The corollary to that thought? Every point on that earth receives the sun at a different angle at the same moment. Every point of view on that planet is different, and they all count.

6

Continuing Education ...

Continued

In our WYNCOM neighborhood, we like to say that school is never out. Today's world of accelerating change, rising complexity and increasing competition means that continuing education is the rule, not the exception. Gone are the days when people lived their lives in three distinctly separate phases:

1. Go to school for 12 to 16 years and graduate with a certain amount of knowledge.

2. Go to work and use your school knowledge to advance as far and as fast as you can, in the process earning as much as you can and trying to store away a financial nest egg.

3. Finally reach your ultimate goal: retirement, a period in which you desperately seek to make up for all the years you wasted in school and at work.

These days, the average person is far less likely than in past years to spend an entire career in the service of one company. Instead, many of us can expect to make at least four career changes in our lives. Some of these changes may be by our own choice; others might be due to mergers, downsizings or other business closings. To be successful, we should view our personal and professional development as a never-ending process.

Whatever our individual roles in the neighborhood, we should seek to maximize our potential by continually increasing our mental assets. When we become — and remain — lifelong learners, we can keep our knowledge and skills current with the growing demands of today's marketplace.

Developmental opportunities for the lifelong learner include activities to strengthen our skills of analysis and interpretation, interpersonal relations, communication, motivation, imagination, cooperation and leadership. They include:

• College courses or seminars

• Constant reading on a variety of topics, from a variety of fields

• Vocabulary building

• Professional or trade associations

• Community organizations

Just remember that whether we achieve our goals of lifelong learning through formal or informal means is not as important as the fact that our education is always continuing.

When East meets West

"The Japanese spouse program I directed at Transylvania University was probably the most rewarding thing I've done in my life. Setting up the program, going to Japan ... it was fun, and it was very enlightening. All I knew about Japanese people was from World War II movies. That opportunity fell in my lap, and I was fortunate to have the support of the university to go for it.

The families coming here from Japan had never been anywhere but Japan, which is a very homogeneous country. They were coming to the United States and leaving behind their entire family support system, which is very strong. Women were having to do everything for the children alone, not knowing the language, not being able to drive a car, not knowing the customs. The husbands got a lot of that education from their companies, but the women didn't. So when we set up our program, Toyota and a lot of the other companies were thrilled out of their minds because we kind of took the burden off of them. They told the families, "When you get there, call this number and Bunny-san will be there!"

One of the reasons I wanted to go to Japan was that I didn't know how they lived. You can't really know until you see it. I wanted to know so that I could prepare them. We got them Americanized. They loved it. They loved the freedom they had, the bright-colored clothes they got to wear. They loved not being around their mothers-in-law all the time! They missed their families, but they got to drive cars here, had to. And then they were going back, to the way it was, and a lot of them had a lot of trouble with that. That would be a great study to follow those people back.

We took them to the grocery store, worked with them on the driver's test, went to school functions, took them to the doctor. A lot of them had babies over here, so we took them to the hospital — having babies here is different than having babies there. The most basic things are different — they had to learn how to cut grass. Most of them don't have houses, but apartments, back in Japan.

They don't have crime there like we do, either. That was the bad thing we had to teach them. It was very hard. When I went to their country, I felt safe 24 hours a day — didn't lock the door, could walk out on the street in Tokyo any time of the day or night and felt totally safe. It's amazing the feeling you get.

Here, we have to tell them you can't drive down this street at certain times. You want to lock your car door, your house door. It was such a foreign concept to them, in every sense of the word. I felt as an American that we should be ashamed of ourselves, that we don't have a culture like they have. If you commit a crime over there, you not only bring shame and dishonor upon yourself, but upon all the family members that have died before you. Even the Japanese mafia doesn't mess with the person on the street. It's just a really different thing.

We had family members get ripped off on cab fares in Washington, D.C. and New York. It's just not done over there. So we had to teach them about life in America. "This is what's going to happen to you. They're not going to like you because you have these kinds of eyes." It was an awful thing, but we had to teach them that.

I would take them to the open houses and make sure that they got into it. They could stay home, and some of them did — they were just afraid. The majority of them had guts, though — boy, did they ever!

I worked with one lady, the wife of a banker, and she had children about the same age as mine. She was learning how to drive, and she didn't want a Japanese car. She wanted a black Trans Am with gold flames down the side! She would drive around her neighborhood. She loved Whoppers, too — she could eat two at a time.

There are a lot more programs like that now than there were when we were starting out. That's another way the colleges are reaching out to the community. It's something those institutions don't have to do, because those people most likely won't ever be college students. They'll either go back to Japan, or they already have an education. They don't need a degree, just help with the language and with social skills.

Ours was a good program that helped them assimilate into the neighborhoods they moved into, and the neighborhoods in return welcomed them, because at the time Lexington was a pretty homogeneous place too.

Toyota was helpful in getting our program started. We met out there sometimes. They helped send me to Japan. The enlightened companies, if they are strong enough financially, will have something like this. They have a kind of "incoming relations" person who helps them get their utilities turned on and stuff like that. I had a whole lot of help. People came out of the woodwork to get involved — it was wonderful, and we didn't have any money.

The program is still going on. It's really nice to have a legacy like that.

— *Bunny Holman*

Finding the answers in Wichita

Chris Cherches
WICHITA, Kansas

In the center of the center of the country,
Wichita, Kansas, city manager Chris Cherches knows
what it's like to leave a legacy. Over his dozens of
years in government and city management, he has had
the opportunity to learn from the pockets of experience
that dot our rich landscape. He has also taught
his share of lessons in those places, gaining as
much from the giving as from the receiving.

"I charted my course in life to go to different types
of communities," says Cherches. After growing up in
Columbia, Missouri, and gaining his undergraduate
degree from the University of Missouri there in
town, he embarked on a many-faceted journey that
has brought him and his colleagues countless
rewards and forged untold connections between
people, sectors and whole communities.

"I'm one of the few city managers today who got a
master's in Public Administration specializing
in City Management. Only two universities in the
country offered it then: Fales in Pittsburgh and
the University of Kansas, which I attended." (Lest
you Big 12 fans wonder where his allegiances lie,
Cherches is a Mizzou Tiger all the way.)

"You spent one year on campus, one as an intern,
and there were only 10 students a year in the
program," he says. "I interned in Glencoe, Illinois,
which was the second wealthiest community in the
country at the time, then went to a small Kansas
community called Holton as city manager.

"That was where I really started to get the real experience. It's like soloing in an airplane — on that first solo flight, with no instructor, it's a scary, eerie feeling. The plane handles totally differently. You think you have all the answers, but then you look around and have a hard time finding them.

"Mexico, Missouri, was next. Then Gladstone, Missouri, which was a new community at the time. We were putting in water, sewers and parks from scratch. Then I went to St. Louis Park, Minnesota, outside Minneapolis. The challenge there was to rebuild an older community.

"A headhunter shortly after encouraged me to go to Great Falls, Montana: It was lovely country, but being city manager was a real challenge. Then it was on to Reno, Nevada. After five years in Reno, I finally found my home in Wichita in 1986. It's my seventh city.

"As you look at these communities, they go from a smaller city and move forward to larger populations, budgets and challenges. They include rapidly growing suburbs to older revitalization challenges in metropolitan areas, then to a community that has 10 to 12 million tourists to the largest city in Kansas. Each city was a step forward in my profession. Each had unique challenges, all with a variety of public services and programs. Each one has been different, with different challenges, and I left a lot of my life in each one of them."

Whew! It tires you out just reading about it. In the course of almost 40 years in municipal government (and we do mean "course"), Cherches has successfully pursued his goal of living in a variety of places, learning and finding satisfaction from each one of them. As he puts it, "I got my master's at KU in 1959, but every day I get a refresher on my certificate!

"During my tenure in city management, I have hired and mentored more than 34 interns, instructed at both the graduate and undergraduate university levels and served as instructor for ICMA (International City/County Management) courses. I have written or co-authored a number of articles on local government's role in groundwater cleanup and community education. Two years ago I had the opportunity to participate in city management with local government in New Zealand.

"Just recently, I went to KU to conduct a public administration class. It was the 50th anniversary of the University of Kansas School of Management. I presented a paper on the future of city management, the new roles we have to play.

"It's good to get my batteries recharged, figure out all over again why I chose this business in the first place."

Cherches does more than sharpen his own saw, though. His accumulated knowledge and experience, combined with an openness to opportunity, have lent a sharpness to the communities he's served as well.

"We started doing this loaned executive program in Reno," he explains. "We needed someone to evaluate the city's fleet maintenance program, so I called the local utility company and asked their fleet manager to come in and tell us what we were doing wrong.

"It was so successful, I've used it constantly and extensively: stormwater drainage and financing, for instance. It was a controversial issue, but because of local involvement the initiative was a lot easier to sell to the community. Having that business name associated with the project dissipates opposition. It's proved to be an effective way to insert private sector thinking into public sector management."

Over the past 20 years, Wichita has been a center for entrepreneurial activity as well as locating large firms. Companies such as Coleman and Koch Industries have a strong presence, as do several major aviation concerns. McConnell Air Force Base is also nearby, and many career military people choose Wichita as a place to retire. This range of career and professional activity gives people like Chris Cherches a ready-made pool of resources and experience.

"Wichita is very cosmopolitan," he says. "There are so many large companies as well as entrepreneurial ventures that bring in various diverse ideas and lifestyles.

"I am a strong proponent of professional development in local government. We have another program called Leadership 2000 that sends young executives into community development. They bring us a fresh perspective on goals and strategies. Because of the large companies, this city is blessed with the ability to be loaned executives — instead of hiring consultants. They come into schools and city government. They serve as facilitators and developers.

"I'm constantly amazed that people don't take more advantage of the talent in their own cities — right in their own backyards."

Backyard University

It's true. Take a look at the flood of consultants pouring into every industry, every community issue. Of course, the initial impetus behind their success is a quest for objectivity in a situation, but there's a point when you have to say "Hey, let's give our local people some credit." Bringing in outside folks is just as politically risky as employing the services of the people already located in the community — perhaps even more so, given the outsider's relatively greater freedom to scram when the going gets tough.

Industry, governments and universities are starting to realize how fruitful their own backyards can be. They're forming partnerships to bolster local economic vitality, research and development, and growth strategies simultaneously — with the happy fringe benefits of stronger relationships and fewer obstacles between the ivy walls, the council chamber and the factory floor. Alfred North Whitehead once said, "The secondhandedness of the learned world is the key to its mediocrity." A harsh assessment of academics, to be sure. But his point will always be well taken: Firsthand, experiential learning, out beyond the towers and barricades we've hidden ourselves behind, is the surest way to attain optimum performance and ceaseless innovation.

We have to mix it up a bit, get our hands dirty and our eyes opened, make decisions right and wrong. Only by going with the flow of action can we realize the worth of all those lessons.

Breathing life into
those hallowed halls

" The tuition-driven university is probably not able to stay alive economically these days, so it's " finding other ways to be economically viable. That's why our concept at WYNCOM has worked so well with colleges and universities, because the arm of the institution that we work with is self-supporting most of the time, and often contributes to the general fund as well. So it's supposed to run like a business, but there are a lot of constraints, starting with being nonprofit.

Almost all schools now have a center for leadership to some degree. Some, like James Madison, take their programs nationwide. Some universities have realized that an education doesn't stop at age 21, so they're going after the lifelong learning concept, which I think is a very real thing. People are taking courses not only for professional development but also for fun and personal growth. There are a lot of people upgrading their personal and professional skills.

Universities are trying to make connections. They're opening up their facilities to community groups, either for a low fee or free, in order to keep those buildings occupied. There are children's programs in the summer, elderhostels. Instead of gates around the campus, with the understanding that "only those between 18 and 22 need apply," now, as one of my community

education buddies says, the university has to be from "the womb to the tomb." If the university is forward-thinking at all, they'll have it from the womb to the tomb, starting with prenatal classes!

— *Bunny Holman*

Learning to work, working to learn

In their captivating book *Organizing Genius: The Secrets of Creative Collaboration* (1997: Addison-Wesley, Reading, MA), Warren Bennis and Patricia Ward Biederman describe one of their "Great Groups" that may have helped to create the notion of institution-sponsored lifelong learning: Black Mountain College in the hills of North Carolina. Perhaps no other post-secondary institution has ever had such a far-ranging and deep effect on the arts in this country. As the authors write:

> Throughout its twenty-three years, Black Mountain was both college and community, a place that drew extraordinary people and brought them into relentless, sometimes bruising contact with each other, far from the distracting options of urban life. It was, as Martin Duberman writes, "an occasional loony bin, a rest camp, a pressure cooker, a refuge, and a welfare agency," but, above all, it was a place where people, whether they were officially faculty or students, learned life-changing lessons from each other.

Black Mountain was host to such diverse artists as writers Charles Olson, Fielding Dawson and Jonathan Williams; artists Josef Albers, Willem de Kooning, Robert Rauschenberg and Franz Kline; dancers Katherine Litz and Merce Cunningham; musician and composer John Cage; and philosopher Buckminster Fuller.

College founder John Andrew Rice was a friend of seminal educator John Dewey. Bennis and Biederman write:

Like Dewey, Rice had a holistic, some would say anti-intellectual, view of education as a process of personal growth. For Rice, the arts and personal evolution were as important as ideas. As he wrote in Harper's in 1937 in a debate with conservative educator Robert Maynard Hutchins, "To know is not enough." (Poet-photographer Jonathan Williams, who was at Black Mountain in the '50s and still lives nearby in Highlands, writes in much the same vein, "Never take know for an answer.")

In many ways, Black Mountain was one long, unending conversation. Discourse and debate were the operative means of learning and experimentation outside of actually making art. Like many such meetings, the talk often wandered far off course, but that was one of the methods of discovery and connection that worked so well for its faculty and students, and affected those artists' ways of living and working for years to come.

What they found was not only that the various artistic disciplines were profoundly connected, but that art and life were equally woven together, driven by such forces as perception, love, philosophy and the limits of the material world.

Forging alliances

It might seem a long way from the monastic atmosphere of Black Mountain to the sprawling, multi-faceted campuses of today. But, except among the rigorously entrenched academics, there is still that impetus to connect. This dynamic has not only inspired groundbreaking interdisciplinary work, but has brought the educational and business worlds into closer contact.

Oh, we're sorry, did we say something wrong? Are those warning sirens going off in the background?

Many people look askance at relationships between industry and commerce and the world of higher education. But those relationships have been around for a long time, often with other names, notably "endowment." While skeptics rightfully question every potential compromise, the overall effect of such ties has been to turn the workplace into a place of learning — a result much more in evidence than the much-feared company-run college research facility. In fact, have you noticed how many companies now call their facilities and grounds "campuses"?

Workplace learning enhances both sides.

The most dramatic recent example of such a partnership is unfolding as this book is being written. United Parcel Service has entered into an unprecedented partnership with the higher education institutions of Louisville, Kentucky, as the shipping magnate prepares to construct Hub 2000 in that city. In a tremendously innovative step, UPS has agreed to construct classrooms and dormitories and arrange unique class times for students who can work their crucial overnight shifts. The students realize a huge savings in pursuing their educations (with no strings attached) and the shipping company gets the flexible, capable workforce it needs in this 24-hour, nonstop economy.

A recent report from the National Employer Leadership Council revealed that internship and school-to-work programs benefit company bottom as students' job horizons. Their survey showed a return-on-investment of anywhere from 39 cents to $5 per dollar invested in such programs.

Companies like McDonald's, Eastman Kodak, AutoDesk and Schwab have had considerable success with bringing students in as interns. AutoDesk's Bob Perlman called it a great investment and an opportunity to practice good corporate citizenship. His company saw a $2.32 ROI.

While the students are exposed to the realities of the workaday world and taught multiple job skills, the firms realize some savings from the occasional subbing in of a $7-an-hour intern for a $25-an-hour engineer.

But not all school-to-work programs work out as planned. BellSouth realized it needed to hire 25,000 workers by the year 2010 in order to keep up with growth, so it initiated a program. But it found that high school students just didn't have enough skills

School-to-work: training tomorrow's workforce

at the outset to turn the corner on a positive ROI. However, the company still didn't consider the attempt a failure. It was a learning process, and an overture to the community that did not go unnoticed.

Materials separation, personal integration

American Saw & Manufacturing Company
SPRINGFIELD, Massachusetts

Perhaps the best known of Stephen Covey's 7 Habits is the one oriented toward self-renewal: Sharpening the Saw. Covey describes how this habit, carried out on physical, social, mental and spiritual planes, encompasses all the rest of the habits, for it is the source of a constantly regenerated vitality.

In addressing the necessary whetstones for that mental saw, he writes:

> Education — continuing education, continually honing and expanding the mind — is vital mental renewal. Sometimes that involves the external discipline of the classroom or systematized study programs; more often it does not. Proactive people can figure out many, many ways to educate themselves.

> It is extremely valuable to train the mind to stand apart and examine its own program. That, to me, is the definition of a liberal education — the ability to examine the programs of life against larger questions and purposes and other paradigms. Training, without such education, narrows and closes the mind so that the assumptions underlying the training are never examined.

In Springfield, Massachusetts, there's a company that perhaps exemplifies this habit better than any other. It's called American Saw & Manufacturing, and in ways both literal and metaphorical, it knows the value of lifelong education and keeping a sharp edge.

American Saw, an international company, is in the business of manufacturing saw blades and related hand tools for separating materials, and providing information and services directly related to those products. Its market is professional users of saw blades.

But since the company's inception in 1915, its leaders have always seen the essence of their business among the people they serve and employ, the communities that sustain them and which they sustain in turn.

Chairman of the Board and company CEO John H. Davis puts it this way: "A company cannot be successful for the long term if it does not give back to the community in which it is situated. A part of any business is to develop and nurture the resources surrounding it."

American Saw & Manufacturing Company began with 10 employees making hacksaw blades under the trade name Lenox. The company now employs more than 650 people, and markets tool and band sawing products in 70 different countries.

The firm has been privately owned and operated by the Davis family for several generations. Over the years, the family has demonstrated an unshakable commitment to excellence. That focus

"People make the company. Receiving the first ISO Certification in the United States in our industry is a classic example of Team Lenox effort."

— *John Davis, Chairman of the Board and Chief Executive Officer*
(pictured right)

"Our Corporate Principles help guide us in every decision we make. Whether we're talking quality or safety or strategy, the Corporate Principles keep us all on target."

— *Stephen Davis, President and Chief Operating Officer* (pictured left)

on quality began many years ago and continues to
be the unifying force throughout every process
in the company. In 1993, American Saw achieved
ISO 9002 Certification, and continues to pursue
numerous internal and external paths toward
community involvement and personal improvement.
Organizational Development Specialist Cleveland
Burton's prime business is sharpening the saw,
whether with individual employees, departments
or outreach programs like school-to-work. Like
the company's executives, like everyone who works
there, his goal is long-term development of people.

"This city is a home to creativity, innovation
and invention," says Burton, a Springfield native.
"It's the birthplace of Winchester and Smith &
Wesson, from Springfield Arms. It's the home of
Indian motorcycles. Springfield made small
biplanes, too. One of the first car manufacturing
plants was here. As the country moved away from
that type of manufacturing, generations of people
didn't stay in touch with the skills and crafts
that those industries needed. So right now there's
a shortage of skilled labor."

Today the businesses in the area are collaborating
with educators to train people in the skills and
competencies needed. It's project-based learning,
for students K-12, in practical applications of
what they're learning in school. It's also a fun
and creative venture.

"This school-to-work effort is a prime opportunity
for Springfield as we get ready for the next
century," says Burton. "We're getting people
together from all sectors — we have to realize
we're all stakeholders. There are more resources

than ever now, but it's not about just money and grants anymore; it's about people: in-kind services, education, measuring the results of investment."

One of American Saw's operative values is a commitment to community involvement. The company calls its community its third "division." Team Lenox members build relationships in education, the fine arts, health, the environment and small business, all in the interest of producing "life signs" as well as dollar signs.

"I chair the school-to-work committee for the county," Burton says. "The kids learn job functions, and also how departments fit into the overall business — how manufacturing needs finance, sales and marketing, etc., to be successful.

"The employees are excited about showing kids what they do. They see the children's perspective, what they know. They get to see the kids' education level, and it creates a learning environment for both parties. Some of our supervisors go out for the educator-for-a-day program and switch places with teachers.

"Our program analyzes how students handle initiation of activity, proactive behavior, health and safety, and responsibility for career and life choices. The goal is to be in position to make informed decisions about their future.

"As the students progress, tangible things are measured: They learn geometry, then learn practical application in saw blade teeth design — how it's applied to the actual world."

But Team Lenox knows that technical knowledge is not the core of its success.

"People training is what resonates the most," Burton explains. "What can you invest in that will make people better at what they do? All training departments need to keep this in mind: 80 percent of any job is dealing with people, whether you're a machine operator or a supervisor. Self-directed people have the core competencies to fit into any department. Personal development and growth is the best way.

"As industry is impacted by technology, our work plan needs to measure 'soft' or people qualities as well: punctuality, neatness, scheduling, working in a team-based environment. We need to learn to listen, accept what others are saying even if we don't agree, understand the value of measurement, and tweak information to meet the needs of a constantly changing environment."

A pretty tall order. But one that Burton and his community (both in and outside of American Saw) seem more than ready to handle.

"This is a very friendly, people-oriented place," Burton says about American Saw. "The owners stay in very close touch with the people who work here and lead by example. We want a long-term relationship with each employee. We appreciate them. The latest survey says that a person will have six to seven careers in a lifetime. Our goal is to have them all right here at American Saw and Manufacturing. Currently, we're adding more structure to it. We give them an understanding of business as a whole. We train in project management, stress and conflict management, presentation skills ... trying to develop a whole toolbox of skills."

To that end, Burton finds that people's minds need to be as flexible and open to possibility as the ever-changing machinery of their trade.

"We challenge people who want to get their foot in the door: What will you do with the rest of your body?" he says. "I was talking to a young lady in the shipping department the other day, asking her, 'What do you want to do five to 10 years from now?' She said something like 'I just pick and pack.'"

"We encourage people to continue their educations, maybe pick up a foreign language. Two years from now, your job may have changed dramatically.

"What I encouraged her to do is open up her perspective. 'This isn't shipping, this is distribution. This is a growing company; there's a warehouse in Singapore. Don't allow yourself to think narrowly.'

"The machine operators of today will be the symbolic analysts of tomorrow, monitoring processes, improving our products. This place is inviting — people can be themselves. There is room to grow, room for new ideas."

Burton himself began as a machine operator in 1973 just out of high school, thrilled to be a part of the company. He went back to school and earned a degree in psychology. At that time, the manufacturer was beginning a team development approach, and the synergy was evident. He became the coordinator for team efforts, consensus building and administration of the TQM system. Now he continues to develop people, which includes ever more emphasis on recruitment as available labor becomes a nationwide issue at the turn of the century.

Indeed, the future is now for manufacturers like American Saw. Which is why its "inreach" is as crucial as its outreach.

"We offer an extensive orientation period of three months," Burton says. "Each new employee is assigned a mentor — after all, this is a 527,000-square-foot facility, and the first things you need are help finding the ladies room, the lockers and the parking lot."

"Mentors guide the new employees through the process of learning internal customers, both upstream and downstream of your particular job. Beginning at our learning center, they learn our focus on personal development and safety. They learn about benefits, about our culture and sense of community. They'll visit a customer to see how products are used in the industry."

Among recent in-house innovations have been new methods for painting and printing the famous Lenox saw blades, developed through collaboration among engineers, designers and operators. One of the ideas was a basic tweaking of a design seen in an engineering trade magazine. The company also recently developed a product for efficiently cutting lottery tickets.

The company's stated Business Purpose refers to "products and related services for materials separation." It doesn't say "hacksaw blades" or "bandsaw lubricants." By allowing their mission to be broadly defined, the company's leaders and team members are limited only by their imaginations and their collaborative energy.

"There are big changes happening in a lot of areas of our industry," says Burton. "We're looking at new ways to think, ways to combine the skills and talents of our design, engineering and tool groups. Our research and development division is looking at these new super alloys, how they might be used in future products. They're like the materials used on the space shuttle — how do you cut that? The materials are getting tougher and harder, so we need a new wave of engineering and design to solve these problems. There's a lot of work to do in dealing with things like friction and aerodynamics.

"We're taking aerospace technology to other areas of the business, too. Things aren't as narrow as they used to be."

The very first plank of American Saw's Value Statement is "People Make the Company." The firm's devotion to such a primary value will be the lifeblood of its future. As John H. Davis has said, "American Saw & Manufacturing Company will become whatever our people want it to be."

That is one smooth saw.

Open-ended

"I know of no safe repository for the ultimate powers of society but the people themselves; and if we think them not enlightened enough to exercise their control with a wholesome discretion, the remedy is not to take it from them, but to increase their discretion by education."

— Thomas Jefferson

"Perfect freedom is as necessary to the health and vigor of commerce as it is to the health and vigor of citizenship."

— Patrick Henry

No slouches, the two statesmen and revolutionaries quoted above. Their erudition was matched only by their fervor: in pursuing ideas, in pursuing meaningful lives and in helping to found a whole new country.

Today, one might be tempted to view educational imperatives sponsored by industry with a jaded eye. After all, what's to prevent them from merely sponsoring the "truth as they see it," with no objectivity or criticism?

But the best education — whether it's training modules, mentoring with your neighbor's nephew, home education or even classrooms — happens when the avenues for exploration are as open as the books.

Companies that try to turn "education" into just another forum for policy and PR have quickly found out just how educated those students already are. The fear that inspires such controlling behavior inevitably comes back to haunt the "controllers."

On the contrary, the most rewarding and innovative learning environments are as open as the day is long. Open book is the closest you can get to everyone being focused on the same thing. By learning the exact and real bottom line and the reasons for it, people learn just how crucial each and every one of them is to the overall operation.

Taking a cue from open book is open architecture, where the workspace or classroom neighborhood is a free-flowing, communicative environment, spilling over with traffic in ideas, relationships and materials.

Finally, the idea of community open spaces or "green spaces" is fast taking over as the model for 21st century learning. After all, the knowledge is there for the taking — it's what you do with it that counts. Spurred by the whiz bang speed of the Internet and its own brand of cyber-architecture, this paradigm has boomeranged back to low-tech pursuits as well: people talking, generations sharing, an ongoing conversation that is literally opening up the wellsprings of experience and insight that are our most precious resource.

Conversation is the linchpin for this process. Even the sometimes obscure vocabulary of computer science recognizes the value of a good talk, albeit one with a machine. Conversation is a word that's all about turning, changing, associating. It's no accident that ongoing conversations are opening up new pathways to progress and solutions, whether the forum is a town meeting, an annual meeting or a class discussion.

You don't have to be an expert to do this. That's the point. All you have to do is open up. The fluid process of learning will sweep you along with a momentum borne of curiosity, limitless connections and a growing sense of the world's continuing immensity.

Watch out. Conversations have been known to start revolutions.

"Without this playing with fantasy
no creative work has ever yet come to
birth. The debt we owe to the play of
imagination is incalculable."

— Carl Jung

7

The Playground

Look through the indexes of those business and organizational books on your shelf. See all those citations under "play," "delight," "game," "fun"? We didn't think so. We aren't supposed to enjoy work, say the puritan habitudes we've inherited. Well, why not?

When we look to the neighborhood, we see a locus, a spiraling place for energetic activity: the playground and the park.

Smooth sailing, easy as pie, nothing to it ... that's what a walk in the park is for, right? A place to fully unwind, relax, let your hair down. Your route may be aimless there, but nobody cares, because they're unshouldering their cares as well. Oh sure, there are the joggers checking their watches, the bikers bearing down on that heartbreak hill, but most park visitors are usually in full saunter.

New York City's Central Park is the ultimate example, of course. Walking along Park Avenue, you can glance up and see the rings of activity from just that one vantage point: joggers and walkers, skaters, bicyclists, horseback riders. Throughout the sprawling green, there are all the various manifestations of rest and relaxation: bench sitting, model sailboating, grass napping, maybe some more bench sitting. Every kind of game you can imagine is played there. There's Tavern on the Green or the hot dog stand for nourishment. There's the zoo. Hey, do we ever have to leave?

In cities like New York, there's also the value of green fields as public space. New York City's Grand Central Partnership transformed Bryant Park on 42nd Street from a "needle park" into a beautiful place of respite. Visit on a mild day, and you'll see dozens of folks ringing the central, roped-off green lawn, just sitting, meditating, looking at that resplendent grass and breathing its rich aroma. Maybe they're reading a book checked out of the magnificent New York Public Library right next door. To non-city dwellers, it is an odd but understandable sight: a roped-off field, encircled like some kind of shrine by people seeking a moment of peace.

You don't walk on such grass there — it's more like a special rare substance that confers peace. In 1997, it was big news that a huge area of Central Park was to be replanted with genuine Kentucky bluegrass.

"Grassroots" organizations derive their special strength from just this sort of organic energy. In their case, though, there's not much looking going on — everybody's too busy doing. But it is the power of an open field of grass, its underlying bed of roots, that makes our home turf such a prized and protected entity.

It's the park where everybody comes out to play. A softball game, a little see-saw time, the always changing guard of dutiful dog walkers. If you're looking for a place of community that's genuine and informal, unplanned, this is it.

Saturn Corporation recognized this back in the early 1990s. So the company came up with a special program, developed, funded and organized completely by its retailers, to supply and install playground equipment in communities all over the country. They called it Kids Kingdoms.

About 100 such playgrounds have gone up in the United States and Canada since the idea was hatched back in 1993 during a Saturn business conference in Tennessee. A playground project was part of the activities. The basic idea was to wear jeans and T-shirts and be prepared to work hard.

Not long after that, some retailers from the New York and New Jersey area found, ironically enough, that they had advertising money left over because of the Major League Baseball strike. They decided to do something that involved the community.

Months of planning went into each project, targeting a weekend and letting the citizens know about it. Saturn owners received special invitations to join the effort. At one site in New York, 5,400 people showed up. Other playgrounds have been built in Chicago, Detroit and San Francisco.

Do you think that may have endeared the company somewhat to people who knew about it? Some look with suspicion on companies "infiltrating" neighborhoods, as if such projects were somehow less than genuine because they involved projecting a positive image for said company. But more to the point, do you think the children playing there cared who built it? They don't have time for such weighty concerns — they're too busy hanging upside down, sliding down the slide and reaching a new record height on the swings.

It's a walk in the park

"The pleasure of life is according to the man that lives it, and not according to the work or place."
— Ralph Waldo Emerson

One odd phenomenon about parks is where the path goes. Have you ever noticed that no matter where they put the sidewalk, people always seem to create their own separate paths? It may be for a reason as simple as getting to the parking lot in a straight line. Or perhaps they want to see a different picture, a new route. Others follow and then veer off on their own new directions, until you have a web of perambulation, purposeful and mysterious at the same time.

That's the great thing about fields and open spaces: They invite our own designs, which change from day to day. All open systems — "open book," open meetings, open houses — invite this kind of activity. The result is a web of human relations stronger than any paved prescription.

Parks are great places to ambulate. People used to call the daily walk their morning constitutional. Before you ever get to develop a personal constitution of values as Hyrum Smith suggests, you have to work with the body and mind you have been given.

A person's constitution is a system of related parts: psychological and physical makeup, body frame, temperament. Getting that system healthy is  a wonderful adjunct to any other aspirations and tasks we hope to accomplish. Like that other constitution, the one that binds our country, it is organic and fundamental to our general well-being as individuals.

Some studies have shown that walking extends life and decreases the severity of some chronic diseases. Today there are an estimated 33.2 million outdoor fitness walkers in the United States; 36.1 million people also use treadmills for exercise. Fitness walking has increased 43 percent since 1987.

So besides being a way to know your neighbors, to actually converse, that walk in the park is a healthy endeavor that can enrich your other activities and your frame of mind.

Organizations are catching on to this phenomenon. One avenue for reaching people with the fitness message is worksite health promotion. The third Wednesday in May is the date for National Employee Health and Fitness Day, when organizations across the nation sponsor walks, health fairs and other fun events dedicated to employee wellness. The event is sponsored by the National Governors' Councils on Physical Fitness and Sports. Since 1989, more than 25,000 companies and 20 million employees have participated in this event at worksites all over the world.

Current studies indicate that U.S. business spends almost half of its after-tax profits on medical care. Obesity and its concomitant medical problems cost the nation $69 billion in 1990, according to a Harvard Medical School study.

Numerous case studies at such companies as General Electric, Georgia Pacific and Bank of America have shown that employee health and wellness programs aimed at prevention dramatically cut into the frequency of medical services use, and thus trim the cost of health care as well. They also boost productivity and performance, while thinning the absentee ranks. More than 80 percent of America's businesses with 50 or more employees today have some sort of health promotion program.

In fact, many companies (Steelcase, for example) have found that the savings realized by reducing the risk among their employees engaged in a wellness program more than pay for the program's cost. That kind of evidence will put a spring in the step of any company leader.

Inc. magazine profiled one such organization, the Center for Creative Leadership, an international, nonprofit educational institution headquartered in Greensboro, North Carolina. "We stress work-life balance in our leadership training programs," said John Alexander, vice president of communications. "It's only fitting that we encourage our staff to maintain healthy lifestyles. We believe a more health-conscious workforce will be more likely to come to work every day, ready to give their best." So they developed Healthwatch, a wellness program designed by the employees.

At American Saw & Manufacturing, they have a Healthy Tuesdays Program focused on eating a nutritional diet. Workers on their breaks are constantly walking around the building, an exact quarter-mile. The company safety department conducts regular stretching exercises. An ergonomics team made up of physical therapists, process engineers and nurses scouts the potential for repetitive motion injuries within the workplace and takes actions to prevent them.

Other companies, Nike being the ultimate example, go all out in providing the latest gyms, aerobics rooms, saunas and other facilities. At the Nike campus, there are 54 separate sports and recreation programs. The company also provides facilities like a dry cleaner, saving employee time and thus reducing stress, a paramount health consideration.

One danger associated with such programs, whether they are within a company or a neighborhood, is that health promotion and new facilities only increase options for the already active, leaving the sedentary still sitting in their chairs. But it's important to remember that you don't have to be an iron man or woman to increase your fitness. Activities like gardening and washing the car count, too, you know. And just 30 minutes of moderate physical activity a few times a week can have huge implications for the individual, the economy and the community.

As with good business, the key is sustainability.

Batter up!

"Playful tinkering requires consciousness. If we are not mindful, if our attention slips, then we can't notice what's available or discover what's possible. Staying present is the discipline of play. Great focus and concentration are required. We need to stay aware of everything that's happening as it is happening, and to respond with minimal hesitation."
— Margaret Wheatley and Myron Kellner-Rogers
A Simpler Way

The great thing about athletics is that every sport works a different set of muscles. And the first time you use a new set ... well, no pain no gain, right?

When you're too tight, you can't really let it go, let things fly. Likewise, there's no freedom of movement in a musclebound organization.

At some companies, you'd become musclebound yourself if you decided to carry around their policy manual for a week. But many companies and organizations are learning that real leadership comes by acceptance, not by decree.

You don't have to get permission from real leaders to pursue your ideas. They surround themselves with the right people, then say, "Go for it!" Real empowerment is about letting people go. Sometimes it's like teaching kids to drive — it's hard to conceal your fear. But people get the message that they are children when you put them under your thumb.

At first, people may be stunned when they are given such freedom. Then, realizing what true empowerment is really all about, they are filled with the energy of autonomy, of owning the power to chase their dreams.

You have the power to climb mountains, fulfill your dreams and reach distant goals!

'You can achieve anything
if you don't care
who gets the credit'

I don't know who said it first, but this has long been one of my favorite sayings. After Kentucky won the 1997-98 NCAA men's basketball championship, I heard Coach Tubby Smith say it at the post-game press conference. It was an especially relevant quotation for him, as he had just taken the Wildcats to a national title in his first year as head coach of the team. He did it with a team that had no real stars; at various times, different players would step into the leadership role and guide the team to victory. It was an unselfish team that truly understood the miracle of teamwork.

But the fact is, I'd heard this expression long before I'd even heard of Tubby Smith. Actually, I think I first heard it from the manager of a local grocery. But it doesn't matter who said it first. In order to achieve great things with our teammates and partners, we must put our egos aside. At WYNCOM, we like to talk about our "collective intelligence," which allows us to maximize our potential. Among ourselves, we've become known as "the quiet company" — a slogan that, unfortunately, another company has already adopted as an advertising slogan. We call ourselves the quiet company because of the way we work with our college and university alliances to promote and produce live "Lessons in Leadership" programs. These programs are generally hosted by the college or university's school of business or its department of continuing education, which gets all the credit and recognition. We essentially stay in the background. It's a win-win situation, of course, as we're benefiting from the school's good reputation in — and relationship with — its local community.

Julius Erving, who as Dr. J became one of the greatest basketball players of all time, earned his nickname from a childhood friend because of the way he "operated" on the court. Yet, as I remember it, he never played for a championship team until his individual point totals dropped and his assist totals went up — in other words, until he became more adept at *cooperating*. And I think there's a lesson in that for each of us, sports fan or not.

— *Larry Holman*

Competition and camaraderie

"We have to be careful, because the application of these many exercises in personal growth can lead to a piety and fanaticism Shivas never intended....As he often said, trying too hard is the surest way to ruin your game."

— Michael Murphy
Golf in the Kingdom

When it comes to building team spirit, nothing beats athletic competition. But can a sport build worldwide camaraderie?

Rugby surely has. Those who play the game call it one of the largest fraternities in the world. You can find a rugby-playing friend just about anywhere, from France to Fiji.

If you're looking for what sets rugby apart from other team sports, look no further than the post-game party. After the game, the home team treats its opponent to a party, complete with food and gallons of the players' favorite beverage (usually of the frothy variety). Fans and family join in the festivities as well.

"It's not like other sports, where you just go out and play and then get in your car and go home," says one longtime player. "You get a good opportunity to meet who you play against."

You'll find the same sense of transcendent sportsmanship in the grueling and graceful world of Ultimate Frisbee. For those who have played a casual version of the game on their college quad, it may come as a surprise to encounter the worldwide popularity of the sport. But it occupies its own niche in the assortment of Frisbee games like Frisbee golf or the ballet-of-the-disc known as freestyle.

Ultimate is played on a large field capped by two end zones between teams of seven self-refereeing players. The object is to propel the disc by various skilled types of throws into the hands of a waiting, often diving, teammate in the end zone, thus earning a score. Games are usually played to 15 or 21 points.

The game is a constant whirl of running, pivots, cuts and all-out effort, best captured by the completely extended dive and catch of a pass, known as "going horizontal." Stamina, hand-eye coordination, speed, leaping ability and disc handling skills all play a part. So do strategy, timing and leadership. The best parallel to Ultimate's flow of action is to imagine a nonstop series of football passes (with no contact in this instance), with the "timing pattern" often serving as a crucial part of the team's strategy. (Yes, Just-in-Time works in a lot of places besides the factory floor.)

Ultimate players, like many niches of people passionate about what they do, have their own colorful vocabulary. The "huck" starts play, as the players converge from opposite ends of the field while one player expertly "hucks" the disc to the opponent in a manner designed to enable his team to hustle down and set up a tight defense. There's the "hammer" throw, a thrilling and quick upside-down pass that can surprise even the most experienced defender. The "skaters" are the long and lean sprinters who can suddenly leave you in their wake as they break away for a long pass.

Two consistently operative phrases are "the spirit of the game" and "winning the party." Even as the sport has grown more competitive, rules and foul calls are made by the players in the heat of action. Sometimes the play of the more serious teams can get out of hand because of this, with endless argument and more endless participation, but most disputes are handled quickly and with a sense of that "spirit of the game" that emphasizes congeniality, fun and fairness.

As for winning the party, well, many teams carry their own proud legacy in this special skill. Some of them even win on the field as well. In business terms, for them it's all about the Process, not necessarily the Goal. That will take care of itself.

Getting to know the people you play with, even play against — not a bad model for the business world. Playing on the company softball team, having lunch with people in other departments or meeting the families of your colleagues at picnics — it's all about getting to know the human, personal side of the people you work with. It can also make your work life a heck of a lot more fun, interesting and fruitful.

In fact, it would be interesting to conduct a study of rugby and Ultimate players to see what they do with the rest of their lives. We could expect to encounter a striking number of entrepreneurs, independent-minded folks who know how to channel their energies in creative ways, including being part of a fluid team.

These games, predominantly pursued by complete amateurs (a word based on "love"), are the ideal embodiments of cutting-edge teamwork in a physical culture, and they do so precisely by not treating it too seriously. The players also recognize the attributes of true sportsmanship, something workplace teammates — not to mention competitors — could use from time to time.

Block party

"I have tried in my time to be a philosopher, but cheerfulness was always breaking in."
— Oliver Edwards

At WYNCOM, we don't just want people to earn a living; we want them to have a good time while they're doing it. Sometimes the fun we're having is the frightening kind, like a roller coaster. But we never got where we were going by coloring inside the lines. The core of all our efforts is enthusiasm, a passion for our mission that is contagious.

What better way to convey that enthusiasm than by celebration? A good old neighborhood block party is one of the best ways to celebrate we can think of. Remember? The ends of the street barricaded with lawn chairs, the grill brigade wafting its aromas, couples and families and pets and always lots of kids making the rounds, a little whiffleball here, a front yard bridge game there, maybe even some horseshoes for good measure. It's like an open house for the whole community: people touring one another's gardens and homes, sharing recipes or concerns, just playing together like the kids they used to be.

It's an almost universal need — the need to lighten things up. If there's a conflict with somebody, it's always good to remember that that person probably didn't get up this morning intent on ruining your day. When there's a productivity push on, there's nothing like a spontaneous get-together to refresh the troops. Sometimes a private celebration is in order, to reward yourself but also to fortify yourself, keep the balance intact.

Bob Nelson sees rewarding employees in this light. His books and programs are great resources, centered on the notion that true motivation and energy happen only when rewards are genuine, personal and public. He cautions against programs that can get out of hand with rewarding every little thing, and notes that the most effective reward and recognition programs usually involve little or no money and very casual organization.

When an organization is writing up its constitution of values, celebration ought to be a priority. We can learn a lot from the block party. Pure and unalloyed goodwill will not suffer to be designed and meted out; it is a natural outpouring that seems to replenish itself. The framework is open and simple. People make their own good times, then carry them home with them, fuller and richer for the experience.

Go ahead — have a little fun.

8

There Goes the Neighborhood

"There goes the neighborhood."

What the heck does that mean, anyway? Generally, when you hear that phrase, it's in a negative context. As in, "Did you see who just moved in next door? It's those crazy Holmans. Well, there goes the neighborhood!"

Did you ever wonder: WHERE, exactly, is that neighborhood going? Are we going to wake up in the morning and find it missing?

Trust us, we're going somewhere with this. For a while — say, for the duration of this chapter — let's look at the phrase "There goes the neighborhood" in a positive light. For example, you might want to picture your entire neighborhood on wheels, trucking down the road (if that crazy image makes you smile just a *little*, you should be able to make the transition rather easily).

The fact is, the neighborhood is on the move, and fast. Or the people who live there are, at least, as they struggle to keep up with the pace in a world that simply refuses to slow down.

No longer is it common for people to accept a job out of high school or college and stay with that same company until retirement. Those who do stay with the same company must often relocate, in some cases multiple times. Many people, of course, choose to move on to other opportunities, taking advantage of more prestigious jobs, better pay, sunnier climes or any number of other perks, such as being closer to family.

Then there are those of us whose jobs require frequent travel, whether to meet with customers, visit sister operations, attend workshops and seminars or perform other functions to help our organizations remain profitable in a turbulent world.

According to the *National Business Travel Monitor*, a record 32 percent of adults made at least one business trip in 1997. (Some of us hit the road significantly more often, though we don't have any figures on it.) Couple that with the estimate that 20 percent — one-fifth — of the American population moves each year, and you can see that we are living in a highly mobile culture. And while, for many people, being on the go is just a way of life, others still find themselves vulnerable to a sort of motion sickness of the spirit.

Wouldn't it be great if we could take our neighborhoods with us? (We're assuming here that you *like* the neighborhoods you live and work in. If not, consider moving.) But what we mean is this: What if that sense of shared purpose, fellowship and community — the kind of environment that thrives in the most neighborly neighborhoods — were something you could take on the road with you?

We think it's possible. And that is what this chapter's all about, more or less.

Pushing beyond boundaries

In a larger sense, what we're talking about is pushing beyond boundaries, breaking free from limiting factors and the shackles of conventional thinking, about finding ways to connect with people, build meaningful and lasting relationships and energize communities — wherever we happen to be at the time. We're talking about expanding our concept of what a neighborhood is, and of what it means to be a neighbor (and a good one at that). We're talking about staying in touch with what makes us human, even in the midst of a maelstrom of technological, social and cultural change, conflicting responsibilities and all-around clamor that is at best disorienting and at worst dehumanizing. We're also talking about maintaining a sense of humor and perspective through it all.

The profoundly perceptive author Alvin Toffler called it "future shock ... the shattering stress and disorientation that we induce in individuals by subjecting them to too much change in too short

Do YOU
suffer from
"future shock"?

a time." That was in a book called *Future Shock*, which came out in 1970. Incidentally, a few years earlier, in 1967, the profoundly perceptive communication theorist Marshall McLuhan had written that "The new electronic interdependence recreates the world in the image of the global village." Then, in 1980, the profoundly perceptive songwriter John Prine sang: "We're living in the future / You ask me how I know /I read it in the paper / Fifteen years ago."

The message? We're not entirely sure, but we think it might have something to do with not taking it all too literally, or too seriously. In other words, engage your own mental process, think for yourself and look beyond the clever metaphors and the hype and the sound bites and the doomsayers and the gee-whiz types, profoundly perceptive though they may be. As our good friend and business partner Tom Peters has said — and, remember, he's not

a man to shy from a u d a c i o u s pronouncements — "Any damn fool who believes everything the business books and speakers say deserves his fate."

Remember that bit about a sense of humor.

Hurry, hurry home

For many of us, the line is blurring between work and home. Some of us telecommute, while others of us leave home every day for the office, only to bring work home with us. Still others among us travel frequently as part of our jobs.

A recent article in The *Wall Street Journal* quoted Vickie Driver, lead researcher on the Survey of Business Travelers, as saying that, among travelers questioned in depth, the rush to get home was the No. 1 factor in selecting business flights. "You think it's going to be the fare or the frequent-flier miles," she said. "But it's always the schedule. They're all trying to get home faster."

In this age of the two-income family, concerns about the family side of the equation are on the rise. Even as more companies begin to concede the notion that employees are complete people with lives outside the workplace, there's a strange irony at play. Some companies that do offer such benefits as emergency childcare have been known to use them to require workers to spend *more* time on the job, not less.

But progressive organizations are beginning to take seriously the need for balance. And, according to a May 12, 1997, article in *U.S. News & World Report*, a number of them are taking steps to redefine the nature of work itself. Among the programs that recognize workers' home lives are offerings like flex time, job sharing and "quiet times" that enable workers to do their jobs without unwanted interruptions. And some managers, like those at First Tennessee Bank, have been receiving training in the "art of flexibility," a breath of fresh air in an area where, in the past, rigidity has been rewarded.

Meanwhile, "director of work-life" is a corporate title that is coming into vogue, reports the consulting company Challenger, Gray & Christmas. The firm surveyed 1,000 workers, more than 75 percent of whom said that having time off to spend with family and friends was more important than the ability to make more money.

For business travelers, there is also relief. Catering to these often-harried souls may well become a leading growth industry in years to come. Here are just a few examples:

- Regus International, based in London, rents fully furnished offices by the day to business travelers in more than 100 European cities. This new "Touchdown Service" also offers access to videoconferencing, multilingual secretarial support and other services.

- A company called Rolling Strong Co. specializes in mobile work site fitness centers for truck drivers. Jeff Abrams, president of Rolling Strong, started his enterprise with six locations on Interstate 40, from Knoxville, Tennessee, to Winslow, Arizona, with the ultimate goal of covering every major highway in the country. Truckers who become members will find a

comforting familiarity from fitness center to
identically designed fitness center, each
featuring the latest in treadmills, cycles,
stair climbers, strength equipment and much
more, including showers and lockers. "Fatigue
is a major concern, and studies show that fitness
is an antidote to fatigue," Abrams told *Inc.*
magazine.

Truckers are also the beneficiaries of a "new breed
of holistic, very comprehensive truck stop that's
sweeping the country," as a friend describes it.
"I've eaten in one of them, and it's pretty awesome.
The thing the truckers don't like is that regular
travelers are using them as much as they are!

Hair dryers and warm cookies: Home on the road

" The way my life is going right now, I'm never at home, ever. My neighborhood is different every day. Tomorrow it will be Houston, the next day it will be wherever. " If airports are any indication, I think a lot of people live that way. You can't get on a plane, they're so packed. They couldn't possibly all be going for pleasure!

They say women business travelers will take things with them to their hotel rooms to make it cozy. Well, I don't stay in one room long enough to take along pictures and stuff like that. I suppose if I had little children ... well, I wouldn't be doing this at all ... but if I did, I'd want pictures of them with me.

Tom Peters talks about the fact that women now make up 50 percent of all business travelers. Many hotels are putting conveniences like hair dryers and ironing boards in their rooms now so you don't have to call down and ask for them. I've also noticed that when hotel staffers come to my room door now, they identify themselves more clearly. Hotels are becoming more sensitive to women traveling alone.

Of course I love the Doubletree because they put two chocolate chip cookies on your pillow — and they're usually warm! I was wondering why in the world I was gaining weight as soon as I started traveling, and I've finally figured it out. It isn't because I eat every meal in a restaurant, which I do, but nobody can truthfully say "I gain weight because I travel all the time" because you can order a salad! But what I do is I crave comfort foods like chocolate chip cookies because I'm not at home. It's nice to find people who understand those kinds of things.

— *Bunny Holman*

"The human side of quality"
(and make it to go)

Jim Percy
MOBILE, Alabama

It's often the little things that can make or break an organization, by bits and pieces. Jim Percy has seen it happen, both in his former job as a chemical engineer for a major corporation and in his current job as a self-employed consultant.

Martha and Jim Percy

"It's a fairly common experience, in the survey world, that somebody will do one for the first time expecting that they already know the answers. Then they'll discover some small thing like how the telephones are being handled, and it's poisoning people's views of their entire organization. Yet they can't see that until it's pointed out to them," says Percy, who has been described as a major player and contributor to quality efforts in the Mobile community.

Talk to Percy for a while, and you get a sense of where the buzzword-endangered "quality movement" is going in the United States. For him and the companies he works for, the answer appears to lie in a three-pronged attack: (1) an increased emphasis on the human side of the equation, (2) the right "tools" and (3) a willingness and ability to look beyond preconceived notions and artificial boundaries — the limiting factors we talked about earlier.

Percy, who has a bachelor's degree in chemical engineering from the University of Illinois and a master's from the University of Washington, spent 25 years with Du Pont in areas including research, manufacturing and site management. After being transferred to Mobile to help develop the organization of a site that Du Pont had bought from another company, he and colleagues "did a lot with quality, teams and self-managing — all that kind of good stuff."

Then, however, came an organizational flattening in the spring of 1994 that left just three layers: the plant manager, the leadership team and "300 people who did good things," Percy says. "That didn't leave much room for middle managers. So I looked around and took the opportunity to start my own business."

That business, Percy Associates, Inc., has in turn given its founder the opportunity to redirect the focus of his quality-oriented work. As he explains: "Basically, what I wanted to do was get involved with organizations that are into what I call the positive side of quality, as opposed to the 'gotta do' side of quality. Somebody comes along and says you gotta do this, and you meet the requirement, but you don't build in the positive, forward-looking, continuous-improvement-with-customer-satisfaction angle.

"I look at customer satisfaction surveys as an entry point because I've found that employees tend to be so far away from customers that they don't understand what they do that is important. These surveys provide sort of a window into the customer's thinking, so employees can learn about it."

Looking for patterns

Percy's work covers a lot of ground. He is active in the state quality award process administered by the Alabama Productivity Center at the University of Alabama. He has been an examiner, trained other examiners and helped clients write award applications. Though most of his clientele is in the business-to-business arena, it covers a wide range that includes government agencies, industrial product distributors, testing laboratories, metal fabrication companies and volunteer agencies such as the Chamber of Commerce.

He is active in the American Society of Quality, having been named membership chairman in early 1995. "I also edit the newsletter and have been secretary, chief cook and bottle washer," he says. The group, which has grown by about 15 percent over the last three years, holds a monthly dinner program each September through May, with topics ranging from hospital quality improvement to how to do a resume to "statistical nuts and bolts programs" to Internet Web page design to managing ISO 9000 compliance programs. With ASQ, Percy has also taught classes in certification training.

He and his wife, Martha, make time for community involvement. That involvement has included coaching, helping build neighborhood playgrounds and leading a family-oriented retreat for members of the rapidly growing Christ United Methodist Church in Mobile. That latter experience, which involved more than 150 people, focused on "providing time for families to get away from it all and reconnect," Percy says. "I'm reluctant to use the term 'quality time' just because it's been beat around so much, but to the degree that it helps foster people living together and working together well, maybe there's some of that."

In the course of his organizational studies, Percy has developed a keen eye for noticing patterns. "You tend to find people who basically can't see what's going on," he says. "Many times it isn't that the information isn't there, but there are often filters in place and the information can't get through. I guess that's why consultants make their money — that's what it takes to get somebody to listen. You've heard the old saying about a consultant: It's just somebody from someplace else. But survey data isn't tainted by opinions inside an organization; sometimes that lets people see things they haven't been able to see before.

"I'm sort of a receptive-oriented person. That's why I like doing surveys, looking for patterns that people don't see. If I have a philosophy, it's oriented to getting people to realize the potential they have that's being wasted. So many times when I see people exert what we recognize as leadership, it's a charge-up-the-hill sort of leadership. What you find is that everybody else feels unable to lead because there's already a leader. But when things happen in the middle of the night, there has to be a leader, even if the designated leader is not around. You have to prepare people for that. What happens if the customer isn't satisfied, or the product doesn't go out? If you overplay the role of one leader, you lose the role of leadership, which we need at all levels."

Let them make decisions

In order to foster that type of grassroots leadership, companies should entrust more decision-making authority to the people close to the customer, Percy says. He recalls examples from both his current and former careers.

"I remember one story about a food service company in the Northeast where they discovered the value of their truck drivers and the role they play in dealing with customers. Since the drivers were the ones making the deliveries to the customers, they knew a lot more about those customers' needs than the people back at headquarters did. When the company let them start making decisions, they were soon stealing market share from their competitors.

"Here's an experience at Du Pont, where we changed front-line operators' roles to enable them to deal with decision makers at other companies. This gave our people the freedom to order the trucks they needed to make shipments. The first barrier was the people at the other end of the line, who didn't believe the operators had that kind of power. They wanted to talk to the foreman!

"The question is: How do you make the connect?"

One "connect" might come in the shifting philosophies among two major camps in the quality movement, the national organizations ASQ and AQP, the Association for Quality and Participation. "ASQ started out on the technical, statistical side, but seems to be moving toward a more humanistic side, with more emphasis on teams," Percy says. "AQP started out with a focus on teams but is moving toward the statistical and numerical side. I think they're meeting in the middle.

"Our experience at Du Pont was if you did team building it was missing something without quality tools, team processes, flow charting and so forth — or if you did quality with statistics but without the people focus, you were missing something too. I think there's been a convergence in quality: making tools available to more people, letting them do things they haven't been allowed to do but have the potential to do.

"There is still potential out there for organizations to engage people, create environments for people. That's what I mean when I say the positive side of quality. It's about creating win-win situations — just like Covey, Senge and a lot of those people talk about."

A neighborhood with no limits

Jim Percy finds the neighborhood metaphor entirely appropriate in the context of quality. The city of Mobile is actually working in that direction, he says, with a move away from centralization. Police, fire, license administration and other governmental entities are restructuring themselves around neighborhoods. Initially, they are organizing themselves around seven council districts; ultimately they will move beyond that. The trend began in the early 1990s with community-oriented policing, as the police department began trying to customize its approach to individual neighborhoods. "What's evolving is the uniqueness of the different city neighborhoods," Percy says. "Each is beginning to get more of what it needs and wants, rather than the city forcing the same thing on everyone." There are lessons here for all of us.

"It seems to me that neighborhoods, be they plant sites, teams or even residential neighborhoods, often limit themselves by the very beliefs that form their common bonds," Percy says. As usual, examples abound:

- "'We are a research (or service, or health care, or education) organization; those manufacturing-based ideas can't work here.'"

- "I twice had the opportunity to expose world-class organizations to some of the safety approaches successfully used in manufacturing. After some initial grumbling, both organizations successfully applied the approaches — and each improved its safety by more than 60 percent within two years."

- "At another location we were very proud of our high-performance teamwork, but dismayed by the lack of new business coming to our site. We found that we had to challenge our beliefs about what was important to our customers. With their help in the form of survey results, we redirected our teams to focus in different areas. The site has gone on to gain new business and take on a key role in the company's product plans."

Percy summarizes: "In these cases, and in others that I have seen, the key to success has been the 'neighborhood's' willingness to take who they are and what they do well and to blend it with good outside ideas. The blending step is critical to improving and to growing the spirit and character of the people involved. That's the role of leadership."

A revolving door, a comfortable neighborhood

" In most neighborhoods, it seems that people rotate in and out every two years. Neighborhoods don't have very long lives anymore, although the one I've lived in " does. People have raised their children there and they die there. It's unique, though. There are a lot of people in WYNCOM who have been with us a very long time, too. It all boils down to the Golden Rule: If you treat people fairly, then you build up that trust and you make an organization big enough and diverse enough to have lots of ways to go, so that people can be a lot of things.

I always tell the people who are leaving, who have been good contributors for a long time, that this is a revolving door — just revolve yourself back in whenever the mood hits you!

By the way, over at the recently opened WYNWORKS building, which houses our registration and printing and distribution operations, employees created their neighborhood after moving from a different building. The new building has twice as much space, and they had some say in designing it: They needed windows cut into the cement block, they had some input on color. I took some cookies over there one Saturday. There were a lot of people working, and they were just so proud to show us all the different areas, saying "Don't you love the floor in here?" and "This wall will be this shade of blue." They were also showing me their own individual areas and cubicles. When you read "Dilbert," you think of a cubicle as the worst possible world, but here they were being creative, decorating their spaces with family pictures or crafts. They've painted the outside and put awnings up so it looks less like a warehouse. They have a big, beautiful break room that looks like a little cafe, and they put some tables and chairs outside.

People are at work more than they're home, their waking hours anyway. So I think they want to make it as comfortable as possible.

— *Bunny Holman*

Hitting the streets

So, as a frequent traveler, how do you fit into the constantly changing scenes that comprise today's ever-shifting neighborhoods, and what do you gain by trying to do so?

Rudy Maxa, host of "The Savvy Traveler" on National Public Radio, urges people to get up and out whenever they are in a new city and experience something that makes the place special — a museum, a festival, a local store or restaurant. He encourages them to talk to the locals and become a part, albeit a temporary one, of the community.

Again, it's important to remember the value of not taking it all too seriously, as Maxa illustrates with a wacky example. Once, while he was watching "quickie" wedding ceremonies in Las Vegas, a wedding party invited him to be a part of the celebration. Experiences like these can be not only highly memorable — providing stories you'll talk about for years — but also excellent ways to make the most of the neighborhoods in which you travel.

You also might want to do your homework before traveling to an unfamiliar city. You can do it the old-fashioned way — travel books (check out the excellent *The Insiders' Guide* series, which now contains more than 65 titles), AAA guides, brochures, maps — or by surfing the Internet, where you'll probably find a Web site dedicated to any major city, and you might even run into a "local" who can give you the inside scoop.

Once you're there, you can take advantage of an organized bus tour to familiarize yourself with the city's hot spots and tourist meccas, but you may also want to hit the streets in search of the out-of-the-way spots where the hometown folks eat. Your hotel concierge should be able to steer you in the right direction. Whatever approach you choose, get out there and explore!

Thanks to nature

Nature — that is, biological evolution — has not fitted man to any specific environment. ... Among the multitude of animals which scamper, fly, burrow, and swim around us, man is the only one who is not locked into his environment. His imagination, his reason, his emotional subtlety and toughness, make it possible for him not to accept the environment but to change it. And that series of inventions by which man from age to age has remade his environment is a different kind of evolution — not biological, but cultural evolution. I call that brilliant ascent of cultural peaks *The Ascent of Man*.

— Jacob Bronowski
The Ascent of Man (1973)

(That goes for women too, of course.)

You bloom where you're planted

Evelyn Lord
BEAUMONT, Texas

Evelyn Lord has been around, seen her share of neighborhoods, made each of them her home. From her hometown in Massachusetts to a seat in the Delaware Senate ... to law school in Kentucky ... to troubled Northern Ireland (twice) ... to two terms as a Texas mayor, she has consistently adapted to new surroundings, never passively but always through active involvement.

"Each place I've been, I've had sort of a different persona," Lord says. "You either bloom where you're planted, or you wither on the vine."

Clearly, she is not the withering type. Now 71, Lord is still going strong, and blooming beautifully. She points with pride to her recent appointment as chairman (yes, chairman is the proper title, and she won't hear of being called a "chair," "chairwoman" or "chairperson") of the Spindletop 2001 State Commission. The commission, one of 14 on which Lord now serves, is coordinating the impending statewide celebration of the 100th anniversary of Spindletop, the oil field that struck black gold in 1901, making Beaumont the first petroleum "boom town" in Texas.

"We just had our first meeting, and I'm amazed at the wonderful people I'm working with," Lord says. "It's a bad day when I don't learn something. If I slow down, I'll know I have arthritis."

Talking with Evelyn Lord, one gets the impression that she doesn't have many bad days — and that even arthritis could not slow her down much. Her enthusiasm for life and her genuine love of people are evident as she recounts her years of service in a variety of neighborhoods and communities. Through it all, she has nurtured a healthy sense of humor and an ability to seek and find consensus among even the most diverse and polarized groups. Republicans and Democrats. Catholics and Protestants in war-torn Northern Ireland. Women and men, for crying out loud.

"There's always more than one side, more than one answer. One side never has it all right," she says. "I've always voted for the candidate, not the party. I voted a straight party ticket only once, when I was a senator and had to take an oath to do that. Later I said that I wouldn't do it anymore — and that I didn't even want some of those people on the same platform with me!"

Lord laughs as she makes this last comment, and it's easy to see how her sense of humor has served her well in each of her endeavors. "I have had a lot of wonderful experiences, and a lot of crazy ones," she says as she relates another tale of her legislative days in Delaware. "I had a baby when I was a state senator, and that was a challenge. Back then they'd say, 'You elect a woman, and she becomes pregnant' — and I did. But I had the best attendance record. I had the baby on Labor Day, which I thought was very clever, and I named him Bill after all the Senate bills we were working on."

Despite the inevitable brushes with sexism, Lord has rarely felt intimidated, never felt held back by others' opinions or actions. "Funny," she says, "but I don't think being a woman has been one of the biggest challenges for me. I haven't really suffered from a glass ceiling. I have kind of a weird sense of humor, and a sense of humor can get you through a lot of things. It certainly helps to have a tough hide.

"But being a woman can be a challenge. I know it sounds as if I'm contradicting myself, but it can be frustrating dealing with groups of men who are not used to women having intelligent ideas. That used to be quite true back in the '50s and '60s, when I was a young woman. I can remember sitting with a group of men in the late '50s, just before I was a state senator. We were trying to solve a problem, and I made a suggestion and nobody listened. I made it again and nobody listened. In the end, they adopted it and somebody said, 'Wasn't that what Evelyn was saying?'"

Times have changed since then, at least for Evelyn Lord. You'd be crazy not to listen to the woman whose lengthy list of honors includes Beaumont's Citizen of the Year Award in 1990 and the city's "Man of the Year" in 1993 (another instance in which she is not bothered in the least by the seeming unfittingness of the title). She's also been honored by the Boy Scouts of America, the Girl Scouts of America, Boston University, the University of Louisville School of Law and numerous civic and leadership groups.

Paying her rent with service

Despite her accomplishments, Lord seems genuinely unassuming, as if she has simply been doing her part, wherever she might be. "I've been very fortunate in that the places I've gone are filled with friendly people who are very willing to let a stranger become a part," she says.

"I think community involvement is a responsibility, but it's also a joy. I give a lot of talks, and one of the things I like to quote is that 'service is the rent you pay for living.' I think Marian Wright Edelman (president of the Children's Defense Fund) is the person who said that."

She has had the opportunity to pay her "rent" in a range of locales. After her husband, Samuel Lord Jr., earned his doctorate from MIT in the years following their marriage, the travels began. First stop was Delaware, where she became a state senator. Then, at age 39 — with five children ranging from high school to first grade — she entered law school at the University of Louisville and earned her degree. While in Kentucky, she also served as administrative assistant under two county judges in Jefferson County and was set to become a professor of law at the university when Samuel Lord's employer, Du Pont, transferred him to Northern Ireland.

In the city of Londonderry, her new neighborhood, Lord soon became active in Save the Children, a worldwide nonprofit organization that works to improve communities where needy children live; and The Women's Institute, part of the largest women's organization in the world, the Associated

Countrywomen of the World (she also belongs to the American version, the Extension Homemakers).

"We had both Catholics and Protestants working together happily in the institute," Lord says. "It was mostly rural women, solid kind of people you might call 'gray-haired gals.' Agatha Christie was always writing about The Women's Institute. In Save the Children, we would have the bishop's wife, the vicar's wife — socially involved people with a sense of obligation. Princess Anne, the international president of Save the Children, would visit from time to time."

Then, courtesy of Du Pont, came another transfer. This time it was to Beaumont, Texas, population 118,000. Once again, Lord quickly made herself at home, winning a seat on the city council in the '80s and serving as mayor pro tem during 1982-84. She was going to run for mayor (a nonpartisan race), but her husband was transferred back to Northern Ireland. A few years later, the couple returned to Beaumont, and it was only 14 months before Evelyn Lord was elected mayor. During 1990-94, she served back-to-back, two-year terms in a job that paid $500 a month. "You don't do it for the money," she says. "In fact, it kind of costs you."

By this time, having long realized that no party could possibly have all the answers, she had developed a staunchly bipartisan philosophy strengthened through her variety of political experiences. "As a senator, I had run on the Republican ticket. In Texas, in the mayor's race, you run nonpartisan. The advantages and disadvantages are pretty interesting," she says. "You don't have the support of the party machine or the party money. You have to get your own. I've been very fortunate to have had a lot of good friends, and we've had good fun. I am 71 years old now, and it's been fun to look back and see the differences in where I was when I started and where I am now. I'm bipartisan in nature, and that's partly due to the training I've received in the League of Women Voters."

That philosophy has come in handy in Lord's dealings with various groups. So have such experiences as the 1950s problem-solving meeting where she found her suggestion ignored — but ultimately adopted — by a group of men. As she explains: "I've learned that it can be good when people don't accept your ideas right off. I have developed a great respect for what consensus is. Even when I have good ideas, they can be changed here and there with input from other people, and we have a better product in the end.

"When you make a cake, if you leave out the vanilla, which is just a little ingredient in terms of the amount you use, you don't have the flavor. We need all those ingredients. Nobody can make the product by themselves."

Evelyn Lord should know. After all, hers is a recipe for success that has been tested, and proven, in a variety of neighborhoods.

9

The "Cyberhood"

There's a new neighborhood in our town and in yours. It's one of those developments that seemed to sprout up overnight, and it's not picket-fence pretty; in fact, there's not even any grass to mow.

It's a totally new concept, like none we've seen before, with limitless possibilities, endless geography and an exploding population. You'd think such a fast-growing community would be full of noise — pounding hammers, barking dogs, humming saws, chattering children and rumbling cement trucks — yet this burgeoning neighborhood is extremely quiet. Even our chats with neighbors are mostly soundless.

Life is different here. You can shop without ever setting foot in a store, visit faraway places without ever leaving your ergonomic office chair, talk with friends in faraway places without lifting the phone. In this community, not only do your fingers do the walking, they do all the talking. And, best of all, it's a place where every day is casual Friday — and if you don't want to get dressed at all, that's OK, too.

Of course, like every other neighborhood, this one has its problems. It's no Shangri-La; there are breakdowns and break-ins, traffic snarls and crashes, as well as thieves, shysters and con men. But still, for the most part, this is a good place to be. And because it covers a big portion of the planet, this new development is one of the most happening spots on Earth.

Welcome to the virtual neighborhood — the World Wide Web — where with the push of a button or two you can buy a book (sorry, no espresso — not yet anyway!) from the world's largest bookstore, check out the references at the New York Public Library from your office in New Mexico, chat with a college roommate who's at home in Tokyo, air your views on recent sightings of Elvis, admire art from the 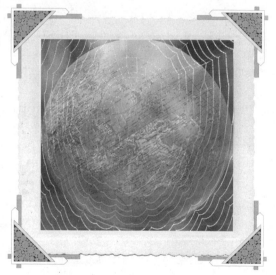 world's finest museums, run errands without ever starting the car or send grandma pictures of her newest grandchild. The possibilities go on and on, thanks to an incredible communication system called the Internet.

Author Dinty Moore visualizes the Internet as a big lace doily, like the one your grandma draped across the top of her mahogany dressing table. Esther Dyson, author of *Release 2.0 — A Design for Living in the Digital Age* (1997: Broadway Books,

New York), told *Communication World* magazine that she sees the Internet as an ocean. "It's something you float in rather than something that has well-defined paths," she said. "It's really an environment in which things happen. It's not a single place; it's a platform for a lots of places."

When we think of the Internet, we imagine computers galore — from Bangor, Maine, to Bangkok, Thailand, all connected in some way — by wires, by telephone lines, by satellites.

The Internet is an amazing feat, but when you think about it, what technology isn't? Every piece of gadgetry we use — from our cellular phones to fax machines — is wizardry to most of us.

That we don't understand all the inner workings of these systems and machines is no crime. The role most of us play in this techno-thriller is that of the visionary. We look for wise and wonderful ways to use inventions. We seek to understand their potential and their possible purposes. Not understanding the Internet's fine points doesn't stop us from using it like crazy. And it sure doesn't prevent us from dreaming of the multiple means in which it can be used.

That's the way H.A. "Red" Boucher, a developer of virtual communities way up in Alaska, operates. Boucher is a seer — his sharp eyes see imaginative ways technology can be used, yet he doesn't profess to be the mechanic who can make it all work. "I like to think of myself as an igniter," he says. "I just point the way, get people motivated and try to get them to do the best they can do. I drive the systems and leave the engines to the technicals."

Boot up your brain

" Here's how I sum up my relationship with technology: When I get hot, I sweat. When I get cold, I put on a sweater.

" It's ironic, because I got my start in teleconferencing, and yet, when it comes to programming a VCR ... well, luckily, I have hired the best technical minds to work with me.

I don't think my lack of mechanical know-how indicates a lack of intelligence. It's a matter of deciding how to spend my time. I identify with a story M. Scott Peck tells in his 1978 classic, *The Road Less Traveled*. Peck, a successful executive and psychiatrist, happened by a neighbor who was fixing a lawnmower. He told the neighbor, "Boy, I sure admire you. I've never been able to fix those kind of things or do anything like that." The neighbor shot back, "That's because you don't take the time."

Peck decided the neighbor was right. Later, he proved he was not mechanically inept by fixing a patient's jammed parking brake. He found that when he concentrated and focused, he could solve a problem that he would have thrown up his hands over before. And the experience helped Peck realize he was not cursed or defective, but that he had made a choice — a choice to spend his time and energy concentrating on non-mechanical matters.

Inundated with information and opportunities, we each must choose where we will focus our attention. We have to face reality — we can't know or do it all.

Regardless of our mechanical ability — or disability — we all have access to one highly specialized piece of equipment, and we do know how to operate it, although we don't always work it to its full capacity. It's our brain. I'd put the Holman 586 up against any box of wires and circuits. We are the intelligence behind the technology. As Denis Waitley points out, "Knowledge is power." If your brain isn't outputting ideas, the size and speed of your computer aren't going to make up for it. In the global economy, ideas are the most valued currency.

Without us, the computer is just a bunch of meaningless wires and chips. Red Boucher is a true fan of technology, yet even he puts the computer in its proper place. "The computer doesn't do anything," Boucher says. "It just turns on and sends ones and zeroes until a man or woman sits down and uses it."

— *Larry Holman*

A chicken in every pot, a computer in every home

If you have a computer at work or at home, there's a good chance it is connected to the Internet. Odds are even better if you live in the United States. Over half of the people in this country have access to the Net, and, if you believe those elusive and often quoted "experts," the other half are probably out buying their computers and getting online right now.

Athough the Internet is new to most of us, it's been around the virtual block a few times. A group of scientists, researchers and governmental types came up with the idea about 25 years ago, and for all but the last few years, they were about the only ones who used it. Then, as with all technology — from pocket calculators to compact disc players — the price of computers fell within the grasp of the average citizen, particularly the average American citizen, who has more expendable income than most. As the computer came home, so did demand for ways to use it, and the Internet and what has become its most popular feature — the World Wide Web — began to spread quicker than kudzu, that creeping green vine that is rapidly covering the American South.

The virtual byway that Al Gore so cleverly called the Information Superhighway has truly become the Earth's main thoroughfare. Internet traffic is doubling about every three months according to the U.S. Commerce Department. The highway just keeps getting wider and wider, with more and more exits along the way. It's an asphalt jungle, without the asphalt.

At this moment more than 100 million people have access to the Internet, half of them Americans. By next week, the number will rise significantly. If you dropped in on a cyberprophet and asked him to stare into the computer screen and forecast the future, he would tell you that the whole world will be networked by the year 2003. On that day, the Internet will become the equivalent of a worldwide community center.

The Internet's seemingly endless flow of information and the tremendous growth and popularity of the World Wide Web — which brought pictures, color, animation and sound to the screen — have left us emotionally tongue-tied. We're not sure whether we should love all of this or loathe it. Are the computer and the Internet miracles or just modern-age Frankensteins in a box?

It's important to remember, amid all the hype and hubbub, that like the car, the computer is first and foremost a tool. It takes us places we want to go, allows us to have new experiences, opens up possibilities for our professional and personal lives. But without the brains behind them — and we're not talking 8-cylinder engines or Pentium processors — the car and the computer are just hunks of metal and plastic. In both cases, we are the drivers; we decide where these contraptions will take us. The cyber neighborhood's advantages — as well as its evils — are produced by those who sit at the screens and manipulate the mouse.

Speaking of drives, how would you like to motor around the Information Superhighway for a little bit, and see the human mind in action, dreaming up ways to put all of these connections to work?

We'll be traveling fast and far — up to Alaska, over to Africa. You might want to bring along a sweater and some sunscreen. Oh, but wait. We forget that in this neighborhood the climate is always controlled. If you are comfortable where you are, it will be just as comfortable no matter where you go.

Adventures in cyberspace

—Our first stop, Africa. Have you ever heard of Timbuktu? The city in Mali is synonymous with the end of the earth, the remotest of the remote. Well, guess what? The computer age has reached this Saharan city of scrub and sand. The wiring of Timbuktu shows us that though many communities are physically removed, the Internet can give wing to the ideas and intellect of their citizens.

Jim Lowenthal is the man who brought the Internet to Timbuktu. He's also establishing connections in other African cities. As he told *New York Times* columnist Thomas L. Friedman, "If you don't factor the Web into your analysis of Africa, then you are going to miss something. We're just two years away from large numbers of people in Africa being able to tell their own story, and that has got to impact politics there."

Having the Web allows Timbuktu to share, for the first time, the extensive archives it has saved from the 14th century when the city was a center of learning. And the computer may also be the yeast that helps the economy in some areas of Africa and other nations rise from stagnation. Friedman points out that, thanks to the Internet's electronic mail feature, many Irish housewives transcribe medical reports for U.S. doctors and hospitals. Soon, perhaps, Africa's citizens will be undertaking similar vocations.

—We journey to tiny Toksook Bay, Alaska, a Bering Sea village with a population of 488. Quite the opposite of the Sahara, the wind chill can dip to minus 80 degrees in this part of the world. Yet, that isn't stopping H.A. "Red" Boucher from bringing the Internet to this and other remote Alaskan villages. Aided by wireless technology that uses satellites to connect people — and computers — Boucher, a former Alaska lieutenant governor, has become the state's leading computer advocate. Boucher sees all kinds of potential for the Net in his adopted state.   Boucher is a story in himself, and we've included a profile of this 70-something live wire and his computer communities later in this chapter.

—Whew! Are you getting Web feet yet? How about a break for coffee or a cocktail? Across the world, Internet citizens are dropping in on virtual "cocktail" parties and coffee klatches, where they meet others to talk about topics as significant as peace in the Middle East or as seemingly banal as bowling scores. Linda Stone, director of advanced research at Microsoft, sees these virtual gatherings as "the important public socializing places of the future." As she told *Forbes* magazine, "I want to talk to people. I think people have the basic need to connect."

What these chats also create for many people is a level of comfort and openness that they don't find in other social settings. There's no question that the Internet and the Web allow relative anonymity. People often become more willing to ask questions they wouldn't ask elsewhere. That can be good when it teaches us what someone's life is really like.

Take, for example, the Web site called "Y?", created by Phillip Milano, a newspaper editor in Jacksonville, Florida. Syndicated newspaper columnist Leonard Pitts Jr. met Milano at a real-life party, and he wrote a column about Milano's site, where people are invited to ask questions about other cultures. The site's full name is *Y? The National Forum on People's Differences* (www.yforum.com). At the site, folks are welcome to ask some questions that we may publicly denounce as silly and mundane, but privately admit that we too always wondered about. Questions like "What would take place during a typical weeknight in a black family's home?" The answers, straightforward missives from people who know, might help blow apart some of our stereotypes and preconceived notions.

—Enough socializing. How about a little higher education? Our next stop is the University of Kentucky, the state's flagship school. It's not just the home of the NCAA champion Wildcats basketball team. UK is an important research center, and its professors, researchers and scientists often make the news nationally and internationally. Like most universities, UK has been using computers and the Internet for quite some time, and by virtue of experience and knowledge, they really know how to make the best of it. Over in the English department, for example, a professor is finishing up on a new CD called *The Electronic Beowulf*, which is a digitized copy of the only original manuscript of the ancient poem.

It will enable scholars to examine the fragile original 11th century manuscript electronically. Over in mechanical engineering, two professors are using computer simulations to figure out how auto manufacturers can make painting cars more efficient. Through highly complex research using computers, another UK scientist is searching for the reasons plaque, a major cause of strokes, collects in our arteries.

—Our next destination is Las Vegas. We're not going to the casinos to research the computer's effects on gambling, although it does have wide use in that industry. Actually, we're going to pay a visit to another university — the University of Nevada-Las Vegas. Anne Tate is director of the Professional Development Center there. Tate's area is a profit center for the university; it behaves like a small business, developing myriad courses for businesses and professionals. The center offers 350 classes a year and administers 20 or so certificate programs. Demand for its services is growing. Yet, like most of us, Tate has much more to do than she or her staff have time for. So when she's starting a new program or needs a speaker for a particular topic, she looks outside her department and the university for help by switching on her computer and heading for a listserv — a computer community of about 225 other people who direct programs like hers. These listservs operate like a community bulletin board. Tate sends a question or message to the group and within minutes, responses to her query or request appear on her screen. "Before, you had to network by calling people you know on the phone or by going to conferences," she says. "Now, you can ask a question one time and get multiple answers.

We were beginning to put together a Family Business Center and I asked, on the listserv, 'What do I need to be aware of, and what are the pitfalls?' I got 10 to 15 answers back."

—Next stop, the hospital. We're not feeling ill, but we are going to visit some children who are. Being in the hospital is a bummer for anyone, so you can imagine how these kids at a hospital in Great Britain feel. But they don't look so glum. The little boy with

leukemia over there is having quite a conversation with a young girl with the same disease who's a patient at another hospital. They are sending lively messages back and forth via e-mail, and they aren't just talking about illness. They're slamming notoriously bad hospital food and cheering on their country's soccer team in the World Cup. Computer links like this one are being used in hospitals in Great Britain and the United States.

—Back to the frozen north, where we will drop in on Russian President Boris Yeltsin. We're going to observe as Yeltsin has an online question-and-answer session worldwide, thanks to MSNBC back in Washington State. Yeltsin is no techie — in fact, during this session, his hands will never touch a computer keyboard. Yet, the world leader apparently realized his gesture will mean a lot to his nation's citizens, who love the Internet and the freedom it gives them to travel outside the confines of their vast but often slow-moving nation. Imagine being able to connect with someone in the U.S. in minutes, from a country where it can take hours and sometimes days to book an international phone call.

More than 4,000 people around the world will "listen," as Yeltsin answers a handful of the 5,000 questions sent his way with the click of a mouse button. Yeltsin's answers, translated to English, are relayed to MSNBC, typed into the Net and dispersed from there.

—And now, for a toy story. Young Christopher Van Allen, who lives in New England, has a humorous nickname. His family calls him Pokey because he's always lagging behind. Christopher's dad got his son a Web site for his birthday and dubbed it pokey.org. Well, it wasn't long before corporate America came calling in the form of Prema Toy Company, maker of that popular rubbery duo, Gumby and Pokey. Christopher was asked not to use the name. Christopher responded by posting this rebellious statement on his Web site: "pokey.org is mine and they can't have it!" The Internet community rallied around, showering Christopher with thousands of supportive e-mail messages and sending a few in a different vein to Prema. The massive reaction made Prema and its lawyers think twice about pushing the issue; they dropped the case.

The case of Pokey is not the only one out there about virtual community support. One of the best examples of a cyber community rallying around a cause comes from Howard Rheingold's 1993 *The*

Virtual Community: Homesteading on the Electronic Frontier (1993: Addison-Wesley, Reading, MA). Rheingold was a longtime member of an online community called WELL (Whole Earth 'Lectronic Link). He came to care deeply about many of the relationships he made there. Apparently he was not alone. When a member of the community fell seriously ill in New Delhi, India, members of the WELL community went to work. Some contacted medical connections; others researched medical evacuation and airline schedules; others started a fund to help finance their friend's possible transfer to a U.S. hospital. The woman recovered and though her doctors credited medications, she credited the good wishes, prayers and advice from the WELL community.

Computercating with the community

In almost all of these cases, and in many others, the Internet is building a community of people — people who are sharing thoughts and information. It's a new way of communicating, what our friend in Alaska, Red Boucher, calls computercating — and it is a valid and vital way to sit down and talk with someone.

Rheingold, who has spent a lot of time studying the dynamics of virtual communities, has found they have benefits for many of us. "People whose physical handicaps make it difficult to form new friendships find that virtual communities treat them as they always wanted to be treated — as thinkers and transmitters of ideas."

You have to realize that socializing in cyberspace runs counter to real life. "In traditional kinds of communities," Rheingold says, "we are accustomed to meeting people, then getting to know them; in virtual communities, you get to know people and then choose to meet them. Affiliation also can be far more ephemeral in cyberspace because you can get to know people you might never meet on a physical plane."

In an article in *InfoWorld*, Robert Metcalfe, who invented Ethernet in 1973, wondered if the advent of Internet communities would mean that Americans no longer feel the need to cram themselves into 271 metropolitan areas. Instead, will they, like Metcalfe and his family, move to more remote areas like Camden, Maine, where computers, telephones, fax machines and express delivery services make it easy to live and work outside the big city?

He says that the Internet has become a tool for community building. "People with similar interests are finding one another online, and thereafter, when they're not getting together for physical meetings, they use e-mail and the Web as tools of community."

Get online and start exploring

H.A. "Red" Boucher
ANCHORAGE, Alaska

H.A. "Red" Boucher is bound and determined to downsize a very sizable neighborhood.

His mission today, as it has been for almost 20 years, is to connect the citizens of his adopted home state of Alaska with one another, with their fellow Americans in the Lower 48 and with the wider world.

H.A. "Red" Boucher, left, is bringing computers to remote Alaska villages.

He's accomplishing that goal with a new company he has founded that uses wireless technology to bring the Internet to the remotest of locations, of which Alaska, the country's Goliath of states — has many.

Alaska's immensity (you could fit Texas inside it twice) and its sparse population mean that beyond Anchorage, Juneau and Fairbanks, there are mostly towns with populations of a few hundred or less. These towns, Boucher says, are perfect for wireless technology, which connects computers via satellites and radio transmission instead of phone lines.

Although he is not a native Alaskan, Boucher is the type of rugged individual you expect to find there. You'd swear that his nickname was the result of his colorful and energetic personality and not his once-red hair. He has served his adopted state in a number of high-profile ways — as its first lieutenant governor and one of the founders of its famous Midnight Baseball League, as mayor of Fairbanks and as a state legislator. He also has his own statewide television show, which celebrates the state's culture.

At 77, he hasn't begun to slow. One of his favorite quips is "retirement is for dead people." Computer connectivity is the latest mission of the man that *Wired* magazine described as Alaska's "most prominent digital evangelist."

He brought the Internet to the tiny village of Toksook Bay in fall 1997, and word has spread to other villages via what Boucher calls "the mukluk (an Eskimo boot) Internet." If a federal grant comes through, 30 more villages could be wired.

Toksook Bay,
Alaska
population: 488

Meanwhile, in Toksook, the villagers, who Boucher describes as "the most self-sufficient people on the planet" are already putting the new technology to work. Children are designing a Web site so that the elders can sell their baskets and other crafts themselves instead of through wholesalers in Alaska cities, resulting in what Boucher, coiner of many phrases, calls an E-conomy.

Wireless technology is also applicable in places like the Russian island of Sakhalin, where Boucher visited with a contingent of Alaska politicians. While there, he met Alexi Okhotnikov.

Okhotnikov is a former member of the Russian air force. His job in the military was to "develop strategies to deliver nuclear packages to us," says Boucher. In the new Russian economy, however, Okhotnikov is an entrepreneur who founded his own computer company and now has 35 employees.

Their mutual interest in computers and connectivity created a bond between the two men. Their friendship demonstrates how the computer may help foster understanding between the nations of the world.

"I'd rather have Alexi put his arms around me than hurl missiles at me," Boucher says. "And I know Alexi would rather have me put my arms around him than hurl missiles at him."

Boucher's interest in computers began in 1980, when he bought his first Apple. Soon, he was subscribing to the Source, a service similar to today's America Online, and then he created his own network to teach his 1,000 subscribers about the real Alaska. He began to take computer courses

— via computer from the first "virtual" college at Colorado Technical College. When he announced his campaign for governor in 1982, Boucher made his announcement from the remote island of Sitka, making history as the first person to file for public office in Alaska using a computer and a modem.

There is no doubt that Boucher is a visionary. When he ran for lieutenant governor in the early 1970s he predicted that the computer's major appeal would be its ability to connect people with one another.

"In our technological plunge toward the future," he said, "we must understand that the greatest hunger of people is not new machines to do less, but channels to each other's hearts and minds."

Computercating with Red

We corresponded with Boucher, appropriately enough, via e-mail, to ask him some specific questions about the use of wireless technology and the building of virtual communities.

Question: You are trying to overcome remoteness, yet isn't that what many hope to find in Alaska? How do you create connections without undermining Alaska's appeal as a frontier?

Answer: *It's all about choice. By providing Internet connectivity to remote areas of Alaska you are giving the villagers the opportunity to gather information from the world around them and still live the lifestyle of their choice. Secondly, there is a lot the rest of the world can learn from the variety of native cultures in Alaska. After all, they have been there for thousands of years.*

Q: Have communities experienced a disintegration of "real" communication when the door to this limitless, virtual community was opened to them?

A: *This is probably quite true in the larger urban areas of Alaska. As for the small villages where we have been setting up systems, the answer is "no." Based on the seven months we have had Toksook Bay up and running, the response has been very positive. Natives know how to sort out information, especially in those villages where a subsistence lifestyle is led. We call it "the native way of knowing."*

It is only when you create a physical presence by outsiders, i.e. oil booms, the missionaries back in the early days, etc., that the problems begin. Bethel, Alaska, a hub community of about 6,500 that serves approximately 40 outlying villages, is a good example. They have daily jet air service along with problems like drugs and alcohol.

Q: Tell us about some of the other "virtual" communities you've established. What makes these the most interesting places to "computercate"?

A: *The most interesting were the early Bulletin Boards (BBS) back in the early 1980s like the Sourdough Network in Anchorage and the Walrus Network in Bethel. At that time communication was letters that flashed across a screen, not the hype, media and sound that is the Internet of today. It was not important what the other person looked like, how old or pretty they were. You could focus on what you were typing and truly go mind-to-mind. In other words, "THINK." Using the epistemological root of learning and exploring.*

Thinking about thinking ... It is a dimension that modern society does not explore enough. We spend a good majority of our lives reacting to what is around us, not exploring what's inside us.

Q: How could our interconnectivity via computer prevent larger problems that we face — dangers like war, pollution, hunger — or can it?

A: *Computer communication, computercating, gives more people the opportunity to synergize, to think, to get more information. A good example was the collapse of communism. They couldn't stop the fax messages from going out and telling the world what was going on. Oppression collapses when it is subjected to a flood of unbridled information.*

Q: How does wireless technology work?

A: *Radio modems are connected to a server (computer) at the base of a satellite receiving dish. The signal is taken from the server and then distributed via radio transmitters wirelessly to the rest of the village. The signal goes from the dish to the server. The server simply digitizes the signal so it can be transmitted in a manner that the receiving radio understands. The receiver then sends the signal along it to another computer and up it pops on the screen as Internet.*

Q: The speed and simplicity of installation of the "wireless" system seems a big advantage in an area where weather conditions can be bitter, to say the least.

A: *Very much so. Wireless connectivity, be it satellite or spread spectrum, is very much the wave of the future, especially in the rural areas of America and Third World countries. It's cost-effective and relatively easy to install.*

Q: How would you describe the optimum relationship between us (people) and them (computers)?

A: *Like any other tool we should not become overly dependent on it. Computercating has allowed me to develop a worldwide network of friends and business associates. However, it has not replaced the day-to-day necessity of relating to friends, family and associates. I love university campuses. There are days when I just set everything else aside and stroll through the buildings of the University of Alaska and suck up the feeling of a new generation learning and exploring the world around them.*

Bear in mind, the same technology that is making global communications possible could turn out the lights on January 1, 2000. I have been tracking the Y2K or millennium bug since it first came on the screen five or six years ago.

We have a major, major problem that is going to take the technical and nontechnical world to solve. The public is not fully aware of the issue, and upper management is still in denial. I wrote an article on Y2K that appeared in the June 18, 1998, Anchorage Daily News (Alaska's largest newspaper). While I have been called a leader in a number of areas, right now I am focusing on developing a forum to let Alaskans and others know that there are bumps, maybe chasms, in this highway and that we need to prepare.

Q: How would you like to be remembered?

A: *Simple. "He created opportunity."*

A few more Boucherisms

Boucher is straight talking and highly quotable, as Doug O'Harra, a writer for *We Alaskans*, found when he wrote a profile of Boucher in 1997. O'Harra's story is filled with Boucherisms such as:

"I strongly suggest that anybody who's over 60 years old should get online and start exploring."

"Some of these politicians don't want more contact with their constituents. They get elected based on commercials. I go to Juneau now, and these guys ask me — today, in 1997 — 'Why do I need e-mail?'"

"One year, if I could, instead of sending out the Permanent Fund, I would send out a laptop to everyone in the state. And we would vault to the top."

"You might say, 'What is its purpose?' The minute you ask 'What is its purpose?' you become a 'late adopter.' There are people who don't try out technology until they find out what it's for. I'm at the other end of the spectrum."

Living successful on-screen lives

In *Life on the Screen: Identity in the Age of the Internet* (1995: Simon & Schuster, New York), Sherry Turkle looked at how technology is transforming the human personality. As Turkle, whom *Business Week* described as the Margaret Mead of cyberspace, says, the Web is "redefining our sense of community and where we find our peers."

It comes as no surprise that Turkle believes young children — those who have grown up with their chubby little digits affixed to a computer keyboard — will make more use of the virtual neighborhood than those who've come before them. "Children from the earliest age have been teaching themselves how to make the most of life on the screen."

Esther Dyson, publisher of a high-tech newsletter called *Release 1.0*, understands that the Internet is a place where both good and evil reside. But like a good citizen striving to keep the neighborhood and community on the right path, Dyson has good feelings about the Internet. "I simply hope to encourage more good people to get on the Net and not be scared. I want to invite nice new neighbors into my neighborhood," she told *Communication World*.

Get on the highway, but drive carefully

Is the Internet friend or foe? Dinty W. Moore, author of the very funny tome *The Emperor's Virtual Clothes: The Naked Truth About Internet Culture*

(1995: Algonquin Books of Chapel Hill, Chapel Hill, NC) took a year to find out. (No, Moore's parents didn't name him after the famous beef stew in a can.)

Moore, a professor, writer and former documentary filmmaker, decided to mimic one of literature's giants, Henry David Thoreau, and spend 12 months not in the woods, but in the jungle of the Internet and the World Wide Web. He says he came away from the experience with "a big headache," but also with the realization that the virtual world is just a mirror of the real one — it has its beauty spots and its warts, its good neighbors and bad, its insightful information and its misinformation.

And so, perhaps like Moore, we should all merge carefully onto this fast-moving thoroughfare, keeping our hands on the wheel, our critical thinking caps on our heads and our eyes peeled for wacky drivers and other hazards.

Because if we choose not to hop on the highway and see where it takes us, we may end up like poor old Barry Byrne, an elderly architect whom Studs Terkel mentions in his 1972 book *Working*.

Byrne, you see, absolutely despised the automobile. "The evil genius of our time is the car," Byrne decried. "We must conquer the automobile or become enslaved by it."

Less than a year later, Byrne was dead, struck down by a car on his way to Mass.

"You must welcome change,
as the rule
but not as your ruler."

— Denis Waitley,
"Empires of the Mind"

10

The "Cyberbiz"

"Of course innovation is risky. But so is stepping into the car to drive to the supermarket for a loaf of bread. All economic activity is by definition 'high risk.' And defending yesterday — that is, not innovating — is far more risky than making tomorrow."
— Peter Drucker, *Innovation and Entrepreneurship*

Let's venture down to the neighborhood business district, run a few errands and see what's happening along the busy streets of our town.

This area sure is bustling. All the storefronts are filled, and the offices up above are peopled with an array of professionals and entrepreneurs — a lot of one-man and one-woman shops. The buildings themselves haven't changed much in the 50 years since this center of commerce was built — a new striped awning here and a fresh coat of paint there. But when we step inside these stores, restaurants and offices, we realize how plugged-in, turned-on and tuned-in the average workplace has become.

Over at our favorite sub sandwich shop, the teen at the counter has pen in hand. He's ready to take your order, while behind him, the fax machine is in overdrive as regulars send in their carry-out lunch orders. Upstairs, in a one-room office, your kids' babysitter has a summer job this year designing Web pages. Down the street at the Catholic church, Father Dan is downloading his day's schedule from his personal computer to his electronic, palm-size personal organizer. Bob, the express mail deliveryman, is checking in with his headquarters. They're using a satellite to try to track down that package of pastrami that was supposed to be here yesterday. At the family-owned jewelry maker that's been around 50 years, the founder's grandson is answering customer questions and queries via e-mail.

Yes, thanks to technology, change is the only constant in business today. It's like that classic Bob Dylan refrain, "The times they are a changin'." And they're changing by the nanosecond. The Industrial Age was a veritable Stone Age compared to the current age of technology. Take the Internet, for example. It captured 50 million users in just four years. It took television 13 years to reach that point, radio a full 38 years.

Wonders of the workplace

Technology came to our office long before it landed in our dens and family rooms. We made way for it, tossing out our typewriters, sweeping off our desktops and making room for keyboards, monitors, mousepads, fax machines, the cell phone, the electronic organizer.

And what's next? To alter Walt Disney's famous phrase, if you can dream it, it's probably in development at this very moment. In *Enterprise One to One* (1997:

Currency Doubleday, New York), Don Peppers and Martha Rogers talk about up and coming innovations — cars that know us; thin pieces of plastic that contain the who, what, when, where and why of our lives; pills that tell us when to take them; packages that open when we tell them to.

"The appliances and machines around us will soon remember us individually and anticipate our needs," they write.

With technological aids, our busy business lives know no boundaries. As a recent ad for an IBM laptop computer touts, we can "Think anywhere. No walls. No limits."

And likewise, our businesses seem to have no limits. Oh sure, we shut the blinds and lock the door at night, but the machines inside hum right along. The e mail is still collecting in the computer's vast memory; the fax machine is still spitting out memos, letters and orders; and the voice mail is still taking messages.

What Tom Peters proclaims is true: "9 to 5 is dead." In its time slot we now have the new formula for business success, what Stan Davis and Christopher Meyer call 24 X 365 (that's 24 hours a day, 365 days a year) in *BLUR: The Speed of Change in the Connected Economy*. You don't have to be a clockmaker to realize that 9 to 5 in Tokyo and 9 to 5 in

Toronto aren't the same. Our technical capabilities have opened the doors of our businesses to the world; our clients want to be able to come in anytime.

"With the reality of today's connectivity, you should be able to conduct your business no matter where you or your customers are," Davis and Meyer write. "This means that you have to set up your sales, service and support systems so that your customers can access them wherever they may be — on the Internet, near a phone, within reach of a fax machine, or grasping their Palm Pilots."

The people we work for and with don't think in terms of office hours and work days any longer. With the advent of online shopping, banking, stock buying and other services, the neon "Open" sign is always on.

This appetite for round-the-clock commerce caused 10 million Americans to buy goods and services on the Web in 1998.

"The spectacular growth of the mail-order industry — and on its heels, electronic commerce — can be attributed largely to the public's hunger for anytime shopping," Davis and Meyer write. "Retail banking customers today would rebel if they didn't have round-the-clock access to their money via ATMs, PCs or telephones. Getting your organization running according to the same we-never-close clock might mean deploying that same kind of automation, letting night-owl customers serve themselves."

Some are concerned that the computer and other high-tech tools of business are destined to depersonalize our lives, but Peppers and Rogers are convinced that technology can make the customer relationship more personal than ever before.

They say that computers allow customers to talk to businesses and enable businesses to keep better track of their "complex, individual interactions with customers," even focusing on one customer from among the millions. And, when information technology is applied to manufacturing, companies can deliver "mass customized products or services tailored to the specific needs of an individual business or consumer rather than to the general needs of a 'segment' of customers." Simply put, Peppers and Rogers write, companies will be able to say to their customers: "I know you. You tell me what you want. I make it. I remember it next time."

All aboard the technology train

But what about the companies that refuse to get on board? Denis Waitley predicts that not only will they be left at the station, they'll be out of business. Are you running a company without a computer and a fax machine? Do you veto express mail because of cost? If so, "unless you are a small, local enterprise in a remote corner of the country, you're probably no longer in business," says Waitley.

Or, as Andy Grove of Intel told Tom Peters, "When it comes to e-mail, companies are going to do it or disappear."

One of the most fascinating aspects of these capabilities is that unlike advances in the past, they are not the exclusive domains of big business. In fact, some of the smartest users of technology seem to be the smallest companies.

"In the end, the information superhighway may become a great equalizer," says Waitley in *Empires of the Mind* (1995: William Morrow and Co., New York). "Ever-cheaper information is of course a boon to big business, but the little guy will also reap many benefits — and some of these smaller businesses are already becoming giant-killers. Armed with ever more powerful computers and high-tech communications — which cost less and less, and can be installed in small, low-overhead offices — legions of individual entrepreneurs are seizing the advantage from bigger companies and also breaking chains of command. Inside the large companies themselves, technology is giving low-level workers power to make decisions that were long reserved for their managers."

The next generation will definitely feel more comfortable in front of their computers, more effective in creating teams in cyberspace. They'll be less likely to hold face-to-face meetings. This whole new approach should lead to more and more contributions from the "regular" employees, Tom Peters says, because the visible traits that cause us to categorize people and their potential will evaporate. It will mean a further equalizing of the business neighborhood, where notions based on appearance, academic background, ethnicity and gender are eliminated.

"I'm not going to know whether you are a man or a woman, whether you are an engineer or an English major, whether you are in Berlin or Bangkok or Baltimore," Peters says.

When technology is too much

Can technology be too much? Can it hurt our business as much as it helps? There are days when it seems so, days our computer has inexplicably crashed, taking our hard work along for the plunging ride into the abyss. At those times, we feel camaraderie with Attorney General Janet Reno, who had this to say about her computer one day:

"It got so confusing, as to what was on the computer or what wasn't on the computer, what was on the hard drive, what was on the soft drive, that it made it easier for me just to do my work with paper and pencil so I could figure out what I had and what I didn't have. At this moment, I do not have a personal relationship with a computer."

There's no quarrel that technology can frustrate us more than it assists us. It can disconnect us. If it is allowed to, technology can depersonalize and sterilize.

Automated phone systems are a perfect example. You know the drill. You punch number after number on your phone keypad, hoping that the next punch will bring a living, breathing, non-recorded person.

These phone systems irk a lot of us, yet companies use them. They are timesavers, conveniences. Never mind that they are as irritating as a Brillo pad to the person on the other end of the line.

Ann Tate, who directs the Professional Development Center at the University of Nevada-Las Vegas, is a believer in customer service. Although her office is a part of the university system, it operates as a small business. It is a profit center; it seeks to deliver the courses and training the Las Vegas business community needs.

And when it comes to phones, Tate believes that it's just bad business not to have a person answering phone calls.

"I said to my dean that it would be over my dead body before they put in a menu," Tate says. "I hate them. There is no customer service involved at all."

It's ironic that one of the country's largest telecommunication companies, McLeod USA, shuns such a system. According to an article in the *Illinois Builders Journal*, McLeod has staked its claim as the only major telecommunications company in the country where a real live person will answer when customers call in for service. Now, that service is not just available from 8 a.m. to 5 p.m. It's 24 hours a day, seven days a week. And they'll answer within four rings.

Keeping in touch

" When you're on the road a lot, scenes from daily life are sometimes lost to you. You miss the little things — when your best friend calls to tell you how, after getting dressed in the dark on Monday morning, she showed up at work wearing two similar shoes, one blue, one red. Or when one of your sons stops by to ask for your chocolate chip cookie recipe because he wants to impress his girlfriend.

I'm a people person — I thrive on others' stories; I cherish the little tales of trial and triumph. I guess that's why e-mail has become so important to me. It's a way to reach out, to preserve those bits and pieces of our average days.

Now that I can take a laptop computer along, I have another option for keeping in touch, not just with family and friends, but also with people back at the office, our university contacts and our speakers and their staffs.

This newfound accessibility to people and information begs another question. Am I opening myself up to information overload? Maybe. Are we doing the same thing in our workplaces with the Internet, Intranet, cell phone and fax? Probably.

But I tend to think we're all a little like kids at holiday time. They tear through the packages, break out the new toys and become completely absorbed in them. But little by little, children begin to pick and choose the toys they like the most.

Doesn't something similar occur when we get a new piece of electronic equipment? For a while, we use it constantly, exploring its features. Then, slowly, we begin to self-edit based on what is most useful to us. What happens, I think, is that common sense kicks in. At least I hope so. I'd hate to think Gertrude Stein was right when she said, "Everybody gets so much information all day long that they lose their common sense."

In our company, we look for people with common sense — people who know when to send a personal note instead of an e-mail message; who recognize there is much to be gained by spending time talking with a client — not always about business, but about themselves and their life; a person who understands that face-to-face communication still has a very important place in every business.

We've chosen high touch over high tech, and as a result, even as the company has grown, we've been able to retain that family feeling. I see technology as a way to enhance our relationships with one another, not to undermine them.

— *Bunny Holman*

The heart of business

Technology has definitely changed the way our businesses operate. You get a real feeling for it if you visit a company like Verifone, a leader in credit card authorization based in Redwood, California, that Tom Peters tours in *The Pursuit of WOW! Every Person's Guide to Topsy-Turvy Times.*

Peters tells us that at Verifone, "Employees get a laptop before they get a desk, internal paper mail is banned and there is 24-hour-a-day, real-time computer networking."

CEO Hatim Tyabji considers his company one without a headquarters. He's on the road 90 percent of the time, and his staff members keep in touch with him via e-mail. Wherever he is, Tyabji simply whips out his laptop computer, and his office door is open.

There's no doubt that Verifone is leading edge. And yet, Tyabji and his company haven't forgotten where the heart of business lies. As Tyabji told Peters, "When all is said and done, no matter how advanced the technology, a company is made of human beings."

Tyabji's sentiment is echoed by others. Many are proponents of technology; they'll tell you your company won't last without it. At the same time, they'll tell you that sleek, speedy computer capability had better be balanced with something warm and fuzzy — some good old-fashioned human interaction.

In his *Keeping the Edge: Giving Customers the Service They Demand,* Dick Schaaf concludes, "In the long run, people are still the ultimate service weapon. Duplication of equipment and programs and pricing is possible; the one bona fide difference is people."

Denis Waitley says, "The competitive edge will belong not to those who use computers but to those who know how to inspire more productivity and excellence from each individual."

The trick is to become a technology user without becoming an abuser. Weren't computers meant to supplement and enhance our personal, face-to-face communication and not to replace it? The minute we neglect the human element of our interactions, we lose our edge.

FM-2030 (not his real name, we're sure), a columnist who teaches long-range planning at Florida International University and is the author of *Are You a Transhuman?*, issued a warning about becoming overly enamored with our tools.

"What good is tinkering with 21st century machines if you are still parked in mid-20th century lives?" he asks in a *Los Angeles Times* column. "Smart machines do not automatically catalyze us to smarter lives. What good is going global on the Internet if your real-time allegiances remain nationalistic and ethnocentric?"

In our lives, we need to look for role models like Sue Dicke who realize that technology is just one of the many materials we can use in building our relationships.

Building bridges to the future

Sue Dicke
PEORIA, Illinois

At Midstate College, where
Sue Dicke teaches computer
courses, many of the
students are adults who
have jobs, kids, bills to
pay and a multitude of
responsibilities. Some are
raising their children alone. Most have returned
to school to improve their lot in life.

Dicke knows that the more she can teach her
students, the more marketable they will be. She's
determined to cram as much high-tech knowledge
into their heads as possible.

"I'm trying to give them a bridge to their future,
really give them their tuition's worth in terms
of preparing them with a skill that's going to
make a difference in their life on the job,"
Dicke says. "When I teach, I can push them to be
all they can be on the computer because I know it
is going to make a difference."

But Dicke realizes also that a computer chat is
nothing like a conversation over coffee with a
good friend; that emoticons can't replace emotions.

So the 47-year-old wife and mother of two has
made her computer classroom not one of clattering

keyboards and mesmerizing monitors, but one warmed by laughter, chatter, smiles and hugs.

"I have real bonds with my students," Dicke says. "The classrooms take on a character of their own. I look upon students as friends. It is so exciting when they come back to see me, and they've gotten a job! They just come in and give me a hug!

"I think it is incredible, what is happening with computers, but what is in my heart is that the most vital link is the human link and the spiritual link. We have to ask ourselves if it (the computer) becomes too much a part of our life. Where are we receiving our nurturing and our hugs?"

Dicke is a decidedly high-touch person, made more so by her firsthand understanding of the fragility of life. She is lively, funny, introspective — and she's living with cancer.

Dicke was diagnosed with the disease in 1991. And even though it has nearly killed her more than once, seldom has her illness stopped her from teaching.

There have been plenty of times when she considered giving it up. Like the days she had to drag her oxygen tank behind her to class.

"I'm sure they thought I was crazy," she says, laughing, when asked what her co-workers and students thought about her dedication. "A bald woman dragging an oxygen tank!"

But she began to realize that her students were learning about the complexities of life, as well as the intricacies of a computer, from her.

"I know that what I'm doing is helping them," she says. "I'm hoping that I'm communicating to them that life is full of adversity, but you can still survive. You can still perform. They are going to find that on the job — they're going to go out in the work world and it might not always be the perfect situation at work or at home. But you can focus. You can just do it.

"When they come in and tell me something has happened at home, I really try to remember whether a child was sick or a parent fell and ask them how that situation is going and let them know I care about them as a human being."

Making laughter the best medicine

Dicke is the master at making you smile. You talk with her a few minutes and feel you've known her your whole life.

For nine years, cancer has been a constant companion for her and her family. Yet, when you talk with Dicke about the disease, there is nothing weary or worn about her long battle. She chuckles at the situations it leads to, and before you know it, you are laughing with her.

For example, one of the effects of her illness is swollen hands. Dicke irreverently calls them "my puffy paws." They don't operate well, she explains.

"My family won't let me hold on to very much, because I'm always dropping things ... particularly items they value," she says, breaking up with laughter.

Her somewhat wacky sense of humor is a genetic trait, Dicke believes, passed down from her good-humored parents. It is a family heirloom she has treasured during her illness.

"I come from a family that has used humor — not as a substitute or as a denial, but as a coping skill. Humor puts people at ease with my illness. It helps people see you as a human and puts it in bite-sized portions and lets you live your life."

Sitting at the oak table

Living with cancer — not befriending the beast or giving into it, but turning the experience into something powerful and useful — has become the theme of Dicke's life. She's taken what many would view as a death sentence and pumped life into it.

Early on in her illness, Dicke dreamed of a place where people with cancer could gather to talk about whatever was on their minds. It would be comfortable, like a welcoming home with a teapot on the stove. Its most important element would be a sturdy oak table, to Dicke a solid symbol of family, roots and tradition.

"It was a place where I would sit at an oak table and someone would come in and say, 'I have cancer,'" she says. "And I would say, 'Well, have a seat at the oak table and I'm going to get us some tea.'"

In June 1998, Dicke sat at the oak table of her dreams and smiled as the Cancer Center for Healthy Living in Peoria opened its doors with fanfare provided by her son's jazz band. Her dream of a place of emotional and spiritual healing for cancer patients had come true. Now, all she needed was some tea bags.

Walking the healing path

Dicke first envisioned a place like the center when she spent a week at a seminar in California about five years ago. The seminar, which she describes as a cram course in walking the healing path, was based on the works of Greg Anderson, an author who has written numerous books on the spiritual, mental and emotional aspects of healing.

When she returned to Peoria, Dicke began meeting with a group of women who had cancer. From this support group, she learned that many other cancer patients shared her belief that medical treatment is only part of the healing process.

The women saw the need for a place where patients and families could gain strength and insight through support groups, where cancer patients could feel the calming effects of tai chi, meditation, visualization, yoga, music and art therapy, and aromatherapy. Where they could express their feelings through journaling, photography and art. Where the troubled or terrified patient could call 24 hours a day to seek the counsel of a cancer survivor. ("You get scared about cancer at 11 at night when everybody else is asleep," Dicke says.)

Dicke and her support group raised $50,000, secured donations of in-kind goods and services from local businesses and wrote winning grant proposals. They dealt with the blows they were handed — the death of a group member and the absence of others who were sickened by chemotherapy and other treatments.

"When one of our group members passed away," Dicke says, "it was very difficult, but that actually empowered us to go on, to do it for Bridget."

The center is exactly the kind of service center the group had envisioned. There are support groups as well as classes

Celebrating the opening of The Cancer Center for Healthy Living

in everything from meditation to journaling. The hotline awaits late-night calls. A resource library is available. There's even a meditation garden in the plans. The center's comprehensive wellness approach has won the approval of the American Cancer Society.

"Doctors are telling their patients about us," Dicke says. "There are about 250,000 people in this metropolitan area. We are kind of holding our breath and hoping we are ready. People are very interested; they are looking for something more.

"I wanted to be a part of something that was a bridge from fear and panic to coping, calm and determination. Hopefully we can help them across the bridge to where they have coping skills and an inner calm and determination. I have this analogy that I use a lot. You wake up in the morning, and you think, 'I have cancer.' But hopefully you can evolve from there to 'What's for supper?' It's not denial, it's saying 'I'm still living.' It's not getting stuck in the 'I have cancer' mode all day.

"Our first purchase for the center was the oak table. It came from a family whose mother had died from breast cancer. And what they said to me was that a lot of people had sat around this table, making family decisions. I told them, 'Well, a lot of people are going to sit around this table making decisions.'"

With one dream down, Dicke has another in mind — a kind of rural branch of the center. She says: "I want it to be a farmhouse, a place in the country with a porch and a swing, a pond, a barn for an art studio and a garden. I want it to be relaxed and comfortable and peaceful."

When life gets abnormal, do something normal

The best dose of medicine Dicke gets some days is the "I love you, Mom!" that Robbie, 13, and Matthew, 17, so willingly shout. "They are a reason for being," she says.

Dicke has found that one of the best retreats from her illness is the normal hubbub and chores of daily life. She explains:

"We have taught our sons that when things are abnormal, you do something normal. My cancer made our lives very abnormal, so we did something normal — we got a paper route. Every Tuesday night we deliver papers for pickup the next morning. We did that with our sons to teach them the value of a dollar. And we are still doing it."

She's found that little things really do mean a lot. Weakened by her cancer treatments, she was unable to drive her son, Robbie, to his drum lesson. When her strength returned, and she and her son resumed their routine, his reaction surprised her. They stopped at McDonald's on the way and got Cokes. When they arrived at the teacher's house, Robbie handed the teacher a Coke he had gotten for him and raised his own cup in a toast. "We're celebrating because my mom brought me to my drum lesson," Robbie said.

Dicke says, "Those are the indelible memories that infuse your soul with strength — and determination."

The desire to live is alive and well

More than once, Dicke has been told her situation is hopeless. When a doctor more or less told her to go home and die, Dicke set out to prove him wrong.

"I had another agenda," she says.

She hasn't always been so seemingly fearless and assertive. Those strengths, she says, are outgrowths of her illness.

"I have learned to live in a 'we'll see' world instead of a 'what if' world. In my life, I have lived with a lot of fear and anxiety. Maybe it comes from growing up during the Cuban missile crisis. I don't know. Some of those issues were indelibly pressed on my mind. But now, when the doctor says to me, 'You just need to go home, I can't do any more for you and don't search for the stars,' I'm saying 'We'll see.' The desire to live is working."

11

The Mix

Banker.

Mayor.   Shoe salesman.

Machine tool technician.

Feminist.

CEO.

ACCORDION PLAYER.

Factory worker.

Programming consultant.

Accountant.

Sailor.   *Counselor.*

Computer whiz.

Breast cancer survivor.

Oh, what a rich neighborhood!

We're not talking about the prices of the houses or the size of the bank accounts. What we're talking about is the rich tapestry of people who are featured in this book. The list we just made is merely a sampling. No doubt your own neighborhood is just as rich in its diversity.

We choose to take a broad view of the concept of diversity. Too often, it is seen as a matter of

black and white, male and female, us and them.
Those kinds of differences are important, yes,
but such a narrow view often seems to produce a
polarizing effect, and/or a preoccupation with
political correctness, both of which are pretty
close to the precise OPPOSITE of what diversity
is all about. As if diversity were an initiative
to be implemented (or some such bureaucratic
balderdash), or even an unknown to be feared,
instead of the vast opportunity for discovery and
innovation and cooperation that it is!

The people listed at the start of this chapter
are all featured in this book, a book that professes
to be about exceptional leadership. These people
all seem rather ordinary, don't they? But, as you
might have noticed, our descriptions of them are,
well, a bit ... one-dimensional.

For example, we didn't mention that the accountant
is also the North American president of a thriving,
high-tech company based in Japan. Or that he
loves to set sail — literally, in a sailboat —
from San Diego to the Catalina Islands. Or that
he and his wife — a librarian, art collector, and
owner and practitioner of one killer recipe for
enchiladas — are the parents of twin teen-age
daughters who, incidentally, share little in common
except their birth date, or at least that's the
way it seems on the surface.

Similarly, there's no way you could have known,
unless you had already read our "There's No Place
Like Home" chapter, that the machine tool
technician will soon be leaving that lucrative
field for the somewhat less-profitable, but more
personally compelling, career of elementary

schoolteacher. Or that his wife's job includes the coordination of live programs featuring such giants of business literature and personal success as Ken Blanchard, Stephen Covey and Tom Peters. Or that he and his wife are the parents of not one but *two* sets of twins, in this case identical (at least physically).

Whoa! Twin daughters ... now *there's* an obvious connection for you: The San Diego accountant and the Milwaukee technician immediately have some common ground. If they ever get together, they'll no doubt have stories, laughter and maybe even a few twin-raising tips to share. There's probably a lot more they have in common as well — who knows what they might discover in the course of a good, old-fashioned conversation.

See, that's the wonderfully exciting thing about diversity. No matter how different you might seem from someone, there are bound to be traits and interests you share. And no matter how alike you might seem, there are bound to be differences. The commonalities are not necessarily to be valued any more highly than the differences, for it is often those differences that help us create magic. This incredible phenomenon can apply to anything from romance and marriage — opposites attract, they say — to friendship to business to creative collaboration. Hmmm. Isn't practically *all* of life, in essence, about creative collaboration?

Call it The Mix. We're talking about that wonderfully rich tapestry of people and personalities and ideas and backgrounds and opinions (meaning, of course, DIFFERENCES of opinion) and flavors and smells and sounds and sights and textures. You could call it chemistry, or even alchemy, because it's powerful stuff. As our friend the accountant and company president says — and this quotation will come up again later in this chapter — "Diversity lies in common people accomplishing the uncommon."

In search of a great team

Perhaps our greatest quest in life is the opportunity to spend that life doing the things we really enjoy doing, with the people we really enjoy doing it with, the people who bring out the absolute best in us and whom we reciprocate by bringing out the best in them. Wow! (As Tom Peters might say.) And, failing that, we find a way to do the best we possibly can with the people who occupy our world. There's bound to be some give and take, but that's life. That's life, indeed!

This is the way Peter Senge sums up that feeling of being involved in something special. The following paragraph, from his classic *The Fifth Discipline*, has long been an inspiration to us and, by extension, to our company:

> Most of us at one time or another have been part of a great "team," a group of people who functioned together in an extraordinary way — who trusted one another, who complemented each other's strengths and compensated for each other's limitations, who had common goals that were larger than individual goals, and who produced extraordinary results. I have met many people who have experienced this sort of profound teamwork — in sports, or in the performing arts, or in business. Many say that they have spent much of their life looking for that experience again.

Senge's name for that experience is "a learning organization." It's a worthy goal for all of us, whatever we might choose to call it. And it might be best attained by finding the magic in The Mix.

Our 'collective intelligence'

"I love to talk about the "collective intelligence" of our organization. Another version of that is my personal mission statement: I want to experience staying in fluid communication with clever people to achieve great things. Senge's paragraph about the learning organization — especially the part about complementing each other's strengths and compensating for the weaknesses — has long held a special place in my heart.

My friend Jack Furlong at Transylvania University likes to talk about "design flaws" in the brain. It's as if each of us has a "stupid section" somewhere in there among all the gray matter. Maybe it's math, or following directions. For me it's a rather wide area that includes the ability to operate machinery or sometimes to concentrate on small details.

You remember the scene at the end of the movie *Jerry Maguire*, where Tom Cruise's title character tells his wife something that the two of them had earlier seen a man on an elevator tell his girlfriend in sign language? "You complete me," he says.

Without getting overly sentimental, I have to say that's what Bunny does for me. She compensates for the design flaws in my brain by keeping me — the big picture, vision guy — grounded at least somewhat in reality.

That's what I mean by "collective intelligence," and that includes emotional intelligence as well as intellect. In a marriage partnership or in a business one, it's a good thing to have.

— Larry Holman

Collective intelligence intensifies our strengths and diminishes our weaknesses.

How many worlds ARE there?

When Cyrus W. Field laid the transatlantic telegraph cable in 1866, future U.S. Secretary of State William Evarts remarked:

"Columbus said, 'There is one world, there shall be two.' Cyrus W. Field said, 'There are two worlds — there shall be one.'"

Today, thanks largely to the onslaught of technological advances in areas such as communications, broadcasting and travel, we are all part of one increasingly "small" and interdependent world. Yet, sadly, at the same time, we are also far too many worlds, characterized as haves and have nots, First and Third Worlds, us and them. The United States, for its part, has become "two societies" — a nation divided economically as well as racially — concluded a recent report by the Milton S. Eisenhower Foundation, an urban policy group.

In many ways, we live in our own worlds. It is only natural that we seek to surround ourselves with people who look and act and talk much in the way that we do. Even those of us who claim to believe in diversity sometimes find that we could sure use a jolt of something a little *different* in our workplace or our neighborhood. We could benefit from a different viewpoint, perhaps, one that hasn't gotten so bogged down in routine and assumptions. We need an idea or a thought from left field, or at least from some source that we wouldn't ordinarily consider. Do you understand what we're saying? Just listen (or, if you've got the hardcover instead of the audio version of this book, read on)...

Out of the mouths of ... whom?

A distinguished university professor, well known on the lecture circuit, had a chauffeur who for years had driven him to all of his speaking engagements. One evening on the way to the lecture hall, the chauffeur told his employer: "What you do isn't so hard. I've heard your routine so many times, I know exactly what you're going to say and how you're going to say it. In fact, I could do it myself."

The professor, who was fighting a bit of a cold and didn't really feel like speaking, decided to accept the challenge. He said, "We're about the same size. It's a big auditorium, so you won't be that close to the audience. Let's just switch for tonight. I'll be the chauffeur, and you give the lecture."

So the chauffeur gave the lecture — and he was brilliant. He gave the full 90-minute presentation without notes, and without a slip. The audience gave him a standing ovation. After everybody was seated again, the speaker asked if there were any questions.

One student raised his hand, then launched into a long, complicated question involving research done years earlier by the professor, before he had been a speaker in demand — and before he'd had a chauffeur. Sitting in the back of the room, the real professor drew in his breath. Was their ruse about to be exposed?

When the student finally finished his question, the distinguished speaker thought for a moment, then said: "In all my years of lecturing, that is the simplest, most shallow question I have ever been asked. In fact, it's so simple that I'm going to ask my chauffeur to stand up and answer it!"

But seriously, leadership ideas, like leadership itself, can come from anywhere, from anyone. Ivan Seidenberg, chairman and CEO of the New York phone company NYNEX, reveals that he learned a great deal from an unlikely source on his first job. His story is related in Daniel Levine's article "My First Job," in the January 1997 edition of *Reader's Digest*.

At 18, he was working by day as a janitor in a Manhattan office building, saving money to go to college at night. One day the superintendent, an older man who tended to say little, told Seidenberg: "You know, there are companies that will help you pay for school," and informed him of a phone company program. The young man applied, took the employment tests and got a job with the company he leads today. Looking back on the experience, Seidenberg says:

> In the year I worked for Mike he didn't say much, but those few words spoke volumes. He gave me a helping hand. If you take pride in your work and do a good job, you never know who might be watching and one day provide a boost.

> Now when I talk to janitors and other employees, I ask, "What's happening?" Invariably they tell me something I didn't know. It doesn't matter if you're the janitor or the CEO, values and performance count — people are watching.

We are not alone

Yes, they are watching indeed ... and many of them are taking notes. For, as we have said, we do tend to surround ourselves with people like us.

In his book *The Clustering of America* (1988: Harper & Row, New York), Michael J. Weiss looks at the United States as a collection of 40 different neighborhood types, or clusters, based on Census data, consumer surveys and public opinion polls. He does so with the help of a target-marketing system known as *PRIZM* (Potential Rating Index for ZIP Markets), which matches ZIP codes with Census and survey data to provide a wealth of information about the characteristics of people who live in a certain neighborhood. This information includes such insights as median income, types of automobiles, eating habits, magazine subscriptions, hobbies, political beliefs and much more.

Despite the concerns that such information might raise — about issues like privacy, security and stereotyping, for example — there is some comfort to be found in such data, Weiss writes:

> It is something in the nature of Americans to shun stereotypes and cherish distinctiveness. As noted economics writer Robert Samuelson has observed, "We favor equality yet clutch to diversity." But while the cluster system disputes the notion of a global village and the "malling" of America, it also reveals that there are hundreds of neighborhoods all over the country filled with households just like our own home, sweet home. However unique we may feel, we are not alone in our lifestyles.

Women's advocate drives 'engine of change'

Sherrye Henry
WASHINGTON, D.C.

"All my professional life has led me to this position," says Sherrye Henry. "Everything I've wanted to do for women has led me here."

"Here" is the U.S. Small Business Administration's Office of Women's Business Ownership. As assistant administrator, Henry acts as an advocate for women business owners in both public and private sectors as well as within the SBA and throughout the federal government.

"This is the only office in the whole federal government that advocates for women businesses," Henry says. "It is exciting."

Her excitement is bolstered by the changes taking place in business. Recent statistics taken by the Census Bureau indicate that women now represent one-third of all business owners. And the National Foundation for Women Business Owners estimates that women are contributing $2.3 trillion (more than the gross national product of most countries) to the U.S. economy. By the year 2000, women are expected to own 40 percent to 50 percent of U.S. businesses.

"This engine of change is going down the track so fast because women are opening businesses at twice the rate of men," Henry says. "Starting this change was not accidental."

One reason for this development is that the Small Business Administration has made "purposeful outreach to women and minorities." Women, Henry says, did not have a level playing field in business. But over the last several years, the SBA has doubled its loans to women.

"We see the pent-up need out there as women try to provide a second income for families, particularly in rural areas and inner cities where there aren't jobs," Henry says. "We also see a need where women are suffering from downsizing and the glass ceiling. This office acts as an advocate for reaching out to socially and economically deprived businesses."

In her position, Henry is responsible for coordinating government efforts on behalf of almost eight million women entrepreneurs. She manages a $4 million Women's Business Center Program for women and monitors the Women's Prequalification Loan Program.

Henry also oversees a nationwide Women's Network for Entrepreneurial Training and mentoring program, which brings together female CEOs with women business owners who are planning to expand their businesses. "What we offer is often the technical experience that so many women need to bring their ideas and creativity to reality," she says.

Henry's background has made her uniquely qualified for her position. She has been both an entrepreneur and a businesswoman. As an independent producer/broadcaster for 15 years, she created the "Sherrye Henry Program" on WOR Radio in New York. She was the creator and host of "WOMAN!" the first television program developed primarily for a female audience. Among the first women in the country to write editorials on women's issues, she won an Emmy award for her television editorials. She is a magna cum laude graduate of Vanderbilt University and holds an MBA from Fordham University.

Henry has also written two books. Her second, *The Deep Divide: Why American Women Resist Equality* (1994: Maxwell Macmillan International, New York), discusses women's political, personal and professional attitudes and behavior. While much change has been achieved, she feels that women still resist putting other women into political and authority positions. For example, she says, out of 50 states there is currently only one female governor, and only 11 percent of Congress is female. "Only by voting our representatives into power are we ourselves empowered," Henry says.

For women interested in the Office of Women's Business Ownership and how they might start their own business, Henry recommends simply "turning on the computer." In January 1998, the SBA unveiled the Online Women's Business Center, an interactive, state-of-the-art web site. It offers virtually everything an entrepreneur needs to start and build a successful business, including online training, mentoring, individual counseling, topic forums and newsgroups, market research, a comprehensive state-by-state resource and information guide, and information on all of the SBA's programs and services, plus links to countless other resources. Information is available in English, Chinese, French, German, Italian, Japanese, Portuguese, Russian and Spanish. The web site is a public-private partnership with major U.S. corporations. You can access the Online Women's Business Center at **www.onlinewbc.org.**

"We have seen the most exciting changes," Henry says, "and we don't expect the momentum to change — only to grow."

Seeing outside of the box

Remember the scene from the movie *Smoke*, in our "Sidewalk" chapter? In that touching vignette, cigar-store customer Paul discovered a new facet of store owner Auggie's personality: his photographic hobby. "So you're not just some guy who pushes coins across a counter," Paul says. Auggie replies: "That's what people see, but that ain't necessarily what I am."

We tend to keep other people in little "mental boxes" by not taking the time to see them as any bigger than the limited dimensions in which we generally see them. The funny thing is, we sometimes do the same thing to ourselves. And when we see ourselves solely in terms of our position, it can create problems not only for ourselves but also for those around us. In *The Fifth Discipline*, Peter Senge cautions about what can happen when people "see their responsibilities as limited to the boundaries of their position":

> Recently, managers from a Detroit auto maker told me of stripping down a Japanese import to understand why the Japanese were able to achieve extraordinary precision and reliability at lower cost on a particular assembly process. They found the same standard type of bolt used three times on the engine block. Each time it mounted a different type of component. On the American car, the same assembly required three different bolts, which required three different wrenches and three different inventories of bolts — making the car much slower and more costly to assemble.

Why did the Americans use three separate bolts? Because the design organization in Detroit had three groups of engineers, each responsible for "their component only." The Japanese had one designer responsible for the entire engine mounting, and probably much more. The irony is that each of the three groups of American engineers considered their work successful because THEIR bolt and assembly worked just fine.

When people in organizations focus only on their position, they have little sense of responsibility for the results produced when all positions interact. Moreover, when results are disappointing, it can be very difficult to know why. All you can do is assume that "someone screwed up."

Obviously, we need to broaden our scope. So why should we see people — ourselves or others — simply in terms of the kind of work they do or where they live or the model of car they drive? Rather than look at the little details that make people different, why not focus on the commonalities, and also on the tremendously rewarding sense of discovery that goes with getting to know someone on more than one level.

There are some incredibly talented people in your neighborhood — and you may not know the half of it. Across the street or in the next department at work, there's a poet or painter or juggler or magician or gourmet cook or home brewer or dressmaker or flower arranger or pianist ... you get the picture. Yet you may know this person only by one facet of his personality: "Oh, that's Joe, the accountant. Number cruncher, you know."

Isn't it funny how we tend to simplify things that really are a lot more complex? Just think of the richness of life we're missing when we don't get to know our neighbors, co-workers and, in some cases, our family in a multidimensional way.

Many companies have discovered the psychic benefits of a talent show. Try it! You'll find that employees will put their considerable creativity to use in ways that may be revelatory to others. Getting to know others as well-rounded, complete people increases your empathy with them. It can break down artificial barriers between departments and "us versus them" mentalities. You might also try it at your next neighborhood block party. (Your neighborhood DOES have block parties, doesn't it?)

Sharing diversity

Sharing is essential to make a diverse workforce a productive workforce. An organization can travel to the ends of the earth to find good people from different backgrounds, but if they don't share common goals and understandings, they won't work together in harmony, and will accomplish very little.

Individuals and teams must learn to communicate and cooperate effectively across lines of function, age, gender, race and other differences. They must find the common ground that unites them, then strive together using proven principles of teamwork.

Here are five ways that sharing promotes cooperation among diverse groups in the workplace:

Share information. Keep information about the organization's progress toward its goals — diversity-related and other — flowing constantly. Information should flow in every direction: upward, downward and laterally. The more an organization understands itself, the more intelligently it can work to achieve its objectives. And the act of sharing helps employees cultivate a sense of ownership and belonging. Shared information can take many forms: spoken conversation, memo, newsletter, e-mail. The medium isn't as important as the message.

Share ideas. As we've already seen, good ideas are not limited to top management. Encourage employees at all levels of the organization to regularly get together with one another and with management to discuss their jobs and how to improve them. A suggestion program can also provide lasting benefits, provided that contributions are actually considered and not just given lip service. Who better understands a job than the person who actually does it? The suggestions that employees produce — especially within an organization with diverse perspectives — can benefit everybody.

Share training. Cross-training across functional and departmental boundaries can create a flexible workforce — and a flexible workforce is a powerful and cooperative workforce. When employees understand one another's jobs and how they are interdependent, they exhibit more empathy toward one another. While they realize the problems that a missed deadline in one area can cause for everyone down the line, they also understand what might have caused the deadline to be missed in the first place. They are more likely to seek satisfactory solutions to such challenges instead of finding someone to blame. In addition, the flexibility afforded by cross-training makes it easier for the organization to take up the slack when someone is sick or on vacation.

Share resources. As employees work at new skills and responsibilities, they need knowledge, tools and — perhaps most important — encouragement. All too often, employees enthusiastically enter a new job or take on new responsibilities, only to find that they don't have the resources needed to do the job effectively. Then their enthusiasm turns to resentment and suspicion, as they begin to question their importance to the organization. They might also question whether the organization is truly committed to the diversity objectives that brought them to the job.

Share incentives. Group incentives reward employees who work together to meet shared goals. In a diverse workforce, employees may find themselves "thrown together" with people whose backgrounds are different from any they've ever encountered. Offering incentives for group performance strongly encourages employees to overcome personal barriers and accept one another as partners on the same team.

Creativity, teamwork and the entrepreneurial spirit

Kyocera International
SAN DIEGO, California

Youth is "in" at Kyocera.

"We try to maintain a youthful vigor," says Rodney Lanthorne, president of Kyocera International, Inc., the North American regional management company for the worldwide Kyocera Group. "But that has nothing to do with the age of our employees. The concept is really about maintaining a

Rodney Lanthorne

youthful zest and seeking what is right. Youth is a state of mind, not of time."

Dr. Kazuo Inamori, who in 1959 founded Kyoto Ceramics (later shortened to Kyocera) with seven colleagues, was "profoundly influenced by the excitement of being a start-up," Lanthorne says. "We try to replicate that by organizing our operations into 'amoebas,' or small business units with their own profit and loss responsibilities. They are small, have clear tasks and are encouraged to implement their own initiatives. Amoebas provide a teamwork mechanism that promotes creativity and entrepreneurial attitudes among employees.

"This company strives to maintain the mentality of a perpetual start-up. We provide high-value-added products and services to our customers, and we aggressively pursue growth in our business and profits. In this way, we can provide greater opportunities to our employees. Everyone in the company has the responsibility to work hard and use their creativity and their God-given abilities."

Lanthorne noted that an amoeba's ability to adapt quickly to change, particularly as demanded by communications and electronics markets, is one of its advantages.

Despite its low profile and humble beginnings, Kyocera now ranks as the world's largest producer of advanced ceramic products. The company ranks as one of Japan's most profitable enterprises and is essentially debt-free. The Kyocera Group operates in more than 20 countries. But while the scale of the enterprise has grown significantly, it has maintained its decentralized, flexible organizational structure.

In 1971, it became the first Japanese-capitalized company to establish manufacturing operations in California. Eight years later, Lanthorne joined the North American operations as chief financial officer. Now, at age 52, he is in his 11th year as president and is one of three Americans on the parent company's board of directors.

"We have been pioneers and, as such, we ran the risk of finding arrows in our back," Lanthorne says. "When Kyocera came to the U.S., we made many mistakes, but we have learned along the way."

The U.S. operations systematically introduced the amoeba concept in the late '70s. Although the system originated in Japan, a homogeneous society, it has been adapted to function effectively in the more diverse United States.

"We have attempted to balance our North American operations with a local focus and a strong identification with the Kyocera value system," Lanthorne says. "With the strong leadership of our founder, we have tried to filter out 'the Japanese way' from our Kyocera philosophy, so that our local members can understand and buy into it. I believe the Kyocera value system transcends national and cultural boundaries and, for the most part, our employees here accept that proposition.

"In the early phase of our development in the U.S., many of our key management and engineers were Japanese expatriates. They made a very special contribution. Now, however, local managers identified as having the leadership qualities and sharing our management philosophy have been assigned the responsibilities to run our North American operations — and they are performing well."

As president, Lanthorne faces the challenge of recruiting, training and developing management who will share the corporate ideals.

"Today we're definitely in the early stages of the Third Wave, the Age of Knowledge," Lanthorne says, quoting Alvin Toffler. "We have to give our people whatever tools they need to satisfy the customer. The diversity of our members in North America gives us a challenge to come up with the training and development programs to arm them with the skills to optimize their creativity. But diversity cuts the other way, too. Diversity is one of the key reasons the U.S. remains as an incubator of new ideas. In the end, we benefit from the variety of ideas that may not exist within a less diverse environment.

"Diversity, like youth, is a state of mind or will. It's defined as the state of being different. We want to set ourselves apart from others. That's the kind of diversity that's important — not your race, color or creed. Diversity lies in common people accomplishing the uncommon."

How about a little common sense?

"Don't blame me, I voted for the other guy."

Ever notice how so many bumper stickers these days have a confrontational tone? It's almost as if lines are being drawn in the sand. Republicans over here, Democrats over there. Meat lovers over here, vegetarians over there. And so on and so on. We simplify our philosophies to sound bites, slap them on the backs of our cars and dare people to disagree with us. (Has anyone ever studied a possible link between bumper stickers and road rage?)

Why do we continue to define ourselves by our differences, as if they are obstacles that can't be overcome? Cabell Brand has strong ideas about that subject.

"The bad thing about the political party line is that it's so strict," says Brand, an entrepreneur and poverty fighter who lives in Salem, Virginia. "I really object to that element of the political system which is so dogmatic that you're going to support one party come hell or high water. I understand why it happens, because they want to have a majority in the Congress, and that's what they have to do, and they take their chances on some of the radicals. But I think the political system would be stronger if there was more flexibility; then people would support the candidate, regardless of a political label."

Maybe, to a large extent, happiness is based on our ability to get along with others, even those who hold markedly different viewpoints. Consider the recent Gallup poll that surveyed 18 nations before reaching the conclusion that the happiest people are in Iceland. Iceland? Yes, Iceland. It's a small (population 267,809) nation with its share of problems — including alcoholism, unwed pregnancies and COLD weather — yet the poll found 82 percent of its people to be satisfied with their personal lives, well ahead of the fifth-place United States (72 percent) and seventh-place Japan (42 percent).

Happiness can be found where you least expect it!

Richard C. Morais, writing in the October 23, 1995, issue of *Forbes* magazine, speculated about how Icelanders could be so happy. A high per-capita income, strong education and healthcare systems, and long lives could be part of the equation, he reasoned, but there seems to be more to it than that:

> Like Icelanders, Americans are individualists. Where we seem to differ is in our sense of community. Iceland, known as the land of "fire and ice," is about living with opposing forces. It is one of the most active volcanic countries on earth, but has 4536 square miles of glacier — heat and cold, co-existing. No surprise then that its society can reconcile another set of opposing forces: individualism and the needs of the community. ...
>
> Tolerance is not a hollow phrase in Iceland. The word for "stupid" is *heimskur*, which roughly means "comes from home" — or as we would say, provincial or narrow-minded. Icelanders believe only a dolt is unable to see the other fellow's position. In this sense, they might find some of what passes for political debate in the United States as absolutely *heimskur*.

Seeking 'pieces of the truth'

Dr. William J. Carroll
LISLE, Illinois

Dr. William J. Carroll, president of Benedictine University, has taken a leadership role in creating a learning environment marked by diversity.

"The measure of how well colleges deal with diversity is the measure of their success in the future," Carroll says. "We are faced with growing populations of minorities demanding access to quality education. Unfortunately, most of us have not been trained to respond to the learning needs of these new students. As a college administrator who is preparing his institution for the 21st century, I recognize that we are in the middle of this sea change. Consequently, and happily, I deal with diversity and diversity issues every day."

Although his activities vary greatly from day to day, Carroll maintains certain habits that increase his effectiveness. One is his early morning swim, which affords him time for reflection, constructing memos and letters in his head and reviewing strategies for the day.

He generally arrives at the office about 7 a.m. Fund-raising calls, board meetings and other responsibilities take up much of his day. But he takes time to be accessible to the people he leads. "I spend as much time as possible in other people's offices," he says, "listening to them and using their ideas, insights and energies to make the college the best place that it can be."

Although Carroll often works long hours, he makes a point of being home every evening for supper, even if he must return to the office. He spends as much time as possible with his wife and two daughters. "A golden rule that I maintain is not to take my work home with me," says Carroll, who also enjoys remodeling and gardening in his leisure time. "Spending time with the family always reminds me of what is truly important. These activities allow me to rest from the daily challenges of the office and to return each day with renewed interest and enthusiasm for the job to be done."

He finds challenges in every aspect of his job, particularly in areas such as fund raising and program development. As president, he says, part of his role is to be a "cheerleader" every minute of the day.

"Success for me," he says, "is measured in the success of the institution — student enrollment, graduates' success, fund raising, building and grounds improvement and so on — and in the morale of the people who give their lives to the institution."

Carroll sees tough chores and crises as "simply steps on the way" that should be dealt with immediately, before they get worse. "I have confidence in myself and my team that we will be able to react successfully to the crisis," he says.

His approach to the job stems largely from his philosophy background. "In reading the many philosophers, I became struck with the realization that no one was in possession of the 'whole truth,' but that they all seemed to have pieces thereof," he says. "Philosophy became for me the pursuit of a puzzle in which I would develop my own world view. I realized that every individual possesses his or her own unique perception of the world and that I needed to listen to everyone in order to make myself 'whole.'

"Truth is like a giant underground river, with many wells seeking its life-giving water. Race, ethnicity, religious affiliation are all wells leading to this underground source. Why not take advantage of the water drawn from each well? We need to create environments that will maximize the realization of our potential. I am convinced that this can be done only in a diverse workplace. Hence, I am constantly reaching out to new populations, developing programs that will serve all students more effectively."

At Benedictine University, Carroll has sought to develop programs that not only accommodate diverse populations, but also incorporate their contributions. Targeted populations have included racial minorities, veterans, college "stop outs" (a more positive term for dropouts) and students who need remedial aid.

"Success is simply the realization of one's potential, whether one be an individual or an institution," Carroll says. "If we enable and empower one another to be all we can be, then we are a success."

12

Citizens of the Globe

How individuals and organizations are giving and prospering

"The enormous needs and opportunities in society call for a great responsibility toward service. There is no place where this spirit of service can be cultivated like the home. The spirit of the home, and also of the school, is that they prepare young people to go forth and serve. People are supposed to serve. Life is a mission, not a career."

— Stephen R. Covey
   "Three Roles of the Leader in the New Paradigm"
   from the book _The Leader of the Future_
   (1996: Jossey-Bass, San Francisco)

Service in our country has almost come to be associated exclusively with customer service. As for service to our fellow man or to our country, the United States differs from many nations by not requiring a period of devotion to community service. Living in such a protracted period of peace has also removed from the horizons of many Americans the urgencies that some other countries live with.

But there is a revival of communitarian ideals in the air, embracing churches, companies and schools. The spirit of volunteerism is sweeping the country like never before, involving young and old, city and country, people from every race and background. Through service to their fellow humans and to the planet we inhabit, people are waking up to the possibilities and opportunities that giving gives back to us.

It's not just about assuaging guilt or accumulating bonus points for heaven. Nor is it a quick image fix for a company's PR department. What people are discovering is the pure joy of good works, the genuine sense of connection fostered by opening up one's mind and heart and giving freely of one's self. It sets off a chain reaction of goodwill that can lift up a neighborhood, and link it more closely to others.

Let's look at one shining example.

Shelter and service: the active mission of Habitat for Humanity

One of psychologist Abraham Maslow's tenets in the hierarchy of human needs is shelter. There is one worldwide organization that has built an unprecedented mission based on this universal need.

Habitat for Humanity's mission is to eliminate substandard housing by building affordable homes. Since its 1976 founding, volunteers including former President Jimmy Carter have constructed more than 60,000 homes in the United States and in more than 50 foreign countries. "We're in the vanguard of a movement to provide everyone with a decent place to live at a price they can pay," says founder and president Millard Fuller.

Many Habitat volunteers enjoy not only the visceral sense of accomplishment that every home builder feels, but also the opportunity to get to know the families moving into them, to meet and talk with people they might not otherwise have encountered.

We will not attempt to portray the full breadth of their programs here, but we can trace one local story and see how far its effects travel. There may be no better illustration of the saying "think globally, act locally" than Habitat for Humanity.

In Lexington, Kentucky, the goal is to try to build about 15 homes a year. Habitat staff have to winnow down a list, numbering more than 100, of eligible families. Then they have to find sponsors. A single Habitat home in Lexington requires $35,000 in cash or in-kind donations. Some homes are built by single sponsors; others are backed by a coalition of sponsors.

The homes are traditional frame houses with vinyl siding. Certain parts of the job are subcontracted, but the framing, finishing and painting are largely done by volunteers. A build can last anywhere from one week to six months, depending on the skill level of those involved. Many groups sponsoring a home organize themselves, bringing in their own construction leaders, while Habitat provides the materials and support.

Future homeowners join in the process by assuming a 20-year mortgage and assisting in the actual building process — what Habitat people call "sweat equity." As a brochure expresses the experience of one couple,

"By the time their home was complete, they had not only a new address, but new friends and new skills as well."

The biggest problem faced by Habitat is available property. The group is also working to get people involved year-round, at the times volunteers are available. Leading the efforts in Lexington is executive director Mary Jo Votruba.

Mary Jo Votruba

Votruba likes the challenge of putting a mission into action. After five years with the United Way and over 11 years with God's Pantry, a Lexington-based food bank that serves 48 counties, she has enthusiastically taken on her role with Habitat.

Votruba knows the nonprofit ropes, and her forthright "let's get something done" nature is immediately evident upon meeting her. She took some time from her many tasks to talk about neighborhood leadership in a Habitat context, the roles of nonprofits and companies in communities, and the personal rewards of being a good neighbor:
I'm involved in the purchasing of properties for Habitat projects, so when I'm out walking in the

neighborhoods, people approach me because I'm not known. They wonder what I'm up to, then they tell me what they like or dislike about Habitat. The things that people say are very useful to me as I prepare to communicate to the larger community what Habitat is all about.

Getting out and talking to people is so important. It's also motivational, because it's easy to get stuck with all the paperwork, and you can go out and see the real people, be more closely tied to what you're doing.

I was visiting a homeowner the other day, but she wasn't home. Her neighbors were out working in their yard across the street where I was parked. The block was not very nice, but their yard was just a showcase. I said, "Oh, your yard looks so beautiful. It's obvious you've put a lot of work into it." They told me about their trees. I told them I was visiting from the Habitat office and the lady said, "Those Habitat houses are really an example to us. We've really been working on our property since Habitat came into the neighborhood because they really set the pace here, and we have to look as good as they look."

They looked out their window and they liked what they were seeing, and it motivated them to make their property look better. I don't hear that very often. When we're talking with government officials, they're concerned about the Habitat homes looking so plain!

I've been living and working in the Lexington community for about 20 years. I'm very blessed because my husband can earn an income for us, and so I didn't have to work. But I'm not very good just being at home, and for my own peace of mind I needed to be out in the community. When we were *younger, I did a lot of volunteer work within schools and for our neighborhood.*

When I started with United Way about 16 years ago, I really got to see the decision makers at work, really got to know the community. I learned a lot about the surrounding communities. Lexington considers itself the center of the universe in this part of the country, but there are a lot of towns around here with a lot of talent and concern for their own communities.

I'm trained as a social worker, and I really didn't want to spend the rest of my life fundraising, so I looked for a way to get back into closer contact with direct service. I became involved with God's Pantry, which at that time was a small emergency food bank. God's Pantry grew tremendously — they probably use more volunteers now than any other organization in central Kentucky.

Lexington Habitat for Humanity is an organization that hasn't ever had a very permanent staffing arrangement — it's all been done by volunteers. Even with that, we're one of the best-producing communities per capita in the nation. We've built 107 homes in this area over 11 years. Louisville will reach 100 sometime in the year 2000, and Cincinnati, a much bigger city, stands at 84 homes.

So, in the overall scheme of things, we've done very well at building houses. But we haven't done a great job of funding them, and we haven't created the structure that encourages people to remain involved for the long haul. For instance, in Louisville, a lot for a Habitat house is sold to Habitat for $1. That doesn't happen here yet. It can, if housing is made a higher priority.

We've used people up, and you can't continue to do that in a community of this size without eventually running into trouble. So we've gone back and put a structure underneath this place.

We're creating an organization that will survive over the long haul ... or until we eliminate poverty housing in this community. We have a long way to go on that, so we're probably going to be around for a while.

Lining up with the bottom line

Keeping our mission in mind, we have to also remember that we are a small business. We are accountable to our donors for how we use their money. We need to treat our volunteers in such a way that they stay with us and continue to support us, and speak well of us in the community. We've done great, but now we're stepping back and firming up our organization.

There is some controversy about the discussion of the bottom line: what's our mission, acting on faith, etc. But if you can't survive, it doesn't matter what your mission is. The vendors deserve to be paid, and the donors deserve to be recognized. Sometimes you have to walk a fine line when you're walking the talk. Sometimes our people feel that things should be handled differently, but agencies that survive watch their financial picture very closely. Those that go down either use their funds inappropriately or just manage things poorly, and people donate to other organizations.

We're trying to bring some of the people who have drifted away back into the fold, because in a community this size, there are only so many places you can go. We don't solicit donations outside our area.

We can't build all the houses we need to build with the Methodists building one house, the Episcopalians building another and the Catholics building yet another. We have to get into the business community. Now, they may not always come for the most humanitarian or even Christian reasons. They'll sometimes come because it's good publicity. So are we going to refuse to be involved with them? No, because there are families who need houses, and those companies' money is as good as everybody else's money. Some people view it as selling out at the expense of the mission. No, they'll help us accomplish the mission. We can't impact this community building just five to 10 houses a year — there's more poverty being created every year than that.

Companies can use their connections to agencies like Habitat to strengthen their own organizations. They create better community relations within their plants and factories by getting people involved in projects like Habitat. We've helped to create better relationships among people of different faiths, by them working together on the same house. It works the same with people coming off of the factory floor, where all they've ever seen each other do is the same repetitive task every day. When they're painting and hammering next to each other, they start to talk about their kids and the other things they have in common, and they see each other differently back in the workplace. Employers understand now the importance of working together as a team, and this improves the team relationships.

Learning the meaning of home

While we're more aggressively courting the business community, we aren't forgetting the churches whence we come. Within Habitat International there are literally hundreds of different congregations involved in some fashion. But what happens so often is that a church will lead us to a business. Several houses have come about this year as the result of that process.

The reason many businesses don't contribute to some of the major charities is that they have no idea what those organizations are really doing. Once they understand that, they become longtime supporters. Habitat is a perfect opportunity for hands-on involvement, because you start with a literal foundation and you watch the house go up and feel that sense of accomplishment. Habitat really has the rare opportunity to make long-range changes in people's lives: giving them stability they never had, giving their kids a permanent residence, giving them an environment where they can study, sleep and educate themselves to be productive citizens. We work at that one family at a time.

We have basic limitations on the houses, but we aren't limited to just houses — we decide what's important to our mission. As we get stronger in our primary mission of building houses, we'll be able to do more in other areas of permanent life changes.

We're already making big strides in that area as we take our families through the pre-education process to become permanent home owners. We're teaching them what it takes to do that: The roof is going to need repair, and you'd better have saved some money for that. If they haven't done this, the property will deteriorate, and the properties will become next year's slums.

Some people have received the mistaken impression that coming into a Habitat home has reduced your housing cost from, say, $500 a month down to $200 a month. We need to help our families understand investment in the future, building equity. They have never had the opportunity to invest in the future — most of them have lived day to day, hand to mouth, by necessity. In today's society, if you're up against it, you do the best you can with as little you have and you do whatever you can to get by. This is an opportunity to build equity, to say at the very least "In 20 years you will own this place free and clear." If they've kept it up and they want to move somewhere else, they can put it on the market, and maybe move up to a better home. But they have the right to do whatever they want to do, just like every other independent homeowner.

Everything comes back to education, and we're concentrating very heavily on educating our families. I think that's one of the most important things we do. Over a long period of time, I think the community will look at Habitat homeowners and say, "Those people know what it means to make the best out of what you have." If we can get the homeowners to think in those terms, what a success we truly would be. They would truly have created something of value for the future and for their children. Our society is so keen on instant gratification. But if you're going to be successful at this and poor to start, you have to latch onto the idea that there's something better in the future if you treat today right.

You'll see cars parked outside of homes that are of greater value than the place they're raising their family. But the other side of that is you have to be careful not to impose your own value system on other people. People have the right to make choices, including bad ones. When people are being given a specific opportunity, though, you would like to think that they would try harder to think long range. I do believe that the key is education.

The key in educating our families is the idea of partnership, with the understanding that none of this works unless they are full partners, unless they catch the spirit of working with other people to accomplish something important, and to do things that benefit not only their family but the broader community.

Right now we're pre-building storage sheds for our houses. Even in that period, we have people building each other's sheds. They get to know one another. There's great variation in these families in terms of background, disposition — they probably wouldn't get to know each other otherwise, wouldn't take the time. People find out that their neighbors have the same hopes and dreams. They come out to help with other people's houses.

What's a neighbor anymore?

I think one of the downfalls of televisions and VCRs is this cocooning trend. I live in a nice neighborhood and I find it more cocooned than many of the neighborhoods where we build Habitat houses. People don't sit out on their porches. Even the kids are inside all the time.

I couldn't tell you who lives in some of the houses. They get in their car in their garage, get back out of their car in their garage, and if they don't do much yardwork or don't go for walks, you'll never see them. I guess they're happy, but I don't know!

I came from a small Minnesota community, where everybody knew everybody else. If you did something you weren't supposed to do, before you got home, your parents knew about it. People paid attention. When somebody told something like this to my mother, for instance, she thanked them for letting her know, instead of telling them it was none of their business. If I complained about somebody's child today, they would probably tell me it was none of my business. I think we've taken a very different attitude about how we relate to one another.

One of the things that happens with Habitat is if there are several homes in the neighborhood, they have their own support system. Sometimes it happens with only one house. We built a house next door to a run-down house where bad things were happening. Now, nothing bad goes on there, because the Habitat owner knows people in the neighborhood.

Making service a priority

I think you have to set priorities, because it's easy to get so busy that some of the most important things in your life get short shrift. It's important to know your boundaries and be able to say "I'm out of time."

The biggest gripe I have with some of the larger volunteer organizations is that you can only volunteer with them between 8:30 a.m. and 5 p.m. because that's when their staff works. Well, a lot of volunteers are not available then because they work, too! I think it's a real change in attitude that a lot of social service agencies have to make. A lot of volunteer organizations are not necessarily volunteer-friendly. That's the only way to get the most out of people. When they know you're making that effort, they'll make the time to help you get the work done.

I think people ultimately find the time to do the things that they feel are important, either for themselves personally or for their community. What's important for us is that when people have a volunteer experience, you give them the best volunteer experience they can have: You're prepared, you give them the proper instruction, you express profuse gratitude, because everybody wants to know they are appreciated. We want them to see that without them, the whole thing couldn't have happened.

Giving back: Success spurs success

"I remember one night over there, it was a clear night with a billion stars, and I'm sitting there thinking 'My God, we're in Africa, in a one-room mud brick house in the middle of nowhere with no electricity and no water — why would we do this?'"
— Patrick Smith

One of Votruba's board members is Patrick Smith, president of Software Information Services, an Inc. 500 company that was recently accorded the honor of IBM Premier Business Partner by virtue of its business results, customer satisfaction and quality measurements.

Only 1 percent of IBM's 1,300 midrange partners worldwide earn this distinction.

SIS offers technology consulting; system, networking and printing hardware; a complete menu of software products for accounting, manufacturing and other applications; and services that

Jean and Pat Smith

include custom application development and system migration. The company represents such industry leaders as Microsoft, SupportNet, GeneXus and DataMirror.

The company has been up and running since 1982, under the guidance of Smith and three other principal owners: his wife, Jean; Steve Sigg; and Greg Otis.

"The importance of relationships is a key to our success up to now," Patrick Smith says. "First and foremost, we want to do what's right for the customer. We want a winning strategy for everyone: our customer, our vendors and ourselves.

"We are willing to accept change and work with our partners for the long term. Our customers like us to have some skin in the game, to share the risk and be a partner in growth, rather than just another supplier."

In 1997, the Smiths followed the example of Habitat founders Millard and Linda Fuller in going on a mission to Africa. What they experienced there has changed them inexorably, bringing them closer to their faith, their family and ultimately their home community.

Pat Smith:

About six years ago, I got involved at Christ the King Church. Every year, the Catholic churches in Lexington get together and build a house. I really enjoy Habitat because it's easy to get work done and meet some people without the commitment going on for long periods of time. In the summertime, we can build a house in six to eight weeks, then go back the next year and do it again.

Last year, Jean and I came up with this idea during Lent that we were going to take two weeks off and go volunteer somewhere and work. I really wanted to go to Africa, and I convinced Jean of this, too. A Catholic nun from the Sisters of Divine Providence came up to Christ the King (church) and spoke of their mission in Ghana and the school that they run. We told her we were interested in going over and doing some work and asked her if there were any opportunities.

After she spent about half an hour telling Jean about the snakes and the food, she realized we were serious about it. She was leaving to go over there in a few days, and said she'd look into working something out for us to come over ourselves. It wasn't real encouraging, because it takes so long to do anything over there and coordinate details. But we said "Give it a try" anyway.

Not long after that, I was working with the church relations department at Habitat. In one of our conversations at Habitat, they were trying to get me to work on the Carter project, and I said I didn't think we could because we were already taking two weeks off to go to Africa. He asked us what we were doing and I told him. He said, "You know, we build houses over there."

So he sent us a brochure from this organization called Global Village (an arm of Habitat for Humanity International), which builds houses all over the world. They're generally two-week work camps. Sure enough, there was a trip to Ghana. Jean and I sent in the application, thinking if the project with the nuns falls through, this will be the backup plan. We had no idea who to turn to and say "Hey, we'd like to go to Africa and volunteer for two weeks. Who do we call?" It's not something you find on the cover of travel magazines.

Well, you can guess what happened next. About the time we heard from Habitat saying "Yes, we'd like for you to go on the trip," within another day or two we heard from Sister Theresa in Ghana saying "Oh yes, we'd love to have you." So here we are with both of them wanting us to go, so we said what the heck, let's take a whole month and do both.

We went with 10 people from the States to build the Habitat house in a remote village called Assasan, in the central region of Ghana, with no water or electricity.

It was a tough, three-hour drive from the airport out to Assasan. There were 14 of us crammed into this van, and all I saw was these little houses and so many people. When you've never been to a Third World country and it hits you, it's almost more than just a culture shock.

Habitat houses there are 20-by-20-foot mud brick, no water or electricity, with a little utility block building beside them that's about 5-by-15-foot, a pit latrine, a bathing stall and a kitchen storage area. You cook outside over an open fire on the ground and don't take any food in the house because of insects.

You mix your concrete right out on the ground. It doesn't take a lot of skills, just a lot of hard work. All we did was move materials the whole time. Water was a quarter-mile away and you carried it in these head pans. The sand was about 200 yards away. So all we did for 70 to 80 percent of the time was go get the sand, go get water, go get bags of cement. If all the materials were there, you could build one of those houses in one day.

There is a lot of erosion, open sewers. You hardly saw anything that was two-story. The only thing left of the old Catholic church was a bell tower. Like everything else, these mud bricks eventually get in such bad shape they just dissolve or cave in.

Jean Smith:

One thing that struck me was how poor most Ghaneans were, and yet they were very happy. Sure, they wanted more, but they were happy.

Pat Smith:

There weren't the haves and have-nots, there were only have-nots. From a purely financial standpoint, they're very poor, but I think they're very rich in their values, personalities, morals and religious beliefs.

One night, three or four of us were sitting there, a few pretty smart people, and I asked the question "Who's better off, us or them?" And we honestly couldn't come up with a definitive answer. We could say we have better food, transportation, lights, water, from a purely economic point of view. But when you look at their values, they seem to be a lot better off. In a lot of respects, they're a whole lot better off than we are.

Faith as a practice

As for religious diversity, Ghana is as multicultural as the United States. There are Anglican, Methodist, Muslim, Pentecostal, New Apostolic, Baptist and traditional African tribal congregations, services and rituals. Christianity is the dominant religion, but is sometimes modified by the neighborhood; for instance, drums might be played as part of the Catholic Mass.

Jean Smith:

When we came back here and went up to Mass, I thought, "Gosh, this is dull." Over there, you bring up the offertory and you dance back— they have a wonderful time.

Pat Smith:

Sunday is Church Day. It didn't really matter which denomination. Services were a minimum three-hour service. They'd die up here at Christ the King if you went and had a three-hour Mass one day!

When the rest of the group left, we went with them down to the capital, Accra, which is about a three-hour drive. Then we drove up to Senyani, which is about an eight-hour drive north, to meet these two nuns. One of them used to teach here at Christ the King from 1954 to 1957. They do two things up there. One is a large church, a diocese, called Cathedral of Christ the King. They run a retreat center there for the religious. The Sisters of Divine Providence also have a school for girls there called Kwasi Bukrum — KBK, they always called it. It was a remote village as well, very similar to Assasan. They did not have any Habitat houses, but very similar mud brick structures.

The sisters have been there about 10 years. They also have schools and a hospital in Madagascar for lepers. I got the sense that it was pretty much of a struggle for them. To me it would be very difficult to do that kind of work anyway, on the long term. They stay a minimum of three years. It's a hard life in a country that's difficult.

Some of the nuns were African. Four or five of the nuns were from the United States. Two had taught in Lexington at Christ the King: Teresa in the '50s and Janet in the '70s. Then there were a couple other nuns from Texas. It's like a network over there of Catholic religious. They've built a lot of schools there, hospitals, churches of course.

I think one of the ways people here can connect to people in villages such as this is through religious faith. I don't know how I would describe my faith. We go to church all the time, but I wouldn't call us strong, devout, praying Catholics.

They're more open with their faith, far more than we are. Everything they would do or say would be centered around some kind of a prayer. Most of the businesses have a religious name. Most of the taxis and lorries were named something like "God Almighty's Transport." It's almost comical — you could do a heck of a photo book on businesses in Ghana that have religious names. But it's sincere — they're so deeply religious.

Different standards, new perspectives

Pat Smith:

We spent two weeks with them building this house. They had two completed houses that nobody had moved into yet, so they put the guys into one house and the women in another. Then they realized Jean and I were married, didn't think it was proper that we weren't together, so they asked another lady in the village and she made room for us in her house by sending a couple of her kids to the neighbor's house.

It's hard to determine populations. I would say a couple thousand lived in Assasan. It's difficult because you could look at a room that's 8 by 10 and there could be from two to 10 people living in that room. So when you look at a structure, it's impossible to determine how many people would live in it. Then they have compounds — a series of rooms, square with an open central courtyard and rooms all around it. You'd have whole extended families owning or living on compounds: grandparents, parents, children, aunts, uncles, cousins ... you could have as many as 100 people in one of those compounds.

We heard drums one night. They were announcing this communal work day that the chief had called. The next morning, they beat them again.

There is a really strong sense of community and communal effort. Family values are very strong. They're all subsistence farmers for the most part, and Saturday is always Farm Day. The entire family walks out to the farm, which could be anywhere from two to 10 miles away, and they work there.

Going home

Pat Smith:

The thing that hit me first was when we got to Gatwick airport early in the morning and I went into the bathroom and there were mirrors everywhere and it was so bright. I felt like it was the first time in a month I'd seen bright light. And then there was the fast food ... there's not a fast-food restaurant in all of Ghana.

It hit me, when I saw all the excesses we have, it hit me like a big brick wall.

Jean Smith:

The one thing I remember, when we got on the road back to Lexington, was the difference between the roads in Ghana, which are mostly potholes, and the interstates here.

Everything about the whole place was totally different from anything we have here. It was total culture shock. It took two or three days before you could look around and start to notice specific things.

The children were another way we connected to such a foreign place. One thing I noticed: They had some type of event or entertainment for us every night, to help us understand their culture and village ... they had dancing and drumming one night, and there were adults who got up and danced, but then a lot of the children got up and danced. You could just see the mothers, you know. I felt like I was up at Christ the King watching my kids put on a show. The girls and boys were laughing, and one had a crush on the other, and they were the same. They're a continent away, but they're just like our kids.

Giving may last more than a lifetime

"A man there was, and they called him mad; the more he gave, the more he had."
                                    — John Bunyan

Jean Smith:

I can't say how, but it's affected my whole life. I think about those people every day. There are so many more options here than there, and I feel like whereas before our business was everything, this has just opened up my life, there's so much more that we can do. It gave me a different outlook.

Pat Smith:

Since I came away from there, I vowed never to complain again — I've done a fair job of it. It drives me up a wall when people complain about them not sweeping the streets or that there's garbage on the ground. A pothole in the road here that people keep calling up the mayor and raising hell over, over there they're lucky to have a road to get from point A to point B — any times they drive off the road because it's so bad. It's just hard to complain about little things here when you see there it's in such bad shape.

I call it humbling. Everybody needs a good humbling experience. You get all wrapped up in what you have, and upset at what you don't have or when something doesn't go right here. So stop and think about that, what's the grander scheme of things ... the pothole down at the corner is not that big a deal, and we have a tendency to make a big deal of it now.

It's also given me a sense of wanting to do more for people. I'm more involved in Habitat now locally. I'd like to do a lot more volunteer work.

I've been involved in the Outreach Ministries committee. There are far more people involved at Christ the King now than four or five years ago. Then, there were only a handful of people doing outreach, which I define as doing something outside those four corners of the church property. A lot of people do stuff within the church and for the church, but their activities are not related so much to things outside the church.

But now there are 200 to 300 people over the course of the year who do things for people outside Christ the King, like serving dinners at the Hope Center on Friday night, or working on a Habitat house, or delivering Meals on Wheels to the people who really have no connection to Christ the King *whatsoever. You see a lot more of that now, and I think that's really good.*

The big outgrowth of this whole project is to try to get more people involved. In the bigger scheme of things, that's the whole purpose of this trip — to help other people over a longer period of time. You can get people to go over and build the church and houses.

Realistically, what would be nice is if the 20 people who may go over this year decide there's something else important they ought to do next year, wherever it is: Africa, Third and Race streets in Lexington, the Salvation Army. That's the bigger picture: to get more people involved in doing things for people who need help.

The next stage

Their work done for that year, the Smiths hatched another plan, one that they have seen through to at least partial fruition.

The Catholic church in Assasan was so badly deteriorated that there was nothing left but the bell tower. The Smiths resolved to try to raise funds and supply American workers to build a new church. Through their efforts at their church and through Habitat for Humanity, they have raised the necessary money for the building and plan to send two teams to do the actual building of not only the church, but five more Habitat homes as well. Without such assistance, the rebuilding might have taken as long as 20 years in Ghana's impoverished economy.

One of the people they met in Ghana was John Osei-Kwakye ("o-say-kwa-chay"), a 30-year-old Ghanean with Habitat of Ghana. Right now, 38 Habitat houses are under construction. More than 1,000 have been built in Ghana since Habitat began its mission there in 1987. While it may cost $35,000 to fund a house here in the States, in Ghana the cost for one of the modest mud brick homes is around $1,000. In Osei-Kwakye's region, which encompasses nine cities, 262 houses have been constructed. Three separate American Habitat groups are making trips there in 1998, including the Smiths' group.

As it happened, one of the Smiths' Habitat colleagues invited Osei-Kwakye to visit the school he teaches at in Florida, Rawlings College, in the spring of 1998. The Smiths quickly arranged to have John visit them in Lexington as well, to help recruit for the mission and to visit their home as they had visited his. It was the first trip of his life outside the country.

During his visit, he shared some of his perspective on the challenges he and his countrymen face and what constitutes community spirit in the heart of Africa.

John Osei-Kwakye:

I think what Ghana needs right now is to invest in ourselves. I think we can use the technological development, but what I think we need to do is not only draw foreign investors, but invest ourselves, plow back what we have into the country's economy. That way not so much would be taken from the country, and the reliance on outside investors might decrease.

John Osei-Kwakye

Gold, diamond, manganese and bauxite mining produce a lot of income in Ghana, but most of it leaves the country. I lived in a gold mining town for six years — my brother is a gold miner. It was very labor intensive, but that has improved. They started this mining over 100 years ago, but they're still working these deposits.

We have the human resources in Ghana. People know what to do. What we are lacking is the finance. It is not easy to get a loan, even if you save with a bank, because of the bureaucracy. But we have the ability.

I ask myself, "What can I do for my people?" Many of the people with Habitat are not able to pay their mortgage because they are not working. So I try to think of what we can do, even if it's as simple as baking bread or farming mushrooms. But no matter what you have in mind, the money's not there.

In Ghana, people come together to do things for their immediate environment on a regular basis: clean and repair the roads, for instance. People also come together in large groups for funeral festivities. Some mourn and some make merry at the funeral. It is like New Orleans, with bands and people dancing and crying.

In Ghana, a neighborhood is the whole community. Our houses are so clustered together. We do everything together. In Ghana, unlike here in the

United States where you can go six months in your apartment without seeing your neighbor, we see each other all the time.

Excerpts of letters from Osei-Kwakye to Smiths:

I have been made the building committee chairman of the church and I see this as a challenge. It implies I have to sacrifice leaving the village for the city to seek some gainful employment for as long as the church remains uncompleted. I've already spent five-odd years in the village seeing to the Habitat program and that has affected me financially, but all the same, I see a call to serve as a divine call and I equally believe in divine providence. Under the circumstances, I have decided to study privately for a post-graduate diploma.

*   *   *   *   *

May God Almighty bless you in your endeavors, for your efforts you are making to assist us in building our church. It will be a dream come true to see you and Jean dedicate our church.

*   *   *   *   *

The Archbishop has agreed to officiate an open air Mass to commemorate the foundation stone laying of the building. The building would be dedicated in September with the last batch. We at Christian Village met to discuss our role in the mission. We are preparing five new houses we have built since August to accommodate the volunteers. We are also preparing a vegetable garden to enable us to get fresh vegetables for the kitchen.

*   *   *   *   *

Thanks a million once again for your efforts made towards getting us the assistance to build our church. May God Almighty grant you the strength to accomplish this missionary work you've started. When I first broke the news of the 50 volunteers coming down to work with us, you can imagine the yellings and spontaneous dancing that greeted it. The only surviving member of the generation that built the old church and who now is 100 years old added an emotional touch to the occasion. His wish is to die after the building he labored so much to put up is replaced. He called your coming down to us a sign of divine intervention. As he shed tears of joy, many were those who could not help but join him.

The chain of relationships that has joined together people from such separate places and viewpoints in this story proves something: There's a connection stronger than any materials. It's the power of human beings doing things for one another.

Volunteering for the future

"Today's business leader cannot justify his existence by profit statements alone. He must also render service to his local, national and world community."
— Dorothy Shaver

You can see how all the participants in the Habitat for Humanity process bring what they do back home with them, whether it's halfway around the globe, or from the Habitat jobsite to their regular workplace. Osei-Kwakye took back to Ghana a newfound perspective on what he does, as well as establishing even firmer relationships with his American counterparts.

As Mary Jo Votruba cited, the effects of community service on a private enterprise can be as profound as they are for the people they're helping. Today's businesses are looking for ways to make a difference, and they're finding them in many places: in the lives of their employees, in education, in donation of labor and expertise, and in an overall spirit of wanting to contribute not just to charity, but to a sustainable community, a sustainable world.

In *Corporate Global Citizenship: Doing Business in the Public Eye* (1997: New Lexington Press, San Francisco), Noel Tichy and his fellow editors provide a snapshot of what's evolving in this arena, assembling in-depth articles and interviews and profiling the companies whose programs and people are making a difference.

At IBM, for example, the Fund for Community Service often donates computer systems to volunteer employees' favorite nonprofits. Whirlpool continues its long-established programs in the Twin Cities area of southwest Michigan, its home territory for the past 80 years. American Express has pioneered a new technique for financing ecologically sound nature preserve projects in Costa Rica, Brazil and Argentina.

For these companies and so many more, the impetus is not compliance or a new way of marketing, it's a genuine feeling of stewardship on the part of their leaders.

And it's not just private enterprise, either. Chris Cherches, the city manager of Wichita, Kansas, cites other kinds of efforts:

"Wichita's experience has been to strongly encourage responsible growth, which means addressing any negative environmental conditions, perceptions of public safety, assurance of adequate infrastructure, including water supply, as well as public amenities, attractions and other quality-of-life features of entertainment, cultural development and recreational opportunities.

"The city government's responsibility is to provide a community which has balance — both in services and quality-of-life features — for businesses to grow, develop and be successful; good schools; quality parks and leisure opportunities; and many other benefits, including community cleanliness and stable, reasonable tax structures.

"Our local experiences include taking the initiative to solve ground water problems (without federal Superfund intervention), beneficial reuse of groundwater contamination from an old landfill, annexing areas with environmental challenges to allow for solutions to be offered and spread over a larger tax base, developing new sources of safe drinking water to extend the area water supply (a new innovation in the making), and a host of other actions. In all of these examples, the city had input of the citizenry and the business community in addressing these challenges in a collective decision-making arena."

Cleveland Burton of American Saw & Manufacturing expresses his sense of involvement with the company's local community:

"More and more people want to make an impact. We can each do something for somebody else, at little or no cost to ourselves. So are we willing to do so?

"All of this comes together to make a business. If the business is properly focused, people have to give back to community.

"Our reputation for community service has been the same since 1915. It goes beyond donations, though like others we give to United Way, Big Brothers, YMCA, Red Cross. For instance, we're working on a leadership development curriculum for employees to give them a well-rounded background. One thing all of our employees learn is that it's expected of you to give something back as part of your job. We let it be interest-driven, and the interests of the community at large derive the reward."

Seeking the abundance mentality

"*The abundance mentality is the idea that there is plenty on this planet for everyone. If we will share what we have with each other, everyone can win. ... This philosophy, in a nutshell, is this: When individuals accumulate more wealth than they need to live well, the difference between what they spend on living well (everyone has a different definition of living well) and what has been created is really not theirs. This excess wealth is a stewardship that has been given to individuals to take care of and do something with that matters.*"

— Hyrum W. Smith,
*The 10 Natural Laws of
Successful Time and Life
Management*

It's no accident that Hyrum Smith saved the best natural law for last: "Give more and you'll have more." Like Stephen Covey's important 7th Habit — Sharpen the Saw — the art of giving of yourself, whether in monetary, labor or educational terms, is a practice that embraces and nurtures all the other facets and disciplines of our lives.

It is our loose collections of individuals — companies, civic groups, associations, nonprofits — that have driven service to new levels, by learning how to give as a team. The members of such steward organizations know what responsibility means, and what rewards each individual can bring away from such experience: fellowship, humility, perspective, awe.

It's not just a metaphor, either. It's quite possible that "give and take" has evolved into "give and accept." The fuller, richer lives of the givers attest to the very real power of the abundance mentality.

13

Paying the Utility Bill

What's the first thing you think of when you hear the word "infrastructure"? A map of the interstate highway system? A circuit board? Your new gutters? Those all qualify.

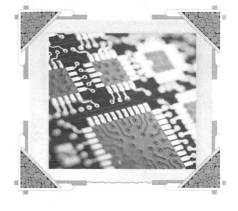

Perhaps only "empowerment" is more widely cited today as a pressing need for successful organizations. You can have all kinds of lofty goals and far-reaching plans, but if the necessities, the backbone of an enterprise or a household, aren't taken care of, all the best-laid plans go right out the window. An infrastructure is literally "what's below" the surface of things. It's the foundation, the grid, the network of connections that supports the activity above it.

We're going to explore ways of establishing and maintaining such a foundation. The outward manifestations of this structure are everywhere: traffic signs, curbs, staircases, fiber optic cables, satellite dishes, waste management ... almost every element of neighborhood life owes at least part of its existence to some underlying skeleton of material or process.

Like everything else, the infrastructure of our country and our world has been undergoing many changes over the last 100 years. Although many basic parts of our modern neighborhoods have only been around for a couple of decades, we can very easily take them for granted.

One thing's for sure. When the phone, electric, water or gas bill comes, it tends to jump to first in line on the payment schedule. The question is: Can we give the same priority to the other building blocks of our workplaces, our cities and our lives?

The neighborhood within

"If you think you can do a thing or think you can't do a thing, you're right."
— Henry Ford

At our company and in our family, if you undertake something with a good heart, you'll have to wait a long, long time for us to second-guess you. That good heart is a power station, and the ability to trust is the transformer.

It's not always what's below, but what's within as well. In fact, like intramurals and intranets, you might call the neighborhood within your "intrastructure." This is the composite of personal utilities that make up who you are and how you interact with the world.

One of the original meanings of "utility" comes from the world of theater (and has been co-opted by the world of baseball): a player prepared to jump in at a moment's notice to play any role. To do such a thing requires the utmost in both basic skills and in understanding of the big picture. It pays to diversify, practice, and study both new skills and even the long-standing ones that might have gone rusty from lingering habit.

While this kind of infrastructure comes from personal initiative, some companies have gone so far as to rotate people in and out of departments and jobs ... a practice as good for the rank and file (probably better) as it is for the proverbial "manager trainee." In fact, the latter method of learning can also be construed as only a kind of sampling. Imagine if everybody were the rank and file, and learned all the necessities of the utility player. There would be no need for special manager trainee programs — they're all right there under your nose!

The dance of priorities and time

Everybody has a planner. Some folks have a computerized one; others have big fat books; still others have human assistants whose duties include steering and reminding them where they need to go next. Scheduling is not only a personal art, but also a niche industry unto itself in this age of "Just in Time" manufacturing. (Actually, some say Just in Time has been around a lot longer than we think, with Henry Ford leading the charge.)

Just in Time, simply described, means the parts get there just as the previous supply is running out, so there's less warehousing overhead and a leaner profile to the action. If you think about it, our prioritization of each day runs the same gauntlet. We try not to overload one particular day, spreading things out over a week or a month. We also use our priorities to weed out those tasks that are superfluous to our needs or the needs of our organizations. We try to balance activity among various areas of our lives.

Hyrum Smith, in his captivating book *The 10 Natural Laws of Successful Time and Life Management*, refers to two fallacies we have about the notion of time:

> The first fallacy is that we think *we're going to have more time at some unspecified future date than we do now*. "Well, I'll do that next week, or next month, or next year, or when the children are grown, or when I retire. Then I'll have more time." The second fallacy is that we think *we can somehow **save** time*. The fact is, you *have* all the time there is. You're given a check every day for twenty-four hours, and you have to spend every last second.

Smith describes the two essential steps for managing that precious time: eliminating "time robbers" and then using those 86,400 seconds of each day to do things that are important to your life. In fact, he describes one's personal governing values, in keeping with our chapter's theme, as the "foundation of personal fulfillment."

Those values might be Ben Franklin's 12 virtues, or the Ten Commandments; they might be drawn from any number of sources, coalescing into what Smith calls a personal constitution. These are the infrastructure that the rest of our lives depend on.

Stephen Covey, along with Roger and Rebecca Merrill, devotes his attention to the time quandary in the book *First Things First*:

Our struggle to put first things first can be characterized by the contrast between two powerful tools that direct us: the clock and the compass. The clock represents our commitments, appointments, schedules, goals, activities — what we do with, and how we *manage* our time. The compass represents our vision, values, principles, mission, conscience, direction — what we feel is important and how we *lead* our lives.

Covey's 7 Habits, in fact, reverberate with this sense of priority and utility. The Circle of Concern differs from the Circle of Control, and that gap translates into what you spend your time doing. Part of Sharpening the Saw is not only increasing the quality and depth of your available time, but also learning how to use that saw to cut out the unnecessary, non-enriching activities that accumulate now and then.

Covey also speaks of a different kind of time from chronological time: *kairos*, or quality, time. In this paradigm, "time is something to be experienced," Covey writes. "It's exponential, existential. The essence of kairos time is how much value you get out of it rather than how much chronos time you put into it."

An important distinction to make is the objectivity of that clock on the wall and the subjectivity of our relation to it. While organizations must have clear priorities communicated to their employees and constituents, one's personal constitution is exactly that — personal. It is tempting for some people to proselytize, to sell their concept of time and their priorities to others. But that domain is so utterly personal that we balk at such intrusions.

It is through our behavior that we "plug in" to shared notions of time, spending that universal allotment in a way as individual as one's fingerprint.

Unlike that fingerprint, though, priorities change. They are part of a journey of personal growth. Every day, we can ask ourselves, "What's my time worth?" And every day's actions will give us the answer.

Weather happens

Well, we have our clock and our compass. Where's the map?

Actually, maybe we need more of an atlas. Some grids are better for one task, some are better for others. Are we looking for mountains to climb, or the quickest pass through them?

Many people think of roads as the basis and emblem for all infrastructure. The building and maintenance of new roads is a constant issue at all levels of government, as growing communities and populations seek out better ways to link, to transfer goods, to move their increasingly mobile selves.

We must be careful however, speaking both literally and metaphorically, to make sure there are still destinations at the ends of those roads. There are times when it seems the crisscrossing lines of navigation only cover up the places that are worth getting to. Perhaps the information highway is the most prevalent example today of this phenomenon: There are a lot of roads to nowhere out there, and if we aren't careful, the pure experience of travel can turn into a circle that spends both time and fuel.

Indeed, the neighborhood, the home that is our base of operations, is perhaps the most crucial transformer in the underlying structure of our lives.

What may be necessary today is to see not only that all roads lead there, but that we are able to take our neighborhoods with us.

Stephen Covey has a similar saying: "I carry my weather with me." It is the ultimate statement of the power and transformative nature of personal growth.

Of course, like that ticking clock, we generally think of weather as something we can't do a whole lot about. But the philosophy of the neighborhood within says, "Hey, weather happens. Now what can I do that adapts to any climate, weathers any storm? How can I store the energy of the sun, the quenching of the rain, the clarity of the air in the dead of winter within my own personal atlas of values?"

What a rich and endless book to write!

Decline in the red tape industry

If there's one thing we absolutely won't suffer in the way we work and live, it's mindless bureaucracy. The traditional repository for scorn of red tape is our various forms of government. They bear the brunt of the reputation for slow, plodding processes, full of forms, waiting in line, departments within departments and then maybe some more forms.

But governments are changing. In many communities, they are leading the way — often in synergy with the business community — toward more open and yet streamlined action.

"Govern" comes from a Greek word meaning "directing a ship." If we see the navigation cited earlier as a crucial part of the neighborhood framework, then government must be, too. Its processes, like all infrastructure, are fundamental and necessary.

Chris Cherches, the city manager of Wichita, Kansas, shared some thoughts with us on how government plays a crucial role in the community's foundation, and not as a red tape dispenser. He reminds us that agencies and departments of governments, while magnets for our occasional discontent, are, like any organization, made up of people. And those people hold the keys to innovation and progressive leadership in governing our communities, as Cherches explains:

There continue to be efforts to work toward diversity in neighborhoods. The most recent example is our Neighborhood Revitalization program, aimed at encouraging private investment and rehabilitation of targeted neighborhoods. The city has also established special incentives for developers to construct and develop housing in the city's downtown business district.

There is recognition by the governing body that development in the center city should be encouraged as the city's ability to construct and maintain infrastructure is stretched with fringe development, along with its ability to provide high-quality municipal services.

Being in government, I hate to be categorized with "bureaucrats" and "red tape" and other typical stereotypes of government officials, but I realize that there are many dysfunctional governments and organizations. We are making a sincere effort in Wichita to change our organizational structure to one of being community oriented; that is, we have set our course to establish more creative partnerships to address community needs — not only with the private sector, but with other governmental units.

To improve service response, we have decentralized many services (into the neighborhoods), making services convenient to the residents. Let me illustrate:

• Assisting the state to centralize its various services in our downtown, convenient to transit stations and other governmental services.

• Establishing the only high school magnet school focusing in law and public service IN CITY HALL.

• Creating neighborhood centers with parks and recreational services, job training, counseling, public health stations and other services made available.

• In cooperation with the school district, creating "lighted schools" by using public school buildings as neighborhood centers to provide services, learning opportunities, meeting facilities, and family activities "after school hours" and on weekends.

• Joining with Cessna Aircraft to develop training and learning centers to provide skill training to welfare clients and guaranteeing them jobs on successful completion of the training, with adjacent services for child care, public housing, etc.

• Establishing community dialogue sessions throughout the city to obtain citizen feedback on services and area needs. We're also establishing special response teams to neighborhood concerns, i.e. nuisance abatements, graffiti removal, community policing, etc.

• Offering incentives to employees who become proficient in other languages to better serve our minority populations.

• Using Internet and fax for services, permitting and other business responses from City Hall.

• Creating neighborhood courts to deal with neighborhood environmental, housing and nuisance issues.

• Hiring special neighborhood assistants working directly out of my office (the city manager's office) to assist neighborhood groups to organize, develop a communications bridge with city government, provide information on service availability and, in general, be available to residents and neighborhood groups having problems or wanting to communicate with City Hall.

• Establishing a special development assistance office to assist small business and to work with developers to assist them in building projects (via a one-stop office), and helping "avoid any red tape" not yet discovered.

Those of us who are fortunate to be involved in public management live in exciting and complex times. *Some of us old enough probably did not anticipate the rapid changes and types of proliferation of economic, political and social interrelationships we are experiencing today in local government. We are seeing vast changes in many areas which are impacting how we manage and lead, changes in information accessibility, technology, diversity, shifting to regional problem-solving and from representative to participatory government.*

These fast-paced changes necessitate that we, in management and leadership positions, understand and be sensitive to them because they affect how we manage. In most cases, they require us to take on new roles, which can best be described as entrepreneurial, enterprising, risk-taking, problem solving and consensus building. In short, they require that we listen and develop methods to ensure neighborhood input into how we operate and spend taxpayer money.

As a city manager, I see my role as one to help find solutions that are "right for the community" and show how these decisions can be implemented — often with the help and support of the citizenry.

Focusing this background into community infrastructure, we have found ways to include our citizens, neighborhood, individuals and organizations into the process of developing our capital improvement programs, which identify, program, prioritize and develop our infrastructure and other needs. All of this requires a certain element of trust and is difficult, but achievable with the added effort required.

In our community there are many competing needs and, as with other cities, limited resources. Taking our available resources and developing our five-year expenditure plan takes time and much effort to plan for equal and equitable treatment to all sectors of the community — our newly developing areas and the inner city— and six council districts. We embark upon our planning and prioritizing by inviting as many special interest groups as possible, especially the developers, home-builders, real estate and others within the business community, along with our citizen councils (representing each of the six districts), neighborhood organizations and our many citizen advisory boards/commissions.

They submit to us what they feel are the needs within the community and within their neighborhoods. Having them involved in the preliminary information gathering has helped our staff focus on what those in the community and in the neighborhoods feel are important. Professional staff then take these proposals and recommendations and place them with those developed by our various departments (i.e. public works, water/sewer, parks and recreation, fire, police and others). By making all groups and individuals sensitive to maintenance and upkeep costs, available resources and growth trends, we are able to bring some responsible recommendations to the table.

Understandably, one of the challenges that we city managers must face is how to balance needs of the community while, at the same time, ensuring some equitable distribution of public expenditures. In other words, how do we assure that there is "social equity" in our programs and that those who choose to not participate are adequately represented in programming public funds in terms of need, demand, preference and willingness to pay? The other challenge, of course, is to address those areas of the community which are growing, and balance these needs with an aging infrastructure within the older, inner-city core.

We are trying hard to bring the public into the decision-making process so that the "perception of mindless bureaucracy" can be defused. By building neighborhood organizations/associations, we seem to be making considerable progress in bringing city hall and our citizens together to work on many issues affecting community life.

Some final comments — government is made up of people and is no better or no worse than the private sector. Both government and business have to overcome perceptions on citizen or customer service. This is an ongoing issue — it requires instilling a work ethic that values the citizen and citizen-customer ... it requires continual training, then retraining, then refresher training. It also requires a system that rewards employees who take risks and finds new and creative ways to improve service.

Government is indeed a vital and dynamic component of infrastructure. For organizations at every level, it's not always a case of the shortest distance between two points, but in finding smooth, open water that assimilates and embraces all points.

Why I like Dennis Rodman

"I love sports metaphors and examples. I've tried to rein them in, but they remain such compelling and accurate illustrations for many points. Indulge me just for a moment:

What's the most underrated statistic in basketball? Why, it's rebounds, of course. (Well, maybe steals run a close second.) The shooters gun for the glory, and deserve it. (Last time I looked, the score was indeed still the only thing that counted at the end.) But the basic skills and tasks of the game could be described as a kind of infrastructure for that scoring.

When I was a kid, I dedicated myself to the specific art of snagging rebounds, studying and adapting its variations and techniques. I'm not the most graceful athlete who ever ran the floor, but I learned the fine art of muscling in under the boards and leaping to the optimum point where my hands might cross paths with that ball.

Say what you want about the ultimate rebounder, flamboyant NBA star Dennis Rodman, but I know one thing: On the basketball court you can't fake rebounds. I think he's really getting them.

An individual passion for the fundamentals — that's a key element in any team endeavor, no matter what extraneous differences exist. The purpose may change or alter, but the *sense* of purpose only grows stronger.

— *Larry Holman*

When no mail was junk

"Companies with strong communications across functions and widely shared information tend to have more productive external relationships. Thus other desirable internal changes include greater cross-functional teamwork and exchange of ideas. ...

"Many businesses fail to realize the full potential from their relationships because internal barriers to communication limit learning to the small set of people directly involved in the relationship."

> — Rosabeth Moss Kanter
> *On the Frontiers of Management*
> (1997: Harvard Business Review, Boston)

Perhaps no single person knows better the intricate values of neighborhood infrastructure than the U.S. Postal Service letter carrier. While some carriers may not even use the sidewalk, preferring instead to increase efficiency by crossing lawns from door to door, they understand better than most of us the importance and true meaning of "everyday." They see the truth coming out in the mundane activity of the neighborhood, the daily rituals that their customers perform.

Look at the changes in the catalog business since that mother of all catalogs, the Sears catalog, debuted in the 1800s. Or the evolution of the Rural Free Delivery (RFD) mail delivery system. (Quick, can you whistle the tune for "Mayberry RFD"?)

A 1994 account of the RFD's birth and growth, from *Stamps* magazine, shows just how crucial communication is to a community's framework. Remember, at the turn of the century there were few telephones, no radios or TV, and the automobile was just coming into fashion. (Our friend Mr. Ford was on top of that one.)

The article reminds us:

> The RFD mail system was lobbied for in Congress by the National Grange in an effort to bring rural families closer to the outside world. With the expansion of RFD mail service rural families now had a one- to two-day delivery of mail-order products, making them equal with their city folk counterparts. The advent of the Sears catalog was the force behind some of the greatest social changes that occurred in rural America.

In fact, the RFD was one of several stimuli for early road and highway construction — the image we most closely associate with infrastructure today. Well before Eisenhower's interstates, the need for better connectors was a constant, prodded by the fundamental need for communication.

The article cites the figures:

> Between 1897 and 1908, local governments spent an estimated $72 million on bridges, culverts, and other improvements. In one county in Indiana, farmers themselves paid over $2,600 to grade and gravel a road in order to qualify for RFD delivery. Beginning with three routes in October 1896, the RFD service counted 44 routes in 1897. By 1902 nearly 8300 routes were in operation, and in 1920 the number stood at 43,445.

Now *that*, friends, is some significant growth. All of it related to the need to communicate, deliver and move.

Living proof

How structure changes over time: the National Rails to Trails Conservancy

Everybody knows how the role of the railroad has in many ways declined over the course of this century. Railroad magnates built and utilized a literal skeleton and circulatory system for industrial America, stimulating all sorts of other growth along the way. Today, while it still plays an essential part in the movement of goods across this country, especially from industrial zone to industrial zone, many of the rail system's tendrils go underused or have been completely abandoned.

Now, a movement called Rails to Trails seeks to transform those valuable and historic corridors into a new sense of infrastructure. Instead of abandonment, this group of interested citizens from across the nation proposes changing the corridors into multipurpose public paths. They follow a gentle grade; they traverse urban, suburban and rural America; and they can be used for everything from bicycling and wheelchair locomotion to in-line skating, walking, cross-country skiing and horseback riding.

In the process, such transformations accomplish so many purposes: environmental greenbelts; preservation of literal utility lanes for power, gas, water and communications; historic preservation; and practical transportation, not to mention the pure joy and fun of community recreation. There's evidence, too, that there are several economic niches along these "linear parks" that can flourish: restaurants, recreational services, lodging and general tourism.

Currently there are nearly a thousand such trails in 48 states, with a thousand more in progress. Statistics show that the average trail user is 45 years old. Most people use the trails for bicycling, walking and jogging. Eighty-five million people used them in 1994.

A 1992 study of three trails — in Iowa, Florida and California — showed that the total economic benefit for each trail ranged from $1.2 to $1.8 million.

Imagine, too, the untold benefits of these trails in terms of community pride, personal health and social interaction.

We can't think of a more dynamic example of how literally infrastructure influences our lives.

On equality and integrity

I'm an equalist. I want everybody to be that way. There are a lot more enlightened folks out there now than there used to be.

We're lucky we're in a very nebulous business and we can make it like we want it. We started it, and we want to keep the character of our business the same as when we started. It's harder, but I think you can be bigger and still keep that.

You can have that sense of unity without having that literal family connection, I think. That's the essence of partnership. Even with our financial partners, though they're understandably bottom-line oriented, they don't tear us down, they try to think of ways to build us up. It's a relationship.

If there's mutual trust and respect among the partners of any organization, and you're coming from the same center and have the same goal, you don't have to be married.

— *Bunny Holman*

Let's get organic

You might be tempted to think of utilities and infrastructure as all bricks and mortar, miles of wire, iron and asphalt.

But when we look at our neighborhoods, we see the living and breathing roots of systems in each other and in the living things around us. The most obvious outward manifestation is the physical patterning in nature: pine cones (whose design elements are part of an entire branch of mathematics, and played a role in code making and breaking during World War II), leaves, bee hives, cloud formations, ripples and reflections. For wonderful explorations of some of these paradigms from the natural world, read Margaret Wheatley's books *A Simpler Way* and *Leadership and the New Science*.

In one another we see the equally outward manifestations of our inner selves. Our patterns of behavior, communication and work derive from that code of values that weaves itself through our very core.

In pursuing our working and family lives, infrastructure is both the trellis and the vine, making it possible for things to bloom within us and within our communities. Organizations are biological organisms. Our job as leaders is to find the humans.

14

The Garage Band

There's a loud noise — what used to be called a racket — emanating from a few doors down the street. The Saint Bernard puppies are hiding beneath the couch as if to escape from what sounds like a combination of dull repetitive thuds, buzzing saws and caterwauling cats.

As a matter of fact, Buzzsaw Caterwaul just might be the band's name. If not, it should be. Next time we see one of the boys out on the street or at the grocery, let's suggest that. They're good boys, really; they seem to have a pretty good sense of humor; and they don't play too late or too terribly loud, for the most part. Somebody called the police once, but now there seems to be sort of an "understanding" among the neighbors. It's about respecting one another's rights, but also not being so uptight with our rules and regulations that we don't allow any room for flexibility, for growth, for allowing people to let their hair down a little, be themselves, make some noise.

It seems to us that a lot of our organizational neighborhoods could use a garage band. If you're in a garage band, we're told, it's best not to take yourself too seriously. After all, you're only making noise in a space designed for a parked vehicle. At the same time, a garage is large enough to hold some pretty big dreams. Just imagine: What if we were to make a recording of that song we wrote yesterday, after we'd taken the time to get the chords right and make the rhythm a little more solid and add some cool harmonies? And then we made a bunch of tape copies and sold them to all our friends for a couple bucks apiece? And then ... well, before too long, we're standing on stage accepting a Grammy award, thanking our parents for encouraging us to follow our dreams and the neighbors for being so understanding about the rehearsals and ...

Make no small plans, indeed!

The great thing about the garage band is that, even if none of that rich and famous stuff ever happens, we will still have had a great time giving it our best shot. You see, the garage band is about having fun and experimenting, saying "What the heck!" and taking a few chances, just jamming together and trying to create something special. It's about staying young, keeping an open mind and playing what you feel. It's about finding a mutual rhythm and dancing to it. It's locking into at least a basic framework together, but then allowing room for improvisation. It's about communication and expression and celebration. It's about making music for the sheer joy of making music, in a world where the pace is so hectic that we often forget to do things for sheer joy. (But in case you were wondering, we DO happen to have some pretty kickin' tunes.)

Our friend Tom Peters, who has long advocated what you might call a rock 'n' roll approach to business, was really in the groove when he wrote the following in his book *The Pursuit of WOW!*

> I think work and business can be creative and exciting. A hoot. A growth experience. A journey of lifelong learning and constant surprise.

(Rock on, Tom!)

We also think this quotation from Fred Rogers is highly appropriate to our theme. "Relationships are like dances in which people try to find whatever happens to be the mutual rhythm in their lives." (In case you didn't know it, the Dean of Neighborhoods is an accomplished songwriter, writing most of the music that is featured on his award-winning children's show.)

So bear with the "racket" and listen closely to the sounds coming from down the street. Somewhere in there is a melody for us to discover.

By the way, does your neighborhood have a garage band? Wanna start one?

Drivin' home to the heartbeat

We love to "shag." In case you don't know what shagging is (and if you don't, you've been culturally deprived!) it's a style of dancing that is especially popular along the Carolina coastline. The music is vintage rhythm-and-blues and soul — "beach music," it's called. Clubs throughout North and South Carolina, and to a lesser extent in other Southern coastal states, are dedicated — and we do mean dedicated! — to the practice of shagging to beach music.

When we are at our beach house in Wrightsville Beach, North Carolina, we often make the trek down the coast to Fat Harold's in North Myrtle Beach, South Carolina. On occasion we have taken WYNCOM employees who are in town with us for a management retreat or planning session, and some of them have taken advantage of free shagging lessons offered by our dear friends Billy and Evelyn Davis, shaggers supreme.

One popular song among the shagging crowd has become WYNCOM's unofficial anthem. The song is called "Drive It Home," though we've adapted it to "Drivin' Home," which also became the name of our weekly in-house newsletter. We're not sure exactly what it means, but we like the emotion that goes with it. On one level, there's the sense of urgency involved with getting home when you've been away from it for a while; that idea harmonizes nicely with the attitude of doing "whatever it takes" to get the job done. On another level, there's the warmth that goes with home itself, which is appropriate because we've always seen WYNCOM as our big extended family, where we love you as you are and give you room to grow.

So when you're drivin' home, you're focused and upbeat and headed for good things.

Anyway, music seems to surround WYNCOM in a lot of ways. It's only natural that the company has become a haven for its share of musicians, as we place a lot of emphasis on creativity. Two employees, longtime musicians, started a new band not too long ago. The original lead singer, also an employee, was forced by impending motherhood to take a break from rehearsals and club dates, and she was replaced by yet another employee. Recently the band, known as Iris, went into the studio and cut an original song called "WYNCOM Heartbeat." The company paid for the recording session and gave tape copies to all the employees. We still haven't heard the song on "American Top 40," but it's at the top of the WYNCOM charts!

The tape begins with a spoken intro: "Whether the subject is employee empowerment, innovative ideas for future business, or any of The 7 Habits of Highly Effective People, our Lessons in Leadership speakers are continually reminding their audiences of the importance of commitment to core values: the standards in our hearts that guide our behavior on and off the job every day.

"As a company, WYNCOM has core values that guide its operation. Those values are the heartbeat of WYNCOM, and just like any heartbeat, it's continuous, 24 hours a day. But WYNCOM's heartbeat is that of a team, not of a random group of individuals. Our company's core values — the values that determine how we approach and carry out our work — will keep our momentum, our company heartbeat, going ... every hour of every day."

Then the band kicks into a driving, hard-rock beat, with lots of soul and meaningful lyrics (and yes, you can dance to it):

WYNCOM Heartbeat
(The Full-Tilt, Optimistic, Positive Boogie)
Lyrics © 1998 Chad Walker

Full-tilt, optimistic, positive boogie
WYNCOM theory, that's the way that it should be
We'll tighten it up so we can turn it loose
This team knows exactly what to do

Its heart keeps beating even when you're away
That's drivin' it home, the WYNCOM way
I'm telling you now, one thing leads to another
You'd better listen to me like you're talking to
*   your mother*

CHORUS
This company's got a heartbeat (you gotta love it)
Twenty-four hours a day (you gotta have it)
This company's got a heartbeat (you gotta love it)
Eight days a week (doing it every day)

We're gonna rock, we're gonna roll, we're gonna
*   twist and shout*
We're gonna shake, rattle, roll ninety-eight right out
We're gonna pick it up and then lift it higher
Beam it out so we can reach much farther

REPEAT   CHORUS

We're gonna raise the roof, roof, the roof is on fire
With all of our friends we can reach much higher
It's a positive vibe with tons of verve
It's a copacetic company creating the curve

REPEAT   CHORUS

"No one can whistle a symphony. It takes an orchestra to play it."

— Halford E. Luccock

Simplicity, sincerity and soul

In a television interview several years ago, the legendary guitarist Carlos Santana was asked to list the characteristics that, in his opinion, make up great music. Santana thought just a moment before replying:

"Simplicity, sincerity and soul."

It makes sense to heed the words of the great guitarist, who arose from humble origins near Tijuana, Mexico, to become a pioneer in rock, jazz fusion and Latin music, noted for his fluid and heartfelt playing style. It has occurred to us that Santana's "recipe" is not limited to music; in fact, leaders could well use it as a guide for leading.

Here, with thanks to Carlos Santana, is a guide to leading with simplicity, sincerity and soul.

Simplicity. "Our life is frittered away by detail. ... Simplify, simplify," wrote Henry David Thoreau in *Walden*.

Obviously, the details are important. But often we tend to make our problems more complicated than they really are. Dr. Kazuo Inamori, who founded the highly successful multinational Kyocera Corporation, writes in his book *A Passion for Success* (1995: McGraw-Hill, Inc., New York):

> We can almost never solve a problem the way it is presented to us. Instead, like untangling a thread, we must find the beginning and try to determine how it became tangled. We trace the problem back one step

at a time until we can understand how and why it became so complicated.

Often, the situation that led to the problem is surprisingly simple — and from there, we can see the solution.

Simplicity should also be the rule when creating organizational mission statements. Can you define, in 25 words or less, your organization's reason for being? If not, it is doubtful that employees at all levels have a clear understanding of what the organization is about. Make sure your organizational mission statement is easily understood and easily communicated — and people will find it much easier to make an emotional commitment to it.

From a musical standpoint, think of the songs that move you, that stick in your mind. More than likely, the "hook," or part of the song that you find yourself humming, is simple. That's why it sticks in your mind.

Sincerity. To a musician like Carlos Santana, sincerity means "playing it like you mean it," creating music that is genuine rather than artificially created in a calculated attempt to cash in on the latest fads or trends.

As leaders, it is our responsibility to be sincere, genuine and honest in all our dealings with employees, customers, partners, community — in other words, with anyone we deal with. Without integrity, how can we create the atmosphere of mutual trust and respect that is so essential to continued success?

In *The 7 Habits of Highly Effective People*, Stephen Covey discusses integrity and what it really means. "Integrity includes but goes beyond honesty. Honesty is telling the truth — in other words, conforming our words to reality. Integrity is conforming reality to our words — in other words, keeping promises and fulfilling expectations. This requires an integrated character, a oneness, primarily with self but also with life."

Soul. What is soul? In his book *The Soul of a Business: Managing for Profit and the Common Good* (1993: Bantam Books, New York), Tom Chappell, president of Tom's of Maine, describes soul as "what connects you to everyone and everything else." He adds: "It is the sum of all the choices you make. It is where your beliefs and values reside. Soul is at the center of our relationships to others, and for me it is at the center of the business enterprise."

Chappell goes on to talk about the importance of running businesses that "seek financial success while behaving in a socially responsible and environmentally successful way." Such a business respects the dignity and worth of its employees, customers, partners and community.

Tom Peters has a slightly different take on "soul." In the "Service With Soul" workshops offered by TPG/Learning Systems, a part of The Tom Peters Group, participants ponder this comment from the company founder: "The definition of service with soul, in part, is something that grabs you. You don't know why, but it's there, and there's no issue about it, and you can leave the electron microscope at home."

Soul à la Peters is about creating products and services that stand out from a crowd of look-alikes, that go beyond merely satisfying customers to actually developing an emotional link which causes customers to love you. It is no coincidence that one of Peters' books is titled *The Pursuit of WOW!* If you can cause your customers to say "Wow!" then chances are excellent that you and your organization have soul.

The challenge of improvisation

While writing this book, we have often listened to Miles Davis' *Kind of Blue*, one of the classic jazz albums of all time. It's a recording that the catalog for the Columbia Jazz Masterpieces series of reissues describes thusly: "Group improvisation at its best ... one of the finest spontaneous performances ever recorded. Miles presents the framework necessary to stimulate individual expression to achieve a sublime result."

In the original liner notes, Bill Evans, who played piano on the pair of one-day recording sessions in 1959 that produced *Kind of Blue*, provides some insight into the project. He begins with an analogy: "There is a Japanese visual art in which the artist is forced to be spontaneous. He must paint on a thin stretched parchment with a special brush and black water paint in such a way that an unnatural or interrupted stroke will destroy the line or break through the parchment. Erasures and changes are impossible. These artists must practice a particular discipline, that of allowing the idea to express itself in communication with their hands in such a direct way that deliberation cannot interfere." This discipline, he suggests, is similar to that of the improvising jazz musician.

Evans adds: "Group improvisation is a further challenge. Aside from the weighty technical problem of collective coherent thinking, there is the very human, even social need for sympathy from all members to bend for the common result. This most difficult problem, I think, is beautifully met and solved on this recording."

Davis, it seems, provided his fellow musicians — Evans, John Coltrane, Julian "Cannonball" Adderly, Paul Chambers, James Cobb and Wynton Kelly — with rough sketches only hours before the sessions. "Therefore," Evans explains, "you will hear something close to pure spontaneity in these performances. The group had never played these pieces prior to the recordings and I think without exception the first complete performance of each was a take.'"

We'll extend the analogy even further — from visual art to jazz to the world of innovation, which applies to business and organizations and, yes, neighborhoods.

Perhaps the bible of innovation is Tom Peters and Bob Waterman's *In Search of Excellence* (1982: Harper & Row, New York). In that seminal work, the authors looked at excellent companies that were "structured to create champions," often in unorthodox operations known as "skunk works." We noticed certain patterns in the skunk works that Peters describes.

They are generally informal in structure and composition, for example, with the number of members varying. They are usually away from corporate headquarters, often spilling over into the homes of participants, who are known to work strange — and long — hours. (Sounds like a garage rehearsal studio, doesn't it? Either that or a mad scientist's lab — and the two may be the same.)

They are usually populated by people who don't fit the corporate mold, who thrive on the unsupervised freedom to experiment and innovate and improvise. Above all, they produce results.

All these years later, despite the fact that many of the "best run" companies featured in *In Search of Excellence* are no longer such paragons of excellence, the book continues to make a convincing case for a "bias toward action." New ideas, risk taking and mistakes are encouraged rather than constricted by policy — and the result can be unprecedented innovation and success.

> I have learned throughout my life
> as a composer chiefly through
> my mistakes and pursuits
> of false assumptions,
> not by my exposure to founts
> of wisdom and knowledge.
>
> — Igor Stravinsky

It's only rock 'n' roll
(but they like it)

Genesis Records
NASHVILLE, Tennessee

The band Copperhead and its label, Genesis Records, are sound examples of making the best of a potentially problematic situation.

That the album *Mint Condition* was recorded in one week, for example, was a matter of simple economics as much as anything else. But it also serves to illustrate the honest and unvarnished straightforwardness of Copperhead's music.

"It's funny how many people have come up to me and said, 'You know, more recording artists should spend just a week in the studio instead of spending several months and several hundred thousand dollars to make something slick, overproduced and without substance,'" says Don Aldrich, president of Genesis Records. "I have to laugh, because it really wasn't an 'artistic' decision. We had an extremely limited budget.

"At the same time, these guys wanted to make something raw and real, something that comes close to capturing what they sound like live. They don't believe in bringing in a bunch of studio musicians and backup singers to make a record that the four of them can't reproduce on-stage in concert. So maybe it was good that we only had a week!"

That "raw and real" performance philosophy extends to the way Genesis Records strives to do business.

From the partners it chooses to work with to the way it resolves potential conflicts and misunderstandings, this start-up company — a bootstrap organization in a multibillion-dollar industry often characterized by excess — believes in getting back to the basics, and having a blast in the process.

"You know, like the Rolling Stones say, it's only rock 'n' roll. We're not working on rocket science or a cure for cancer. Our main purpose is to entertain people," Aldrich says. "But within that framework of entertaining people, we have certain ideas about how the business should be run. Yes, it's a business. Yes, we want to make money. But we want to do it the way *we* think it should be done. It has to be fun for us, or why do it?"

An evolution of events

While the name Copperhead is relatively new, the band's four members — Wayne Turner, Billy Earheart, Ray Barrickman and Bill Marshall — are anything but starry-eyed newcomers to the music business. For years they have been known as the Bama Band, an award-winning ensemble that has recorded and toured extensively with Hank Williams Jr. and also released its own albums.

Copperhead
(Turner at right)

But "this is the first time we've been able to make the record we've really wanted to make," says Turner, whose 18 years supporting Williams gives him the longest tenure in the band. As Copperhead's lead singer, guitarist, principal songwriter and bandleader, he is also the band's unofficial spokesman. Turner says the freedom of working with a small, independent label allowed the band to record the songs it wanted to record, songs that reflect a variety of styles and influences: country, Southern rock, blues, R&B, gospel and straight-ahead rock 'n' roll. (The label has dubbed the approach "multi-format." Turner, on the other hand, has suggested a number of tongue-in-cheek descriptions for the band's unique blend of music, including "combat country," "rock 'n' roll with overalls" and "a cross between the French Foreign Legion and a fraternity party.")

Why the name change, from the tried-and-true "Bama Band" to the untested "Copperhead"? Much as Genesis Records' name suggests a new beginning, so did Turner, Earheart, Barrickman and Marshall want to — as Tom Peters would say — reinvent themselves. But the total plan came gradually, piece by piece, rather than in a sudden flash of inspiration. In fact, as the band and the tiny Genesis staff will attest, in many ways they are "making it up as we go."

"Genesis Records was not an initial thought; it was an evolution of events," Aldrich says.

The chain began with a phone call from Turner to longtime friend Aldrich on December 15, 1996: Bill Marshall had left Survivor, the veteran arena-rock act that he had joined in 1993; Billy

Earheart had left the Amazing Rhythm Aces, the Grammy-winning group he had helped found back in 1974, maintaining occasional membership over the years; and the guys wanted to get back together and do another project of their own. Three weeks later, they were in the studio, along with Barrickman. (As it turns out, the band members had already been writing songs — particularly Turner, who had written several in the previous five years with Aldrich.)

Aldrich and another friend, Bobby Feltz, formed Professional Artist Management and signed a management deal with the band members, who had decided their new music warranted a new name. About the same time, Aldrich and Feltz, with help from a few other partners, had started a songwriter critique service, which was soon to evolve into a worldwide web store.

At this point, none of the principals could have known that Hank Williams Jr., father of a new baby, would decide to take a yearlong hiatus from the music industry and spend time with his family. When that happened, the members of the Bama Band faced the cold reality: Touring pays the bills; not touring means getting a "real job." It was time to hit the road — and get the new CD out in stores and, if possible, on the radio.

Aldrich and Feltz tried to pitch the recording to the major labels in Nashville. They soon realized that the powers-that-be in the music industry were not particularly ready for the stylistically diverse collection of music that the band had recorded. Because it does not fit easily into any one genre of music, the reasoning went, it's difficult to market. So the artist managers expanded their vision.

"We evolved past the point of management," Aldrich says, "when we realized the labels in town did not 'get' the multi-format approach of the album. We realized we had one option: Form our own custom record label to market and distribute the product, get a booking agent, get the band out there in a transitional mode, going from 'Hank Williams Jr.'s Legendary Bama Band' to 'Copperhead' by way of concerts and club dates."

("Transitional mode" meant simultaneously embracing the past while moving away from it. While the band was eager to develop a name as Copperhead, it had a well-established base of fans who instantly recognized and responded to the Bama Band. Therefore shows were billed as "the Legendary Bama Band, now known as Copperhead," or "Copperhead, also known as the Legendary Bama Band.")

Another development around this time was increasing dissatisfaction on the part of many music lovers with the current state of radio. The recent upswing in popularity of country music, which had coincided with the rise to fame of Garth Brooks, had apparently peaked, and many listeners were grumbling that the market had increasingly been saturated with formulaic, cookie-cutter pablum.

People who had grown up on rock and Southern rock in the '70s, then discovered country, found themselves looking back wistfully at bands such as Lynyrd Skynyrd and the Allman Brothers, and times when radio stations had wider, less restrictive playlists.

"We saw the writing on the wall," Aldrich says. "The face of music was changing, especially country music. We were looking for ways to get a wider audience appeal, a bigger demographic. We hadn't cut the album with multi-format in mind; it just fell into place. It was one of these things that ran its own course, then we recognized it when it was done and realized what we had."

'Wonderfully, deliriously crazy'

"Genesis Records is the Heinz 57 of entertainers and creative people who are all wonderfully, deliriously crazy — but good at heart," Aldrich says. "We embrace those types of people because you need to embrace the creative process to implement it. I'm a firm believer that when you sell a product, you need to know it inside and out to become a good salesperson."

Of course, it's common knowledge that such creativity is sometimes accompanied by a lack of focus. Aldrich considers his label fortunate in that regard. "It's hard to find someone who is both a business person and a creative person, who understands both processes and is able to merge those elements together. We have been fortunate enough to have found some of those people, and we have embraced them. As a result, we have a small group of people running this operation, basically five people."

Because of the label's budget, however, not all of these relationships would be considered conventional, from a business standpoint. Bartering has played a key role. The publicist, for example, agreed to come aboard on an unpaid, part-time basis until the fledgling company could attract some investors and thus be able to pay a salary. In the meantime, bandleader Turner is providing some free song demos in exchange for the work of the publicist, a songwriter himself. Aldrich and Feltz are also providing some insight into the development of the publicist's own business plan.

"You might have no money in the budget, but there's always a way to trade and barter and help each other out, and still get the job done," Aldrich says. "And there's not really a downside. As long as everybody maintains what he or she is doing, and does it with an open mind and an open heart, with all the cards on the table and no hidden agendas, it will work."

The overall business approach of Genesis Records continues to evolve — "just like everything has evolved to this point," says Aldrich. "There have been no hard-and-fast rules. We've allowed ourselves to make a plan, but we've also allowed ourselves the flexibility to make a change in midstream. We have kept things lean and mean. We keep a low overhead. The majority of our money that comes in is earmarked for marketing and promoting the act. But we're not just promoting the band — we're also promoting our record label and the concepts behind it. So we're trying to raise visibility and awareness across the board. In our single-mindedness, we still have diversity. Being flexible is a real big key."

As a small, independent label, Genesis can also afford a more realistic perspective than its more bottom-line-oriented, instant-results-obsessed counterparts. "Booking and visibility are our key focuses right now," Aldrich says. "Visibility builds awareness of the band and gets bookings, and the bookings in turn keep them sustained and making an income. We can sell product that way. We may not hit a home run on the first album, in the first year, but we'll most certainly have made some tremendous strides in the right direction. It's a three-year plan."

Aldrich says the philosophy behind the band and the label is very simple. "It's based on the insight 'Do unto others as you would have them do unto you.' We try to treat everybody fairly, at whatever level. We're honest and up-front with people. If we're in a position of making a decision, and we see it's going to hurt somebody, then we will not make the decision to do that. We have made a pledge to maintain our integrity in a business in which that can be very difficult to do.

"We've walked away from opportunities where we could see that somebody was going to get screwed over down the line. But when we walk away from a relationship, we walk away knowing we did everything we could to make that as positive as possible. Sometimes we bend over backwards. I don't do that so I can sleep at night — I do that because you *have* to maintain the full scope of that philosophy. You can't say you're doing this, then turn right around and do something different. Consistency is what makes it work."

"A neighborhood is a group of houses that are next to each other. The people of a neighborhood work together or watch out for each other. They form groups to raise money for a playground or something like that. A neighborhood is not just a group of houses. It's a lot of people helping each other and giving things to each other."

—Tara, age 10

15

The Neighborhood Association

Crystal clear wisdom, courtesy of a 10-year-old. It would be difficult to pen a much better definition of neighborhood than the one Tara gave to the editors of *Cartouche Architectural & Design Review*.

Tara's answer appears in Richard Louv's essay "Tara's Neighborhood" in *The Web of Life: Weaving the Values that Sustain Us* (1996: Conari Press, Berkeley, CA). Of all the answers Cartouche received to its questions, from people such as politicians, architects and schoolchildren, Tara's seemed most insightful because she realized that a neighborhood is not a collection of homes but a collection of the souls within those homes.

Or, as Jim Engelke, dean of the architecture school that produces *Cartouche*, said, perhaps a neighborhood is not so much a place, as it is "a state of mind."

These associations of people — people with geography as their common thread — can take many forms. Neighborhood associations exist all around us, not always within the confines of a city block or two. This type of informal association

— of people sharing a common space and a common goal — pops up in an office tower in downtown Minneapolis, where a group of officemates decides to walk as a team to raise money for the March of Dimes WalkAmerica; in an inner-city neighborhood in Philadelphia, where two tenants start a petition for a slower speed limit on their street; or in a rural farming area in Kansas, where farmers meet over coffee in the downtown diner to discuss a trip to the state capital to talk with legislators about ways to save the family farm.

Journalist Bill Moyers conducted a series of interviews with enlightened leaders in all types of fields — science, politics, the arts, education, history — which were compiled into a book, appropriately called *A World of Ideas* (1989: Doubleday, New York). Among those he interviewed was sociologist Robert Bellah, who had this to say about the importance of gathering together, to unite to fix the problems that plague us:

> *We can only solve our problems through the tough process of becoming involved in our neighborhoods, in our local communities, in the larger public issues, and even in the world issues that face us.*

Surrogate neighbors

" Larry and I recently moved to a new neighborhood, but we've maintained our ties with the old one, where we'd lived for a number of years and developed some close relationships. " It's a very tight-knit neighborhood, one that believes in having block parties and other get-togethers, and our old neighbors have gone out of their way to include us back in when we're in town.

So we're still surrogate neighbors in our old neighborhood. That was one of the contingencies of moving into our new house — we had to be within walking distance of our old neighborhood. Our friends told us there was actually a bidding war for a house there, with the final price significantly higher than the asking price. The house there sold within the first hour of the open house. So people must value that sense of community.

Neighborhoods are becoming more important again. They were when the country was young, and in Europe it's still that way. Now people are constantly mobile all week. On the weekends, I can't wait to be home, to see people I know, walk the dog. You see a lot more people doing that now, and it seems that it's a lot more important than it was even just 10 years ago. I think it's because so many people are not physically living at home, they're coming home after it gets dark and getting up and going first thing in the morning.

One of the reasons we've been so successful at WYNCOM and have been able to work with the caliber of speakers we have is that we make them feel part of a family. We'll have three or four people on our traveling team, so sooner or later the speakers will get back to the same people they were with before. They recognize them, know their personalities, greet them by name, which makes our people feel really good: This very famous person knows my name, knows how I like my coffee. We work so closely on these trips, we know a lot of stuff about these speakers, some that their own organizations don't know because they don't live with them 24 hours a day and we do!

I think we create that neighborhood feeling on the road; we bring WYNCOM feelings and characteristics along with us everywhere we go. We go to the same schools two to four times a year, so we get to know them, know how old their children are. These people become part of our family too. So in a sense, when our traveling teams go out, we do have a neighborhood: our speaker, the school representatives and us.

— *Bunny Holman*

Great teams of people exist all around us — on our block, in our cities and towns, in our companies and in our communities. They come together to reach goals, and when they do, some magic occurs. We've captured some of that magic in the three following stories about groups of people who have turned around a high school, a company and an entire town.

Class of 1998
White Swan High School,
White Swan, Washington

Ambassadors of hope

Gary Fendell
Don DeVon
WHITE SWAN, Washington

Gary Fendell hadn't been the principal at White Swan High School long when a group of students converged on his office. They posed a question to the school's new leader.

Gary Fendell

"They asked me why I had come here," Fendell remembers. "I said, 'I don't understand your question.'"

There was a long pause. The students looked at one another. They looked at Fendell.

Finally, a student spoke: "The kids out here have a feeling people only come to White Swan when they can't get a job somewhere else."

"Well, how does that make you feel?" Fendell asked.

"It makes us feel like we're not worth much," the student replied.

"Well, I can assure you that is not the case with me," Fendell said. "I came here because I wanted to be here."

That exchange almost 20 years ago was the conversational equivalent to pouring gasoline on a sputtering flame. It was the fuel that ignited the transformation of White Swan, a tiny public school on the edge of the vast Yakima Reservation.

Back then, about the only thing White Swan High School was noted for was its dropout rate, one of the highest in the state. The majority of the school's students (68 percent) were members of the Yakima tribe. An additional 20 percent were Hispanic, mostly the children of migrant workers who toiled in the area's orchards. The area was economically depressed and the school was a reflection of that. Most students were from poor families; unemployment was high; teen pregnancy was a big problem.

Then Fendell arrived. He was no naive newcomer, having taught and served as a principal in a nearby school district. As bad news often does, word of White Swan's woes had traveled his way. But until the students visited his office he had no idea of the depth of their discouragement. It surprised and moved him.

Not long after the students left his office, Fendell called an impromptu assembly. Standing before the school's 350 students and its teachers, he told the students that they were not lost causes and that they deserved to be taught and taught well, by conscientious and caring teachers. He added that any teacher who did not share his feelings should perhaps think about teaching elsewhere.

As many teachers nodded in agreement, students stood en masse, applauding strongly.

A different story today

Today, White Swan is a much different school, thanks not only to Fendell but also to a student-oriented school board, a dedicated team of teachers, and a persistent and tireless guidance counselor named Don DeVon, whose office is plastered with signs broadcasting a singular message: "Never, ever give up."

An average of 75 percent of White Swan's seniors graduate each year. Of those graduates, about 80 percent continue their education. Each year, students at the school are awarded from $300,000 to $700,000 in college financial aid. White Swan can now boast of the 17th lowest dropout rate among the state's 297 school districts.

White Swan graduates have gone on to be leaders at their colleges. One recent graduate was named multicultural student of the year at his school. Another is on the student Senate. Still another has been named president of the American College Students Association.

So many White Swan students enroll at the University of Washington that when new president Richard McCormick arrived at UW three years ago, he decided he must see for himself the small school that was sending so many students his way.

His visit was a historic one for White Swan, marking the first time the president of a major college had come calling. And the school made sure its guest knew he was a special one. The band played UW's school song. Native American students did native dances. McCormick met with leaders of the Yakima Nation. Television crews did news reports. "It was a good boost for our kids and teachers," says Fendell.

McCormick isn't the only notable who has been intrigued by White Swan. Microsoft has donated computer equipment. IBM, which scours the nation for 40 interns each year for its science and engineering programs, snapped up three students from White Swan.

Two decades of change

No institution changes overnight, particularly one with as many problems as White Swan had. Fendell clearly recalls a conversation he had with his wife after his interview at the school. "I said, 'Man, that place is full of problems!' and she said, 'Well, you like to solve problems. It sounds like it's right up your alley.'"

Fendell knew she was right. So he took the job and went to work, chipping away at problems little by little, like a determined miner in search of an elusive vein of precious gold.

Like any wise strategist, Fendell had multiple targets with his plan. First, he wanted to show the school's teachers that he valued them and needed their input. He pursued grants for seminars, workshops and retreats so they could learn the latest about topics as varied as student discipline and computer software. And, when teachers volunteered to work on projects, they got a handwritten thank-you from the principal.

Like the students, the staff members were so jaded that they weren't quite sure how to interpret Fendell's gestures at first, he says. "A real good teacher came in to my office and she said, 'We want to know what you want.' When I asked her what she meant, she said, 'Every time we volunteer, you send us a thank-you note!'"

When Fendell explained that no underlying motive existed, the teacher seemed surprised, and relieved. "She said, 'You just have to understand, we've been treated like cattle for so long out here.'"

As he slowly won the respect of the teaching staff, they began to work together to tackle the school's biggest challenge — creating programs that would work as safety nets and springboards, catching students who were in danger of falling through the cracks and propelling them toward a fruitful future.

Everyone realized that far too many promising students were letting their education end at White Swan. But how do you convince students that college is a part of their future, when no one they know is headed in that direction? Fendell and his staff developed summer programs at area colleges and universities. They reasoned that once students set foot on a college campus, they would realize that it wasn't an unattainable goal. By 1997, almost 70 students were participating in summer college programs each year.

Of course, it would be unrealistic to expect every student to go to college. But even those who didn't could have a bright future if they had marketable job skills. So White Swan worked with a nearby vocational school to create a program that allowed its students to learn various job skills. Military recruiters were also welcomed on campus. "Back when I was in high school, students were considered cannon fodder for the army. But now we make sure kids get a guaranteed educational package through the military," Fendell says.

Students who were falling through the cracks because of discipline problems were funneled into an alternative school, where the curriculum mirrored the regular classroom, but the smaller class size allowed for more individual attention. And instead of allowing teenage mothers to become dropouts, the school created a program for them that included parenting classes and free child care.

"He has worked to build a system for our students where we have all types of support systems to get them through school," says DeVon. "We just don't accept failure. If one plan doesn't work, we'll come back and try it again."

Of course, not every innovation has been met with applause. Fendell remembers the flak when the program for teen mothers was established.

Don DeVon

He never flinched. "Those kids are going to need their education more than ever," he reasoned.

None of the programs was aimed at making education easy, just so White Swan could hand out more diplomas at year's end. As every new program was introduced, the school's board was there to scrutinize and to ask its favorite question: "How will this benefit students?"

"I tell the kids every year, we'd rather work them hard for four years than have them be behind the eight ball for the rest of their lives," Fendell says. "High school is going to be hard, but it is going to pay off. Besides being teachers, we have to be ambassadors of hope to these kids."

Shows of support

As students, teachers and parents began to see the difference the programs made in their school, they began to line up behind the straight-talking man who had vowed to give honest answers, even if they weren't always the answers hoped for.

The Yakima tribal leaders, who had given no quick approval to the new principal they called "white man," began to warm to him. Soon the Yakima were calling him "Mr. Fendell" and, eventually, "Gary."

Students, too, began to believe not only in what Fendell was doing but also in what he would do in the days ahead. One student's handwritten note said simply, "Thank you for everything I know you are going to do for us."

Another student, who had been a troublemaker, left White Swan for another school in the area. Before long he was back. "He told me, 'They don't really care what we do down there,'" Fendell says. The student's brief stay at the other school seemed to make him appreciate White Swan more. He became a role model, stepping in to break up fights on the school grounds and volunteering to organize a blood drive.

The solidarity began to show, even in social events. A skating party planned by Fendell drew such a crowd that it caught bus drivers by surprise. Notified that more buses were needed to take skaters to the rink, the driver shook his head in amazement.

"We've never had enough people to fill one bus before," he said.

A springboard for success

Although Fendell provided the spark to ignite White Swan's turnaround, he is quick to tell you that he by no means deserves all the credit.

The credit goes to collaboration. White Swan has done exactly what business author Rosabeth Moss Kanter says is essential for success. As Kanter says, and White Swan proves, "Lining up allies and partners extends your reach and provides more resources, opportunities, and ideas."

The alliance begins at the school with Fendell, DeVon, the teaching staff and the school board. But it doesn't end there. Across the state and region, White Swan has developed binding relationships with college and university staff who've come to care as much about the students as the White Swan staff does.

Fendell credits DeVon, the school's counselor, with creating the strategic connections.

"He knows all these people on a first-name basis at all these colleges," says Fendell. "And he has the respect. People listen to him."

DeVon's respect has been hard-earned. Throughout a teaching and counseling career that has spanned 36 years, DeVon has sought the toughest places to ply his trade. When he wasn't teaching and counseling in some of Washington's most remote and poor areas, he was teaching prisoners on death row at a state penitentiary, building one of the country's leading educational programs in the corrections system.

Only once did he succumb to the temptations of working in a school district where students weren't struggling to overcome the disadvantages of poverty. It was in Palm Desert, California, and though DeVon liked his job and loved the area, he realized that he missed the satisfaction of helping kids for whom success was not a given.

"I realized I like to work with the poor kids — the kids who grew up like I grew up," he says.

In developing his vital network with colleges and universities, DeVon sought out people like himself, who hadn't had many advantages, who had to pull themselves through school, who hadn't forgotten their roots.

"Overall, I've found that there is a common thread with the people I work with at these schools," he says. "The common thread is that most came from humble to modest beginnings and have risen from there, but they didn't forget where they came from."

DeVon thinks of Gene Magallanes, who directs minority science and engineering programs at the University of Washington, Michelle Whittingham at Eastern Washington University and Bruce Carter at Columbia Basin College.

These school contacts will work with White Swan students individually. Instead of having students register by phone, they may have them come in to register in person.

"They really look after our kids," DeVon says.

DeVon knows what a difference such caring attention can mean. He had been told that he was not going anywhere, but his baseball coach took an interest in him and became his adviser.

"He started me off in low-level classes and it allowed me to develop some confidence," he says. "We have good strong support people who really look out for our kids. We have, over the years, through our contacts had the opportunity to find the colleges and universities that will work with our students and give them the same support we have here."

Going the extra mile, literally

Dedicated staff members like DeVon are commonplace at White Swan. Fendell knew that if his school was to succeed, it would need teachers and staff who had students' best interests, and not their own, in mind.

"The teachers who have been hired here hold high academic expectations of the students," says DeVon. But how has White Swan been able to entice good teachers to such a remote location, particularly when teachers seem to be in such short supply?

White Swan goes the extra mile, literally. When it hires staff, it doesn't have a "We'll take what we can get," settle-for-second-best attitude. Fendell and others travel as far as Alaska and Oklahoma to learn more about job candidates.

And when they visit a job candidate, they don't just sit in on a class. "We talk to the people at the school, to the schoolchildren, to parents, to people in the grocery stores," Fendell says. "We want to know what type of people and teacher they are. It is easier to spend that money up front than to try and get rid of someone who is incompetent. We are trying to get the best teachers for these kids."

Returning as leaders

Because of the school, life in the area is destined to improve. Although many successful graduates are still being lured to other areas by jobs and money, many are returning to the White Swan area. A recent UW graduate is now working for the tribe's fishery. Another biology graduate is tackling environmental issues on the reservation. A White Swan valedictorian has returned to work at the high school.

"They are gradually coming back and becoming leaders of the tribe," says DeVon. "I believe we will see more and more as time goes by."

As Rosabeth Moss Kanter has written, "The lesson is clear: Success belongs to those who persist and persevere. To convert imagination into useful results, leaders need not only vision, they need patience, flexibility and persistence."

Patience and persistence are the bywords at White Swan. Fendell admits he wishes he had more of each.

"It is hard for me to be patient. I like getting things done right now. But sometimes, it takes years. You just keep working at it."

When it comes to the value of hard work and persistence, he often thinks of his father-in-law. "My father-in-law had a huge garden. He was out working in it on the hottest day of the year. I said to him, 'Charlie, you're going to work yourself to death!' and he said, 'No Gary, you work yourself back to life.'"

White Swan High School staff Christmas party

A rebuilding project

Karen Lillie
PUEBLO, Colorado

For Karen Lillie, coming to Pueblo Diversified Industries five years ago was a little like moving into a once-charming but slowly crumbling neighborhood: The blooming lilacs and irises are pretty, but they can only mask the sagging porch and the peeling paint for a  time, and then you realize that the only thing that's really flourishing is a growing feeling of disintegration.

That's sort of what Lillie discovered shortly after becoming president and CEO of PDI, a three-decade-old nonprofit that provides jobs and job training for the disabled and disadvantaged.

Lillie's previous job as vice president of operations for Goodwill Industries of Detroit, a $13 million organization, had been her passion until a new president came along who did not share Lillie's fervor for serving others.

"Every day was miserable," she remembers. "There was no heart there for what he did."

Lillie had already made up her mind to leave when she picked up a trade publication and found her ticket out of Motor City. A place in Pueblo, Colorado, was looking for someone to lead an operation similar to Goodwill Industries. She and the job description were a perfect fit.

So Lillie made a move that would make Tom Peters applaud. She LEAPED and then looked, packing up and moving to Pueblo to take a job at a place she knew little about. And maybe that's why Peters' contrary logic is often not as backward as it sounds. If Lillie had looked a bit longer at PDI before she made her leap, she might not have made the move at all. And in hindsight, both she and PDI would have suffered.

About a month into her new job, Lillie began to realize that PDI was a very troubled organization. Opened in 1967 to give the Pueblo area's mentally and physically disabled population a place to work and learn job skills, PDI seemed to have forgotten its purpose.

The mammoth desk her predecessor had left behind seemed symbolic of the detachment and distrust that were destroying the company. "From the current management style, it was the most offensive of all possible desks you could have," Lillie says. "It told everybody, 'Don't you dare come near me and my space.'"

As she sat staring across the monstrosity, Lillie took an accounting of the troubles she faced. The plant's management was a shambles. Run in an autocratic and dictatorial fashion for many years, the organization had crumbled during the former president's long illness.

"When you have a top-down-directed organization, you have to keep your thumb on it all the time or it becomes totally dysfunctional, which it had," she says.

The staff was one very unhappy bunch, split into warring factions. "They were in unarmed camps and they hated one another," Lillie says.

To top it off, the company just had lost "tons" of money when a major contract was badly executed. "We were bleeding red ink. The company had been going in a negative direction for a number of years," Lillie says. "It was a real critical time for the organization."

As if the internal problems weren't enough, PDI was also facing foes outside the company — state vocational rehabilitation experts who were dead set against workplaces like PDI because they believed the disabled should be working in what it deemed as more traditional and diverse settings. To some degree, Lillie realized, the state had reason for its skepticism of PDI's value. The plant had not been aggressive about winning new manufacturing contracts and there was not enough work to do. Instead of learning job skills, the disabled workers sat idle much of the time, passing their time working puzzles.

No turning back

As the gravity of the situation sunk in, Lillie realized there was no turning back. She and her husband had packed up their belongings, their house had sold, and he had resigned from his job.

"At that point, I had nothing else I could go back to," she says. "I thought, 'OK, sweetie, you thought you were pretty good; now, we're going to find out.' And I had to face the fact that it was very possible I would fail."

Lillie has never been averse to hard work. In the small town where she grew up just north of Detroit, work was a given. "Everybody worked," she says. "Definitely the Protestant work ethic was part of who I was. My father worked 60 hours a week. He placed value on who you were as a product of what you did. I'm sure that's about as fundamental to who I am as anything else."

Luckily, Lillie was well versed in organizational change. She'd been fortunate in her previous job to have as her mentor W. Del Wisecarver, a forward thinking man who realized that though he was beyond changing his managerial style, Lillie wasn't. Wisecarver, former president of Goodwill Industries of Detroit, sent Lillie to the Planned Change Institute at the University of Michigan. In the intensive yearlong program, she stepped inside organizations that were in the midst of change — places like Ford, GM and Chrysler — and absorbed the lessons to be learned about how to transform a company.

That experience had taught Lillie some hard, but invaluable lessons about corporate change. Like an inner-city urban renewal project, the reviving of PDI would not be pretty in its preliminary stages as she made some radical and unpopular moves to salvage the company.

The most major was a 20 percent layoff of the staff. The purpose was twofold — to stanch PDI's cash flow problem and to split the factions that were tearing the company at its seams.

As she did whenever she was faced with such a tough situation, Lillie called Wisecarver. "For the first three years I was here," she says, "when I'd get in one of these situations, I'd run it up the flagpole and ask him, 'Does this make sense?' He'd always ask some appropriate questions and make some suggestions that I may have thought of or not. I really valued his opinion. He had taught me a lot."

Lillie also made it clear to her staff members that from now on, they would be held accountable. "I had to say, 'Look, you're accountable for what you do here and the outcomes you get.' And that was very frightening," she says. "Back a few years ago, you never talked about accountability in human services — you just did warm, fluffy, muffy stuff."

Developing a devoted team

From her experience at the Planned Change Institute, Lillie knew a devoted team was essential to PDI's transformation. She decided to eliminate existing layers of management and chose one person from each of the company's six major departments to serve as directors and become her management team.

She looked first for people who believed in PDI's mission, people with attitudes like that of a retired military officer who now runs the company's management information systems. Before he was hired at PDI, he had told Lillie, "All my life, I've had to do what I've had to do. I'm now in a position that I can do what I want to do. And I want to do what you do."

"That's the kind of person we look for," Lillie says, "a person who brings the skill base and expertise that can help us move forward through all our challenges. You thrive here by having the opportunity to do something you can really commit your heart to. It's not about earning a paycheck. It's about making a difference in somebody else's life.

"The staff we have now, I would put up against any Fortune 500 company. They are incredibly talented, incredibly good.

"People who work for me, in many cases, have 10 times the experience I do. What a stupid person I would be not to understand that and use it. In the new world, the role of the CEO or leader of any team is greatly minimized."

She and her team make an effort to choose new employees who add something to the mix — whose talents, opinions and ideas are not just like everyone else's.

"One of the first things I want to be very careful to avoid is that we hire people who are all the same," Lillie says. "It is real easy to do. You always want to hire somebody who is just like you because those are people you are comfortable with. And that does not make a good organization. It makes a very lopsided organization."

Taking pride in their team

Lillie remembers when she told the team about a new person she had met that she wanted to hire. The team immediately said, "We want to talk to him first."

"They all had their chance to talk with him," Lillie says. "They all have their one vote. And it is important to them to be involved with the interviewing and hiring process because they have to work with these people on a daily basis.

"We are very proud of the team we have put together. And they will fight to preserve the team. And so the interviewing process is very much a part of that. We all put in a lot of hours and we all work real hard. No one wants to risk making a bad decision if we can avoid it."

By building a team with diverse talents and dedication to the company, PDI has made significant advances. It has expanded the types of work it does, giving its 150 mentally or physically disabled clients and its 40 welfare-to-work clients a wealth of job training opportunities. PDI does metal and vinyl fabrication, packaging, and electronic and cable assembly. In addition to its manufacturing arm, it also offers foodservice and janitorial services. Its clients range from Fortune 500 companies to the General Services Administration and the Department of Defense.

When Lillie arrived, gross revenues were $1.8 million, including almost a million dollars almost a million dollars in local funding. Today, gross revenues are over $3 million and there is a potential to reach $8 million in the next 18 months if the company wins a new contract through its expanded plastics plant. The new contracts will help the plant decrease its reliance on dwindling government funds.

There are still challenges to face. "We have some real significant challenges with our facilities themselves," Lillie says. An HVAC system must be replaced, restrooms do not meet guidelines for a barrier-free environment, and a roof is leaking. To fund the needed improvements, a multi-phase capital campaign has begun.

Patience is a virtue, and it is definitely a necessity for those like Lillie who are leading an organization through a radical revamping.

One of the principles that Lillie learned at the Planned Change Institute was that organizational change takes five years: "When I was learning it, I said, 'I don't see how it can take that long.' And now, being in year five, I can say, yes, it takes that long."

Making principles the underpinning

Louisiana State University at Alexandria
Hibernia National Bank
ALEXANDRIA, Louisiana

About a decade ago, Alexandria was shaken to its foundation when the federal government announced that England Air Force Base, the city's major employer, was on its base closing list. The base meant almost 4,000 jobs to the central Louisiana area — 3,000 of them military. In a tremendous show of concern, more than 5,000 of the city's 50,000 citizens attended a public hearing on the proposed closing.

The base did close in 1991, and when it did, Alexandria made the news again, but the story wasn't about a woebegone American town, devastated by a federal government decision. Instead, Alexandria was being lauded for the redevelopment plan its citizens had created, which eventually transformed the base into a multi-use area that has become a model for communities facing the same situation. Today, the base is home to an industrial park, an air strip, an assisted living community, a school and a golf course.

Instead of paralyzing Alexandria, the base closing invigorated it. Inspired by that project, the city's leaders began to look around for other places where this newfound spirit of cooperation could make an impact. The evidence of their continued work is evident as you drive through Alexandria today. The city's art museum just reopened after a major renovation and expansion.

A new studio for community artists is under construction. And plans are under way for an $8-10 million performing arts center.

"In a four-year span, there's been millions of dollars in new development," says John Newhouse, publisher and president of the *Alexandria Daily Town Talk* and its printing company subsidiaries. "And it's all been done by different groups."

There's no doubt, Newhouse and others say, that the base closing made the city look at itself in a new light. "It just gave everybody the confidence that if we can do that, we can do anything," Newhouse says. "If you can turn a whole base around, it's no big deal to build a $6 million museum."

Sometimes, these waves of progressive spirit tend to ebb with the passage of time. That is unlikely to happen in Alexandria, though. Instead, the city seems to be on the crest of a new wave of enthusiasm inspired by a new project sponsored by Louisiana State University at Alexandria and Hibernia National Bank.

The LSUA/Hibernia Bank Leadership Training Partnership is bringing Stephen Covey's 7 Habits and Principle-Centered Leadership seminars to the Alexandria business community. Its intent is to build upon the spirit of cooperation that grew out of the base closing and to provide an underpinning to support further collaborative efforts. Wayne Denley, city president for Hibernia, and Reba Harrington, director of short courses and conferences at LSUA, developed the program.

Already, the partnership has sponsored three Covey seminars, and several more are planned. The partnership has also received a grant from the local private Rapides Foundation that will fund 20 scholarships for nonprofit leaders whose organizations could not otherwise afford to send them to the 7 Habits training program.

"We've put a total of 73 business people through the program," Denley says. "We've touched the larger employers in the community as well as many small businesses, professionals and nonprofits.

"In the case of 7 Habits, it's really a lot easier to live them if the people you are doing business with are living them also. It's a lot easier to think 'win-win' if the other guy's not thinking 'win-lose.' We're trying to change the culture of the community so it is more conducive to the prosperity and to doing business in a principle-centered way."

Denley and Harrington had worked together through the years as members of the executive committee of the Central Louisiana Chamber of Commerce. They began talking about their enthusiasm for Covey's principles at a Lessons in Leadership teleconference that LSUA hosted in fall 1996. Covey was one of the speakers for the teleconference.

Harrington had attended a four-day Covey program in Texas a year earlier. Denley had just returned from New Orleans, where he had attended a Covey program. Because of his excitement for Covey's materials and the possibilities they held for the bank and its employees, Hibernia had decided to send him to the Covey Institute in Utah to be trained as an in-house facilitator for Hibernia.

At the teleconference, Denley and Harrington began to talk about the effect the 7 Habits could have on their community as a whole. They realized that, working together, their organizations could bring the training to the Alexandria business community.

The programs offered through LSUA/Hibernia Bank Leadership Training Partnership are strictly break-even propositions. "We decided early on that this was not something that either of our organizations had to make money on, even though that is what

Wayne Denley and Reba Harrington

both of us do all day," says Harrington. "We just believe strongly in this program."

Supporting the program is a logical choice for Hibernia, which has made a tremendous commitment to bringing the Covey principles to its rapidly growing organization. Hibernia is the largest bank headquartered in Louisiana, and during the next three to four years it plans to send all 5,000 of its employees through the 7 Habits and Principle-Centered Leadership workshops.

The bank believes doing so will allow it to effectively bring authority to the local level so each of its banks can operate and deliver services as a community bank would.

"We tried to implement an empowerment initiative about four years ago and it completely flopped," Denley says. "One of the reasons it flopped so badly was that we didn't know how to do it and there wasn't trust in our organization. That's why we backed up and went to the Covey Institute to start over again."

Denley's and Harrington's work on the partnership has been both personally and professionally gratifying. One of the most enthused groups to take the training is the management staff of Newhouse's newspaper. The cooperative spirit that has resulted has allowed the newspaper's staff to develop and roll out a major new product — a real estate marketplace guide — in less than 60 days.

Denley says: "I've had people within that team come up and privately give me a big hug and say it has made a tremendous difference in their personal and professional life. There's been some spin-off that has been very positive. Three companies have already contacted Covey about bringing the program in-house."

Among them is St. Rita Catholic Church, whose priest, Father Bruce Miller, attended one of the Covey seminars. The seminar had such a dramatic effect on his work and life that he decided he wanted others on his staff to enjoy the benefits.

"Anybody would tell you I work very hard and play very hard — but now that's twice as true," Miller says. "I work harder in a sense of getting more accomplished, and I work smarter and I take even better care of myself."

He sees great potential for Alexandria as a result of the Covey training.

"I think it is going to make a difference in everything we do in the community as it filters down and we are working toward the goal of becoming a principle-centered community," Miller says. "I think if you align your actions with principles, good is going to come from it in the way of synergy. We are going to see one plus one equals three all over the place."

Hibernia's determination to bring the training to the community is "a great sign of community leadership," Miller says. "I can't imagine a corporation expressing its care for the citizenry in any better way. It speaks volumes about their corporate culture and how the 7 Habits have caused them to make those deposits to the emotional bank accounts instead of people just contributing to the bank's financial accounts."

Through the chamber of commerce, Denley has helped seek new businesses for Alexandria. He always felt the community's response to the question "What's different about your community?" was rather typical.

"We'd say, 'Our people are what make us different.' It's not like everybody in the country isn't saying the same thing," Denley says. "If you really want to be able to say that, you need to be able to point to something like this. If you could say that 500 people in Alexandria have taken 7 Habits and Principle-Centered Leadership courses and that they believe and follow those principles, you could really point to something that makes your community different."

16

<u>The Limits of Design</u>

Inside the J.B. Speed Building, a Louisville landmark on the National Register of Historic Places, sits the office of the Louisville Community Design Center. At the center of the Center is a man named Jack Trawick. His work, like that of his many cohorts over the past 25 years, has traveled many of the roads explored in this book.

If we're looking for street smarts in building a community, it's to warriors like Trawick that we need to turn. We'll just let him tell his story:

The Design Center was created in 1972 as an outgrowth of a movement that actually began several years earlier with an architectural service. Of course, it was on the tail end of the epic of community involvement and community change

Jack Trawick

and social ferment resulting from the Vietnam War internationally, but more locally the civil rights movement.

In 1968 the civil rights leader Whitney M. Young, Jr., who was also a native of Simpsonville, Kentucky, delivered an address to the National Convention of the American Institute of Architects. And in a highly empowered, eloquent way, he challenged the architectural community, as represented by the AIA, to get off their lily-white duffs and start to do something meaningful for a change, to start to address the incredible social ills that were burning down America's cities and, in particular, to address the civil rights problem, which at that time had reached its crescendo, because he addressed the AIA just a few months after the assassination of Dr. King.

The architectural community got shaken up a bit by that. And at that time the architectural community was lily-white and it was male and it was fairly conservative. And yet there were, as there always are, young people coming out of architectural schools who were all full of vim and vigor and vinegar. And they were the ones to really raise the flag and begin working — or begin what became the Community Design movement.

They began to volunteer their services to community projects. It wasn't really clear how they could get involved — they just wanted to get involved. So they started to do this and that: community parks, things that were largely decorative and cosmetic in nature but, at least, gave people an opportunity to get involved.

In 1972 a couple of architects finally got around to taking what had been a volunteer community

committee-based activity, out of the local chapter
of AIA, and decided to incorporate and create the
Community Design Center and were able to get some
volunteer staff members to run the place. There
was a fair amount of involvement from graduates
of the University of Kentucky. And it continued
along those lines for a couple more years, just
sort of a tattered band of architect guerrillas
trying to do good in the community, but without
any particular focus or any notion of empowerment.

In 1975 we received a grant from the city out of
the Community Development Block Grant Program,
which had just begun a federal revenue-sharing
program targeted for local community development.

The Design Center received an appropriation and was
able to hire a real executive director who was an
architect. He established, using VISTA (Volunteers in
Service to America) volunteers, a kind of a pro bono
public service architectural firm that provided
design systems directly to the city on a variety of
community development projects, especially in the
design of community centers and community facilities.

The easiest way to describe the VISTA program,
like AmeriCorps now, is the domestic Peace Corps.
Rather than going to Somalia to try to revive a
community, you would work in either a depressed
inner-city neighborhood or a coal town in Appalachia.

The funding disappeared in '78. We maintained the
board. We didn't go out of business. And in 1980, the
board was able to align itself with a guy in
Atlanta who was with another community design
center and was putting together an innovative
grant to the Carter administration, to create a

network of community design centers in the Southeast. It was through that grant that they hired me. I was 28 and had been working for five years for a downtown development organization called Louisville Central Area, a downtown planning and promotion agency.

I had been learning about urban revitalization through that program and had served as the liaison from that organization to neighborhood groups because there was a proliferation of neighborhood groups that grew up during the '70s. The organization that I worked with viewed those neighborhood organizations as potential adversaries. So they sent me out to kind of keep an eye on the potential enemy. I actually found it to be the way that I learned who my friends really were.

But I shouldn't put it in ways that make it sound so adversarial. It was more a case where I really enjoyed getting to know people out in the neighborhoods and also felt like they were in need of development assistance as much as downtown was.

Downtown received an extraordinary amount of attention, an extraordinary amount of resources, because there is this powerful romantic notion about revitalizing the downtown to what it had once been. And, yet, downtown was only one downtown neighborhood. There were many downtown neighborhoods that needed revitalization or professional assistance.

When the position at the Design Center came open, it was the right time and the right place for me. And I jumped at the opportunity to be able to have my own shop, my own organization, to do just that. I was not an architect and I am not an architect. My degree is in comparative religions from a small liberal arts college in Ohio called Kenyon.

So I found myself here with really a brand-new organization because we had gone out of business. That was good because there had been about a year and a half there when there was bad blood. The bad blood went away, and I had no history with the organization. I had no history with the movement. I had no history with anybody and was just the new guy on the block.

So ... what is it you do exactly?

The critical thing about the Design Center has always been that everyone knows that what we do is important, but if you ask them, "What does the Community Design Center do?" they would have to think about it for a while.

On the one hand, we are known as a technical assistance provider. But, on the other hand, we're known as an intermediary organization. I used that expression that I think it was BASF used to use in their TV commercials about "We don't make the sound; we make it sound better." And that was the same thing for us: We have tried to provide counseling, consulting, one-on-one relationship-based counseling to neighborhood-based nonprofit organizations in trying to enable them to accomplish what they believe in, what they want for their neighborhoods. We try to enable their inspiration.

I don't want to get misty-eyed about it. But it's really just working with people who want to get involved, who want to be a part of their community and, thereby, help to make their community. Because, you know, community is not community without people getting involved, people knowing each other, people working together. It really is a team-based kind of thing.

The writings of De Tocqueville are probably over-emphasized and over-romanticized. But he did recognize that there was something unique about America and the way people associated with one another. I think that the voluntary associations and trade organizations helped to contribute to the vitality of America. That is something that has always been underlying for me. I'm only now realizing there were three things for me that were the root of why I've committed some portion of my adult life to this work.

I was in Boy Scouts and, you know, this may sound simple-minded, but Boy Scouts actually did really provide me with a lot of lessons in working with other people and in self-reliance, especially.

I attended in 1975 a Democratic National Committee event here in Louisville that was a mid-term convention — basically a warm-up convention for the 1976 presidential convention. And at that convention were all of the major candidates who were running for the Democratic presidential nomination: Jimmy Carter and Mo Udall and Sargent Shriver and Fred Harris and a couple of other people. And there was also a lot of discussion of issues. It was called an issues convention.

One of the real strong themes of that period and of that convention was something they called participatory democracy. That sounds redundant — or it should. But it was a very powerful theme at that time because they were really trying to encourage people just to get involved with the party and with politics, not to get a Mayor Daley elected or to buy into some kind of monolithic power but, instead, just to represent the diversity of thinking and opinion in American culture.

That was very exciting to me, because I was just out of college. I had come from living in Vermont — if I were ever going to be a Republican, I would be a Vermont Republican. What I view as a Vermont Republican is an individual who is very involved in his or her town and town politics and attends the town meeting every month to know what's going on and to keep the civic dialogue always going. That really to me represents what democracy should be all about. It's a high level of personal civic involvement. It's like in the Norman Rockwell painting, there's a guy standing up in the town meeting and having his say.

That may all sound too romanticized. But if there's anything important about my biography, it's the influence that those experiences have upon me that brought me to be here and to be doing what I do. It also explains why, after I came here, the Design Center has been shutting down its design capacity in favor of its community focus.

I found early on while I was here that there were a lot of people who wanted to get involved in one way or another personally. They had it in their hearts, but it would get lost in the incoherence of the world, or of community, of how to work with other people — how to even find other people to work with; how to basically be effective with what they wanted to do but, also, how to satisfy their yearning to be involved. And there are two sides to that.

The satisfaction is really important because if you can't get any satisfaction around your desire to be involved, then you get frustrated and you become cynical or, at least, you give up and do something else. Then your energies get channeled in a different direction. But worse than that is that you might get cynical, or burned out, which is kind of a subset of cynicism or just kind of psychic exhaustion. People get burned out a lot of times, take a break and then come back in a different form doing something else similar. But people get cynical, just become less and less capable of doing anything positive.

So there's the satisfaction aspect and then there's also the effectiveness aspect, the ability to not reinvent the wheel, to not give up when a door is closed on you because you don't know that the doors are going to be closed on you.

All of these things inspired my organization — with, I guess, some leadership from me — to create this Neighborhood Institute program that we started 10 years ago. The institute has always had many purposes, many agendas. But it, in part, was to try to decipher for people what the system is, the system that we always rail against, and in some ways describe what the meanings of personal and local initiative are. Maybe to begin to reinvent civic organizations as they probably once existed before people became entirely dependent upon government.

Finding a human architecture

I think that there is a big problem with big government and, unfortunately, all forms of government, down to county government and city government. When I say "big," I mean that they seem totally impenetrable and, therefore, not particularly accessible on the one hand. But they also have created this chronic dependency among the citizenry where if you have a problem, you say, "Well, why don't they do something? Why doesn't the city fix that?"

One of the stultifying facts of the growth of big government since the '30s has been the retardation of self-reliance.

Primarily through the Neighborhood Institute, we've been trying to re-establish a culture of self-reliance and to create a safe harbor, at least a healthy home, for the notion of self-reliance and the practice of self-reliance by neighborhoods.

The way that we've done that is through a core course we've designed that touches on a little bit of everything. In fact, if there are any problems with it, it's too general. It's a 12-week, 30-hour course. In 30 hours we try to touch on every imaginable topic or every topic that the class is interested in discussing.

We believe that the Neighborhood Institute could be its own separate entity. But we have never had the financial resources to make it more than it is. One of the reasons we've had difficulty accumulating financial resources for it is that it's a radical idea. It's a radical idea because it bypasses the government.

I read recently that "radical" derives from either a Latin or Greek word that means "roots." So very literally the Neighborhood Institute is a radical concept, because it's trying to get to the roots of the community, the people who make the community happen. The nice thing about it is that we've always found that there are still a lot of people out there who are very involved.

There's a French word, charrette; it actually means "little cart." It's from a college of architecture that was first created in the late 19th century in Paris. And they would do these compressed design problems called charrettes. Those lovely pen-and-ink and watercolor renderings that you see of the classical buildings in ancient Rome and such or Greek classical revival buildings were designed by those people and tended to be designed in three days.

The professors would say, "Here is the program for a coliseum which would seat 38,000 people and have 15 exits and restrooms to accommodate 1,500 people at a time, and a viaduct to run in the water for the mock sea battles and cages for the lions and whatever. And now you design it and plan elevation and perspective and be ready to present it in three and a half days. And we will send around the new charrette in three days to pick up your drawings."

The charrette would come around and the architecture students would chase after it, not having slept for three days, and throw their plans in at the very last second, and have their professors then judge them and grade them.

Well, several years ago, our mayor borrowed a corporate planning tool or problem-solving tool that was being purveyed by General Electric. It's a modified quality circle team-based method of addressing particular management or operating problems or just any kind of particular problem that might exist within an organization. The approach is much like a charrette.

GE donated some professional staff to help the city to download that into the city's overall management structure and created something called City Work.

They do frequent problem-solving within city government using teams that are almost randomly selected from numerous agencies at different levels. And they really involve city employees in trying to figure out how to be more efficient, more effective, better at customer service in dealing with simple problems to fairly complex problems.

It always concludes with the mayor at the end of maybe two and a half days. The mayor attends the report out, the teams make their recommendations to him and he says "Yes," "No" or "We'll look into it."

They train city employees to be facilitators for the process. And then it's almost like these people become the lay priests of the City Work method. They get their "certifications" in facilitation. And then they are called upon at regular intervals to facilitate a City Work on, say, how to handle illegal dumping in alleys.

We've actually done one that was a neighborhood City Work where a neighborhood organization working with some city agency representatives sat down and addressed problems that were being faced by a particular neighborhood to try to develop a series of recommendations to the mayor. That was an effort to try to do a first pass, a more collaborative problem-solving model as opposed to an entirely internal organization problem-solving exercise.

Associations in action

The larger effort that we've tried to make over the last several years has been to try to make neighborhood associations be more the external agencies or agents for the services that city agencies can provide to neighborhoods. So in effect, the neighborhood figures out what it needs and then it plugs into the array of services available from the city to make sure that it is getting the services that it needs.

Basically the neighborhood association becomes the

planner and the broker for the services. Then the agency provides those services. That might mean something as mundane as a more effective solid waste management or garbage pickup and recycling program.

Volunteers sweep the streets in Louisville, Kentucky.

The notion is that these individual neighborhood associations, small governments in and of themselves, could come in — rather than individual citizens and the neighborhood being passive/reactive by complaining to government, and then having government become bureaucratic and indifferent. There would be more collaboration, correspondence, between the service and the citizen, or the organization that represents the individual citizens.

That's kind of the base of what the neighborhood organization could do, should do, because then you get into more customized revitalization strategies, to address much more intangible community problems.

The most pressing and difficult challenging community problem in this community right now is gangs and drug-related crime. It has to do with the import of street-grade cocaine, which is highly addictive and very marketable and ... it's like a cancer.

I told you I was a Boy Scout when I was a kid. I can see that street gangs provide a lot of the same kind of opportunity for self-definition that I got from being in the Boy Scouts. But the thing about Boy Scouts is ... even when I was mentioning it to you, I was a little ashamed to admit that I was a Boy Scout because it was viewed as, you know — "What a nerd!"

Street gangs are probably just the opposite of that. It's adolescent super macho to be a part of one. You're tough; you're cool; you're with it; you know, you're where it's happening and you belong.

I've only tried to figure it out because it is having such a devastating effect on some of the neighborhoods where we work. It's kind of like Maslow's hierarchy of needs. In a community setting my feeling is that personal safety is a base of the hierarchy of needs. And unless you have a sense of personal safety, nothing else is important.

What we've been wrestling with is how community organizations can really tackle this, but also — and this is much more challenging — how community organizations can replace the sense of belonging that is provided through the gangs. It's almost like competing with gangs. How can you compete with gangs? I don't see anybody with even a vague notion of how they can, really. How do you compete with that whole macho thing? How do you catch that testosterone and really channel it in constructive and community-building directions rather than in such destructive directions?

You know, what I've heard is by the time they're 15 it's too late; that it's really between 11 and 15, or 11 and 13, that you've got to save them or they end up with a mind that is so hardened and so angry and destructive and self-absorbed.

That might be a key word, self-absorbed, versus self-relying. You know, it's like two opposite ways to deal with an individual streak.

Probably the best thing you could do is pick them all up and take them all out into the middle of the Wind River Mountain Range in Wyoming and tell them to find their way home.

It's almost like putting people in touch with what's real. And the problem is that people are so out of touch with what's real any more. We just live in a world that is so synthetic.

I don't know what to do about that on the one hand. But I do think on the other that what you do about it is you encourage people to begin to talk to each other again. One of the things that we emphasized this time in our class that we really hadn't before was "You all aspire to be neighborhood leaders but how many of you can name who lives two doors away from you? How many of you know your neighbors?" Unless you know your neighbors, unless you have some kind of contact with them, unless you have some kind of society with them, then you're no different than any of these subdivisions that you rail against as not being real neighborhoods.

The other thing that I have become more interested in just recently is churches. Churches, especially in the black community, have always had a strong organizing action, a strong social function but also strong spiritual function. Our generation is a little uncomfortable with that, because that falls in with the notion of evangelism.

I've worked with ministers trying to work in the community. Some of them are worth their weight in gold. There's a church in Louisville, St. Stephen Baptist Church, and the pastor, Kevin Cosby, is charismatic, he's powerful, he's brilliant and he's also brave. On certain days he puts his life on the line trying to deal with troubled kids.

And there are other people: Albert Polly, a long-time board member; a woman named Edna McDonald who has begun to study for ordination in her church. She's the director of a community center in a very low-income black neighborhood in the southeast city. And she's had days when she's had to call kids down who if she pushed them one step too far would go back to their apartments and get a gun and come back and, as she so simply puts it, "pop me."

I could never, ever do that. But she is endowed with a faith that has helped her to see past all that, see past the fear. The way that she has put it to me is that, if it's her time, it's her time. At the same time, she has practiced love in a way that kids like the one I'm talking about, she's gotten through to, maybe not to turn those kids' lives around but ... at least he didn't go back and get his gun and come back and pop her. He's still very troubled. But now when she sees the kid, she gives him a hug and he hugs back.

I'm not a person of deep religious conviction. I told you that I majored in comparative religions. But all that did was confuse me about religion more than set anything straight.

I read something once about addicts who have been convicted of crimes related to their addictions. They were treating themselves through monastic contemplation and prayer. And it was as though their addiction was a substitute for spiritual peace. They recognized that if they could find some spiritual peace, that might be the best cure for their addiction. And I only thought of that because I was thinking of this problem of crime, gangs and cocaine. It seems there is a correlation between the three variables: Where there are drugs, there is crime and there are gangs. Or where there is crime, there are gangs and there are drugs.

You can't rid yourself of the gangs or the crime unless you rid yourself of the independent variable, and that's the drugs. And you can't rid yourself of the independent variable unless you go to the source of the problem, which is the addictive nature of the drug and why or how people get addicted to it in the first place.

People want to be together

I think that, getting back to our original founding, we discovered very quickly that physical design was 15 percent of the problem and that the real problem is in all of the factors that make or unmake the community. And that we had to be able to both understand those factors and affect them in some positive way, individually as well as collectively; that we needed to be able to facilitate community. But in order to do that we needed to know what it is and why it's so important.

We go from the hypothesis that community is important and then try to figure out how it works so that it is important. But every once in a while we know we're going to have to turn back and ask ourselves, "Why is it important?" People talk about community all the time but how much community is there anymore?

Have we have forgotten how to live? I don't know what the answer is. I know that there is an underlying social pathology out there that suggests that we may have reached the crown of creation, but we don't really have any more good reasons to live than before.

I think a lot of what underlies things like the New Urbanism is a desire to return to some kind of a human scale in our daily living. But, unfortunately, as long as the scale is pretty much confined to subdivisions and not to total communities, then, at best, it will be kind of moderate to weak replicas of places like Savannah.

The thing that I loved about Savannah is that it was a total place where you would live on the square, perhaps go to church on Sunday, walk to work on Monday through Friday, and then go to the market on Saturday, and never go more than four blocks from a place. In doing so, you would know everybody or know a third of the people you encountered in some way or another. There was familiarity there.

Maybe that's a key word in all of this: familiarity. In a lot of respects it seems like what New Urbanist communities do is they conjure up that sense of familiarity. But unless they can also deliver real familiarity after a period of time, they end up smacking of artificiality.

A couple years ago we were doing a plan in that same neighborhood where Edna lives. Maybe you've seen a bunch of guys standing around a street corner in front of a liquor store. To some people that is unsavory behavior. It's loitering. It's not quite criminal but it's just not acceptable. And so there will be an effort to put up big signs, "No loitering." And cops come by every once in a while and shoo people away. Somebody at a meeting said, "What they don't understand is that in certain subcultures, in neighborhood culture around here, hanging out on the street corner is what people do."

When you try to impose upon this neighborhood what you would like your neighborhood to look like ... first, you have no right to impose that on them. And, second, by your trying to flush it out, you are putting a negative spin on a positive activity. You're criminalizing something that is really good, people just wanting to be together. What's wrong with that?

17

The Frontier Town

Ssshhh. Listen for a moment. Sometimes, late at night, when all is quiet around here, if you close your eyes and listen closely, you can tune in to another time. This used to be a frontier town, you know. Can you imagine what it was like back then?

There were great men and women in those days, some of whom walked these very streets. Here in Lexington, Kentucky, one of them was Henry Clay, a man of personal conviction who said, in an 1850 speech to the U.S. Senate, "I had rather be right than be President." Despite his fiery eloquence, Clay was known as "The Great Compromiser" for his ability to bring opposing groups together.

Each of our neighborhoods and organizations — as well as our cities and states and countries — has individuals and groups who paved the way, who laid the groundwork for the great things to come. Those who have gone on before us bear much responsibility for our condition today, much as we bear responsibility for not only ourselves but also future generations. We have learned from the progress and the mistakes of our forebears, making improvements to their breakthroughs. Sir Isaac Newton, the great scientist, mathematician, astronomer and all-around thinker, acknowledged his debt to two of his influences — Rene Descartes and Robert Hooke — in a 1675 or 1676 letter. "If I have seen further (than you and Descartes)," he wrote to Hooke, "it is by standing upon the shoulders of Giants."

While we look to the heroes of the past for inspiration, keeping alive the lessons their lives teach us, we should bear in mind that the history books never paint the entire picture. For every gallant general — or almost any brilliant CEO or organizational strategist — there have been the unknown men and women in the trenches, carrying out the directives, making things happen, fighting the everyday battle for survival.

In this day and age, we recognize that the battlefield comparison can be a risky one — after all, these are supposedly the times of kinder, gentler management, when the trend is to replace the generals with coaches. But our organizations still need the general. There are times, for example, when quick, decisive action is required and there's no time for consensus, or when the troops must be rallied to meet a particularly tough challenge. We need the general, the visionary, the pioneer, the explorer ... and each of them, truth be told, could use a strong support group.

Later in this chapter, we'll meet three people who have, in their own diverse neighborhoods, blazed some trails. One has helped pioneer a highly effective nonprofit organization serving a large urban area. Another has made progress in the frontiers of children's television programming. Yet another has worked to unify Japanese and American automakers behind a common goal.

Across the great divide?

To many, the word "pioneer" conjures romantic images of the rugged individual single-handedly blazing trails through the unknown wilderness. Even in the modern world, we still need brave pioneers who are willing to risk failure in their search for new frontiers. But so do we need people supporting them, whether from the trails or from the home front. The reality is that, despite the mythology, very little is accomplished entirely alone.

"Community life is by definition a life of cooperation and responsibility," writes Wendell Berry, who stresses the absolute necessity for the existence of real communities with shared interests and shared lives. He warns, "if you are dependent on people who do not know you, who control the value of your necessities, you are not free, and you are not safe."

That would imply a need for involvement, interaction, two-way (at least) communication, trust. Know your customer and your partner and your supplier and your neighbor. Ask questions, and actually listen to the answers. Build a relationship around your shared goals.

If M. Scott Peck has anything to say about it, we will find a way to bridge the gap between "rugged individualism" and interdependence. In *The Different Drum* he characterizes individualism in terms of isolation and suppression of emotions, while he equates "interdependence" with a sense of community, openness and sharing.

Many people, Peck adds, live trapped between their "fear of community" and "fear of isolation."

Yet both community and isolation are important at their own times, he says, citing a person's spiritual journey as one part of the road that must be traveled alone.

The presence of community is not the absence of crisis, mind you. Witness the Amish, who are widely  known for their strong sense of community and cooperation. When someone's barn burns down, for example, all the men come together to rebuild it, usually within a day, while the women and children gather to watch and lend emotional support.

Many communities exist only in times of crisis, then lose their purpose once this trouble has passed. We should not shy from crisis or downplay our own ability to thrive amid it, Peck further advises, pointing out that the Chinese word for crisis is two characters: "one representing danger and the other symbolizing hidden opportunity."

One especially poignant example from recent headlines is Oklahoma City's response in the aftermath of the bombing on April 19, 1995. There are countless stories of dedicated volunteers and rescue workers who risked their own lives while searching for survivors amid the death and destruction. Perhaps more incredible, to the jaded among us, is the fact that there was no looting in the wrecked downtown area, and the crime rate dropped for several days. Then there's the incident involving the thousands of dollar bills that the explosion scattered to the winds from the vault of the Federal Employees Credit Union. For several days, money was returned — and when it was counted, it was more than had been lost.

Tom Brokaw, who covered the Oklahoma City scene for a week, spoke of the experience: "Oklahomans may feel more vulnerable now, a little disoriented by what's happened to them, but in their response to this madness, they have elevated us all with their essential sense of goodness, community and compassion."

One of the lessons from such events is that we not underestimate our own capacity for making a difference. We potentially have much in common with the great ones of the past. In Peck's words: "We are more important than we think. We are responsible for history."

The gold-rush town

Our friends Ken and Belle Davis have seen WYNCOM grow from a handful of people to an international corporation. (We're still a small business today, but we were *tiny* in those early days.)

Ken and Bette own and operate Komei, Inc., a successful global communications consulting company, from their home base in Indianapolis.

During a time of rapid growth in our company, marked by considerable growing pains, Ken shared with us a marvelous metaphor that really helped us understand what we were going through. With Ken's permission, we have paraphrased his remarks to a small WYNCOM group in a crucial meeting. Consider whether the metaphor might apply to changes in your own organization or neighborhood.

While driving to Lexington recently, it occurred to me that organizations — and particularly companies — are like towns.

Ken Davis

I grew up in Seymour, a farming town of 800 people in rural Iowa. Most people's families had been there for three or four generations. Everybody knew everybody else. Everybody knew what you made and what religion you were. You knew where everybody stood because of the long tradition that had been built up.

The upside of that was the security. The downside was the lack of flexibility, opportunity for growth and freedom to really be yourself. Today, that town is dead, almost literally. The population has dropped to just a few hundred. Most of the businesses have closed, just like in The Last Picture Show. *When the farm crisis hit in the '70s and '80s, Seymour, Iowa, was one of the victims.*

It occurred to me that in many ways, WYNCOM has been like a gold-rush town. Bunny and Larry Holman struck gold with the concept of "Lessons in Leadership." They found a vein of gold, and very quickly this town grew up around that find. As in a gold-rush town, people got thrown together.

Most of us just happened to be in the right place at the right time, walking in the door the day that a job needed to be done. And so all of us come with different values, from different backgrounds, with different business experiences in different kinds of companies.

Resources have been used fairly freely, as in a gold-rush town. The upside is the excitement, the energy, the freedom, the flexibility, the opportunities that are available to people. And the downside has been that, because everybody has come together suddenly to form this community, people have been rubbing up against one another, invading the "claims" that others have staked. Territorial disputes break out when someone's "turf" is trespassed upon.

WYNCOM is at a point where, as in a gold-rush town, the inhabitants decide it may be time to elect a mayor, hire a sheriff, bring a schoolmarm in from the East, build a school, put up a church. As in those Wild West gold-rush days, we're going through the transition of settling in, being better stewards of our resources and figuring out how to build a community that will last. We're keeping the same freedom, the same adventure and sense of excitement, but going for some staying power, some long-term results.

Our challenge is to develop a supporting structure without losing that sense of adventure and freedom that made the town so exciting in the first place.

Rodney Lanthorne, president of San Diego-based Kyocera International, Inc., makes a similar observation: "This company strives to maintain the mentality of a perpetual start-up."

The risks of pioneer
... and NOT pioneering

Another quotation from Lanthorne is relevant here. Like the previous one, it is also contained within the profile of Kyocera in the "Mix" chapter. We like both statements so much, we decided to use them twice.

"We have been pioneers and, as such, we ran the risk of finding arrows in our back," Lanthorne says. "When Kyocera came to the U.S. (from Japan), we made many mistakes, but we have learned along the way."

There are perils involved with being a pioneer. One is that you will get lost and look foolish. Even worse, you could be wounded or even killed in the marketplace. Competitors might stand on your shoulders and subsequently improve the technology that you invented.

It can also be dangerous NOT to pioneer. Not pioneering can mean missing out on excitement, discovery and new solutions. It can mean being left behind, bogged down in bureaucracy and routine while the neighborhood grows stagnant and competitors steal market share.

Louis Gerstner, president of American Express, has a sign on his desk that reads: "A desk is a dangerous place from which to view the world."

Indeed it is. That's why our advice is to get out on the frontier and EXPLORE.

From volunteer to full-time feminist

Karen Perkins
FORT WORTH, Texas

It took Karen Perkins a year and a half to realize she had changed careers. In her spare time, Perkins, a literature teacher at Texas Wesleyan University, had been working as a volunteer in a fledgling program to provide a variety of services for women. One day she had a revelation.

"It just slipped up on me," she says, remembering the 18-month period of volunteerism she began at age 35. "I do remember a moment where I heard myself say in my subconscious, 'I wish I could get somebody to pay me to be a full-time feminist.' And then I forgot it and kept teaching. I started The Women's Center, never thought about it anymore, and then one day I looked up and thought, 'My goodness, look! I *have* changed careers!'

"So I sort of accidentally stumbled into this business."

Thus did spare-time passion became full-time pursuit. The preliminary work that started in 1978 culminated in the official 1979 opening of the Women's Center of Tarrant County, Inc. Perkins is executive director of the nonprofit, multiservice organization, which serves an urban area of a million-plus people in Arlington, Fort Worth and other cities around the Dallas/Fort Worth Airport.

The Women's Center offers one of the largest, most comprehensive rape crisis programs in the country. It also provides general counseling, problem-solving and intervention. It works to help both women and men not only get jobs but also, through extensive pre-employment preparation, advance on those jobs.

"We do what I lovingly call headwork and then job-search training and placement," Perkins says, citing a placement rate that, since 1982, has always been higher than 70 percent and typically tops 80 percent. In 1985 the center began working with welfare women to get their lives turned around. "We help them build personal skills that are prerequisites to success in both life and work. We then help them move into the labor market, and then we will stay with them a very long time so that, hopefully, they move out of poverty and not just off welfare."

The Women's Center menu of services includes the training each year of more than 40,000 children from ages 4 to 17 on how to reduce the risk of sexual assault and abuse, and how to seek help if they are victims. That training, done primarily through area schools, also teaches school staff, parents and youth workers how to recognize the signs of abuse — "to hear children who are trying to 'outcry,'" in Perkins' words — and how to work with victims.

As the self-described "founding mother" of the center, Perkins makes no bones about its origin and inspiration. "You understand, this is women's movement stuff," she says. "There's not a battered women's shelter or rape crisis center, or anything that calls itself a women's center, that does not come out of the women's movement in the '70s. Others may have been spawned after that, but you don't go back and find a place like this, say, in 1955 — or even '60."

'We're going to be here for a very long time'

Now that it's here, Perkins doesn't see the work of The Women's Center being completed any time soon. "Not in my lifetime!" she says. "Not in yours, either. With the level of violence we're seeing in the news, especially around women and children and certainly with the way women are still behind in the labor market ... I think we're going to be here for a very long time."

Part of the problem, says Perkins, mother of a grown son and daughter, is the stereotypical messages that girls and women continue to get — "things like 'You don't have to worry your pretty little head about it, honey' and 'Be a good girl and don't make waves,' all that kind of stuff. It has been around for millennia, and it takes a lot of undoing. You literally have to shift away from dominance and toward partnership. That's a big trick! Women are still too often defined as genetically, generically less — less smart, less capable, less entitled — along with minority people. Of course, all that's called bigotry. And it takes a long time to undo those old vestiges, especially when they're linked to power." There is good news, on the other hand. "The labor market *has* opened up. More women are going to school and college. I think more women are moving out and taking charge of their lives, and they have a different kind of permission to do that. I think women have raised sons who see that women are supposed to make decisions. We're going to have these new women; we gotta have new men to go with them! (laughs) Boys have seen their mamas growing up to be working people, and their dads sharing more of the childcare and being more of a parent.

"So families are shifting in terms of roles and responsibilities, although women still do what everybody calls that 'second shift,' and go home and bear most of the burden of that. But we see more stay-at-home dads now. The 'Norman Rockwell family,' where Dad went to work and Mom stayed home and kept the children, is only 7 percent of American families now. Just the economics of what it costs to live today are driving  women into the labor market. When we look at what houses cost, we see that it's very difficult these days for a woman *not* to work. Families depend on that second paycheck in many cases.

"The problem is, as a country, we have a public policy that's way behind. So we're not into doing things that support those kinds of families. You know, there's a big political conversation about this, and a lot of conservative agendas that float around it, but we're having a very difficult time discussing, for example, childcare policies."

These are indeed challenging times, not only for The Women's Center but for institutions in general: churches, schools, banks, other nonprofit organizations. Perkins sees leadership and vision as the key to overcoming these challenges. "It's not just about management," she says. "In the corporate sector, those who have strong leaders and a sense of vision, and who do their business with absolute ethics, and can make that work exciting — those people will have an advantage.

"And passion helps. Passion fuels vision. You can see it sometimes when a nonprofit will be very sleepy, just kind of grinding along, and all of a sudden a new leader steps up, and everything changes and gets exciting. So leadership empowers — whether it's from the volunteers who work with organizations like this, or the staff people, it's critical."

In her nearly two decades with The Women's Center, Perkins has formulated a few other ideas about what it takes to succeed — that is, to find one's purpose in the neighborhood and fulfill it. These ideas are applicable to for-profit corporations and nonprofits alike:

Know and focus on your mission. "You can't be all things to all people," Perkins says. The Women's Center has recognized this from the start, managing to stay focused while gradually expanding the scope of its services. Even today, Perkins sometimes finds herself identifying the center as much by what it *isn't* as by what it is. It's not a battered women's shelter, for example, and it doesn't provide specific training in job skills such as typing.

"We never have done that," Perkins says. "We find that there's so much that women need, and training is available elsewhere. Our community colleges in America are some of the very best training entities. We don't need to replicate that. We need to do the things that nobody else knows how to do as well as we do, that turn out to be the transformational things that make women's lives work."

Support your community. "Now, at the end of the century, is a rich time for communities to come together and begin rebuilding themselves. Especially given the present rhetoric about not wanting the government involved. People need to get a sense, again, that they all need to pay their civic dues. I don't mean just in dollars. It can be individual help, not even through an organization.

"We have a very nice little program here called Citizens on Patrol. Typically, it's older people who are trained by the police department just to drive around their neighborhood and notice if they see strangers or cars that shouldn't be there. That has really made a difference in our town and, we think, in the crime rate.

"At every level, in any way you can name, there are opportunities to do that building. It's very important that we do that."

Enlist your community's support. Similarly, Perkins has discovered that, when you need help, financial or otherwise, it's hard to beat the help that comes from within the community. "Grants come and go, but your community cares about the work that you do," she says. "We work very hard to generate support in our community. We feel like that is the best money we have, because it's the most reliable."

Still, diversity is important. Funding for The Women's Center, with a budget that grew from $20,000 in 1979 to $1.4 million in 1997, comes from a variety of additional sources: the United Way, which provides about one-third of the center's money; state and federal grants; local government entities; and special events. "We have purposely, over the 18 or 19 years that we've been in business, built a very diverse funding base. Because we feel that security — whatever security there is in a nonprofit — lies in that diversity."

Do your "headwork." "Headwork" is Perkins' shorthand for what she calls "an interior, internal mental and spiritual transformation process." Here's how she explains it:

"I figured out early that the key thing for women was — because of the cultural messages that impede their thinking and their development, generally — to shift from a passive to an active stance toward life. And to believe in themselves. So we began to look at a lot of research and began to devise training programs that would teach *living* skills.

"It's a charade to talk about self-esteem to women. Women begin to build self-confidence as they develop real skills, begin to use them and win. So at the center of our philosophy of service is that kind of personal empowerment. If you teach people real skills, self-esteem takes care of itself, as you grow and change and become active rather than passive."

Use prevention and systems advocacy. "You can drag people out of the river forever, but you need to go up the river and see why people are falling in." This philosophy is reflected in The Women's Center's focus on prevention, as well as its emphasis on systems advocacy: "changing the way the big systems work with people, which itself can cause problems in life."

Perkins cites the center's work with the Arlington police department, which as late as 1982 routinely polygraphed every rape victim. "We did some community organizing, in a very positive way, and got not only rape exams decentralized out of the central county hospital, where the wait was nine hours, but we also got that polygraphing stopped. Those are systemic issues, especially in an area like sexual assault. One of the reasons that reporting has historically been low is that people feel re-victimized by the criminal justice system. So we've worked very hard in our community to breed a more user-friendly criminal justice system by building coalitions."

Be proactive and entrepreneurial. "We're always willing to try something, and if it doesn't work, we stop doing it. We believe in trying and learning, and building on what works."

This approach extends to marketing efforts, Perkins says. "The American public gets bored real fast and loses focus. So our challenge is to keep the messages out there about the emerging roles and needs of women, children and families. We have to keep those issues before the public, and keep them compelling. We need to re-create those urgencies anew every few years. That's marketing.

"You know, we really do have a short attention span. All of us have to be willing to pay attention to the marketplace, and collaborate with other organizations, to combine, to be entrepreneurial. There are still an awful lot of nonprofits that don't understand the need to become entrepreneurial."

Say yes to opportunity. "One of the things I've learned from all of this is that it's important to say yes to opportunity. Sometimes the opportunities identify you. And this is one of the things that we try to teach women: Don't be afraid to take a stance. You can always back up.

"My totally unplanned career change really illustrates that. You say yes to opportunity, and other things open up. You can always turn around and come back, but nobody much does."

Passion for job benefits children, educators and broadcasters

Karen Jaffe
WASHINGTON, D.C.

"I felt there was a missing link between educators and the broadcasting industry," says Karen Wise Jaffe about her decision in July 1984 to create KIDSNET, a not-for-profit clearinghouse for children's television, radio, audio and video programming.

"Television was becoming big in classrooms at that time, but teachers didn't know what programming to access or how to facilitate the process. There was a great deal of distrust and anxiety separating the education and media constituencies. Without cooperation, both sides suffered from missed opportunities. Our integrity and credibility with these groups enabled KIDSNET to bring them together in a relationship of mutual respect and trust."

As executive director and chairman of the board of KIDSNET, Jaffe was uniquely qualified to create this computerized, international service that recommends programming for young people to schools, libraries, regional media centers, state agencies and other subscribers. For nearly 10 years, she had been a communications specialist with the National Education Association, after a decade involved in all aspects of the broadcast industry.

Although her position as "chief cook and bottle washer" for KIDSNET means that work is almost always on her mind, Jaffe appreciates the opportunities it affords her to combine business with parenthood. Even if it means putting in extra hours at night or on weekends, she has the flexibility to adjust her schedule on behalf of her 15-year-old daughter, Sara, who often offers her mother valuable input.

"Since my work affects children, I welcome Sara's honest evaluations. Her involvement with some of our projects also brings us closer together." For instance, when KIDSNET collaborated on a bilingual public service campaign to make children aware of the nutrition facts on food labels, Sara was asked to participate in the kickoff campaign, which gave her the opportunity to meet KIDSNET's partners in the project — Secretary of Health and Human Services Donna Shalala and Food and Drug Administration Commissioner David Kessler.

After getting Sara to the school bus stop at 7:10 a.m., Jaffe is off and running. "While I don't have a specific daily routine, I'm constantly thinking and writing. I make different lists for different purposes and reprioritize regularly. I keep notepads in my car, the bedroom, anywhere an idea may strike. This can happen in the middle of the night or even in the shower, where I've gotten some of my best ideas. I write random thoughts on large stick-on notes, which can be attached to a pertinent paper or file. I have often found that incidental thoughts can lead to something big.

"If I'm near a phone and get an idea, I call the office and leave messages in my voice mail for myself or a staff member. Our password for something that requires immediate action is 'hot.' We have 'hot' labels that we affix to phone messages or other paperwork, and a 'hot' box that can be checked off on our fax sheet."

In addition to her small but dedicated staff, Jaffe relies on freelance subcontractors for research, writing and design. "I thoroughly believe in delegating. It unclutters my mind and allows me to focus on the next item at hand. The down side to this is that people sometimes hesitate to come to me with problems that arise from their assignments. I have to remind my staff that I'm available to help solve problems. Our biweekly staff meetings are also helpful."

Among the methods Jaffe uses to assess her progress is feedback from others. "It can be hard to stop and smell the roses when you are ultimately responsible for an entire organization," she says. "At a cable series premiere, I was presented with an award from Showtime in recognition of KIDSNET's 10th anniversary. The honor was entirely unexpected, and it illuminated for me some of the contributions we've made to children and education.

"I have an ongoing concern about being able to continue doing the work I believe in. I always tell new staff members that the nonprofit world is not the place to be if you're looking for luxury. You have to be totally passionate and committed to your mission. Every successful person must have a vision of something in the future he or she wants to accomplish, while taking care of all the details and hard work it takes to make that vision a reality."

Finding new worlds across the ocean

Satoshi Tachihara
TOYOTA CITY, Japan

"I don't think I can tell our story very well because of my English level, but I will do my best," says Satoshi "Ted" Tachihara. The American nickname is courtesy of his secretary — "easy to remember, to make friendly," he says.

As it turns out, Tachihara does just fine with English. That's not surprising, because he has played a major role in facilitating Toyota's growing presence in the United States. Therefore, communicating across cultural differences has been a crucial aspect of his job for well over a decade. Since 1986, Tachihara has been involved with the location of Toyota plants in Kentucky, Indiana and West Virginia. But most of his time in the States has been spent in either Kentucky or New York — two vastly different locales.

The genesis of Tachihara's American adventure was in 1984, when Toyota started its first U.S. manufacturing operation: New United Motor Manufacturing, Inc., in Fremont, California. Toyota and General Motors equally share in the ownership of the plant. At that time, Tachihara became interested in overseas projects and sought to move from Toyota's System (Computer) Division in Nagoya, Japan, where he had worked since joining the company in 1979. After applying for, and being accepted into, a program that allows employees to study business management abroad, he was set to begin studies at Illinois University.

In January 1986, however, while he was busily preparing to study at Illinois, there was a change in plans. The general manager of human resources informed him that he would be dispatched not to Illinois but to Kentucky, where a new manufacturing project was in the works in Georgetown, a small town near Lexington. He would be an MBA student at the University of Kentucky. "You can easily guess how much I was surprised at the time. I was at a loss and wondered why me," Tachihara says. "That was a big turning point in my life. I have been involved in overseas project for a long time since then."

One of the company directors explained the strategy to him:

Although Toyota had several experiences in the United States, those had been limited to big cities: New York, Washington, Los Angeles, San Francisco. So the new project in little Georgetown, Kentucky — population about 11,000 at that time — required a different approach for the automaker.

(Before Toyota's selection of Kentucky for the new plant, Tachihara says, "There were few people in Toyota and in Japan who could tell the location of Kentucky in the U.S. map, and who could tell its topics other than Kentucky Fried Chicken.")

Therefore, the first step was learning as much about Kentucky as possible, paving the way for Japanese understanding of the company's newest hometown and helping to build a strong relationship between the two countries. "You have a really big assignment to input us about Kentucky," the director told Tachihara. "You can see a different world in Kentucky as a student there. Make good friends as much as possible."

A new beginning

Tachihara's family was the third from Toyota to be sent to central Kentucky. The move to a foreign culture was as much an adjustment for the family members as it was for the employees.

"It was a really challenging job for me and for my family," Tachihara says. "We and other Toyota families started real new American life in the new world for us. For us, it was the start from almost nothing, the new efforts between Japanese who have few experiences of U.S. life and Kentucky people who don't know about Japan and Japanese."

(It was around this time that Tachihara met Bunny Holman, who had started an English as a Second Language program at Lexington's Transylvania University for the Japanese wives of Toyota employees. For a look at that program, see our "Continuing Education ... Continued" chapter.)

Toyota's mandate to build relationships with the local people was clear, and it was about more than money. As Tachihara says, "Toyota's big investment can make local people happy because of big economic impact, but we always keep in mind we need to become a part of local community and to be regarded as good neighborhood and good corporate citizens."

His own local involvement included accepting an offer to be a Japanese tutor at the University of Kentucky, as well as attending small parties as a guest to introduce Japan and Toyota to the community and talk about the differences between the two cultures. He relished his role. "I was happy that there were people who would like to study Japanese and to know about Japan," he says. "I remember I had to learn about Japan and even about Toyota to provide correct information. It was good for me."

Georgetown has also benefited from the Toyota Camry plant, the Japanese company's first wholly owned U.S. manufacturing facility. Since the first vehicle rolled off the line in May 1988, the original $800 million manufacturing facility investment has grown to more than $2 billion through an expansion plant and the addition of plants to produce power trains, V-6 engines and Toyota's flagship vehicle, the Avalon. In August 1997 the site, which employs more than 7,000 people, added the Sienna minivan (which uses the same vehicle platform as the Camry) to its lineup, thus becoming the first North American manufacturing plant to produce two types of vehicles on the same assembly line. Meanwhile, Georgetown's population has increased to 14,000.

Another city, yet another culture

Tachihara's Kentucky assignment lasted three years, after which he returned to Japan. There he continued to assist long distance with the overseas project in areas such as pricing the Camry and introducing the Avalon to Kentucky.

Then in summer 1995 came a new assignment: Go to New York and become a member of the site selection team for a new truck plant and engine plant in the United States. Because of U.S. restrictions on Japanese imports and pressure to correct the trade imbalance between the two countries, Toyota was seeking to expand its North American operations. Tachihara's role was to contact the governments of several states that were candidates for the new plants, letting them know Toyota's questions about the communities being considered. After a study of almost one year, the company selected Indiana for the truck plant and West Virginia for the engine plant. Both were scheduled to begin production in late 1998.

Tachihara remained in New York until the end of 1997, then returned to Japan as a manager of the Overseas Project Division, the job he holds today.

His experiences in Kentucky and New York, as well as with Indiana, West Virginia and other plant candidate states, have illustrated for Tachihara one of the main challenges for his country in dealing with the United States: the homogeneity of the Japanese culture as opposed to the diversity of American life.

"Japan is a small island, a single culture," he explains. "In the United States, it is very different. We should be careful; we cannot tell about the United States for business. There are cultural differences between states, from Kentucky to Indiana or West Virginia. We have to know about local people."

Differences in local or state traffic laws or other regulations can also pose a challenge, as can levels of government bureaucracy. In the

United States, a foreign company must communicate with local, state and federal government to obtain various approvals. Although Japan has 50 prefectures, each with its own government, a higher percentage of decisions is made by the national government, Tachihara says.

The cultural difference between New York and Lexington, Kentucky, is significant, he adds.

"In New York, if we want, we can spend daily life without speaking English. It seems to me New York is not a melting pot of many foreigners from many countries. There are separate communities such as Chinatown, Korean town, Little Italy, and many groups living separately together. As a matter of fact, some Japanese feel comfortable to speak only Japanese, eat Japanese food and have only Japanese friends. But we, my family, thought our Kentucky life was more interesting, exciting and even comfortable for us.

"New York people have a lot of information about Japan and no interest to become a friend with Japanese. Most people don't need to make efforts to be regarded as a member of local community.

"New York was an exciting city, though."

Cooperation with the competition

Today's auto industry, much like many other industries, is undergoing a transformation in which competitors are also partners — the merger between Germany's Mercedes-Benz and the United States' Chrysler being a recent example. Tachihara, as a manager of North America Group #2, is in charge of Toyota's joint ventures with GM. The two companies are working together in various areas, including development, manufacturing and sales.

"All automobile manufacturers are now studying how to cooperate with other competitors," Tachihara says. "Of course, we are thinking our strategy with a careful eye to the movement of other companies. You can imagine how busy we are now.

"It is very difficult to explain the relationship between GM and Toyota. Because GM is our biggest competitor and also it is our good partner on the other hand."

It is widely known that the Japanese culture typically puts more emphasis on building relationships and on long-term results than do American businesses, which tend to focus on immediate results. Japanese manufacturers make a substantial investment in both time and money to foster their relationships with suppliers and educate them about their KANBAN system of parts delivery, which drastically reduces the need for warehouse space at a plant. In the much larger United States, the logistics change, thanks to differences in such areas as distance and parts defect rates.

Perhaps the greatest lesson to be learned from the partnerships, mergers and joint ventures is that nobody has all the answers. That's a lesson that has come from experience, Tachihara says.

"Many years ago when we first landed in the United States, some Toyota people tried to adjust themselves to the U.S. culture in any event to become Americanized as soon as possible, and some people tried to put the Japanese culture and way of thinking to the U.S. to be a pure Japanese company," he says.

"Now we have to know the local culture and local people first and try to find a mixed way, a hybrid way of Japanese culture and American culture in the business area. Our way is not almighty. We have to modify our system to find the best solution to grow and to become more competitive as a good corporate citizen."

18

Growth and Preservation

Let's take a little drive around town and see what's happened since we passed this way last week.

Main Street just keeps getting longer and busier, doesn't it? Remember when all this land was covered by alfalfa and timothy instead of blacktop and buildings? Yes, this town is, as the Chamber of Commerce likes to say, a city on the grow.

Another new restaurant, this one a branch of a Chicago chain, just opened this week. A new mall is under construction just a few miles from the old one. Wonder what will happen to the old mall when the new one opens up?

Downtown, construction workers are taking a break, having their lunch by the fountain in the city park. These guys are renovating the city's first skyscraper. Built at the turn of the century, it's a whopping 15 stories tall, dwarfed by the 30-story, glass-fronted office tower constructed next to it in the 1980s.

A few blocks from downtown in a historic district, tourists are lined up, waiting for a docent to lead them through one of the city's first homes. It was saved from the wrecking ball in the early 1960s.

Now, visitors to the city tour it daily. The house is a solid-brick link to the past.

Sometimes the wrecking ball goes smashing along. A crumbling old building that no one but the preservationists thought was worth saving is now a pile of bricks and broken rafters. By next week, it will be a parking lot.

Saving the past, savoring the future

Cities and businesses have a lot in common. They both have histories, stories from the past that made them who they are. And both are growing entities, constantly changing shape and form. Or at least those that survive do.

The question of how to grow without losing sight of what made us what we are is one that communities and our companies wrestle with constantly. Our cities and towns and our companies and corporations grow so quickly that we wonder, "Are we losing what keeps us from being 'Anytown, U.S.A.' or 'Any Business, U.S.A.?'" If we opt not to keep pace with the rest of the world, do we risk becoming boarded-up businesses in ghost towns?

Cities, Elizabeth Wilson said, should be "spaces for face-to-face contact of amazing variety and richness. They are spectacle — and what is wrong with that?"

Our businesses, too, should reverberate with personality and teem with a spirit derived from appreciating the past and leaping with both feet into the future.

At the same time, we have to avoid the potholes and ruts caused by being too closely aligned with previous successes. In *The Pursuit of WOW!*, Tom Peters warns that success sometimes spells stagnation for small businesses: "If they are successful, they tend to get stuck in a rut — pounding yesterday's ideas into the ground."

In *The Circle of Innovation*, Peters quotes Dee Hock, the creator of Visa, as saying: "The problem is never how to get new, innovative thoughts into your mind, but how to get old ones out."

Preservation need not be the stuff of musty old books and reassembled bones. It's not about pickling our companies and putting them on display in glass jars. Our histories can best be preserved through the telling of stories that illustrate that our companies are human and have suffered their share of ups and downs, successes and failures, laughter and tears. Our company histories shouldn't be glossy, four-color fairy tales. They should exalt our foibles as well as our fame, our mistakes as well as our magnificence.

Mistakes are our Miracle-Gro. By sharing the error of our ways through the recounting of our history, we teach our current and future employees not to fear mistakes. For as Tom Peters says, "Mistakes are not the 'spice' of life. Mistakes are life. Mistakes are not to be tolerated. They are to be encouraged. (And, mostly, the bigger the better)."

Growing wisely

Communities, and our companies, will continue to grow. And, they can, as author and entrepreneur Paul Hawken says, be grown wisely and wonderfully. It just takes wisdom, vision, planning and fortitude to grow without losing character.

The real hazard is in standing still, in becoming rootbound. Denis Waitley summed up the danger well in a column for our *Lessons in Leadership* newsletter:

"The real risk in life is doing nothing. If you confine yourself to the boundaries of safe, familiar ground that is totally secure, you put overwhelming limitations on your opportunities for happiness. But when you break out of the old routines and shatter obstacles with a no-limitations approach to reaching goals, you open yourself up to all the bounties of life."

Our history can give us a positive identity, a foundation that helps us feel rooted and stable. Often, it is the simplest ties to our past that mean the most. Take, for example, a recent movement in Los Angeles that gave neighborhoods a positive identity by restoring their old names.

By putting up new signs and letting citizens know their neighborhood had a new "old" identity, a measure of stability was restored to eroding communities. The feeling of anonymity that pervaded many of the older, disintegrating neighborhoods was diminished.

As one government official said, "We're harnessing history to lift people's spirits and make them see Los Angeles in a new way."

It's difficult to preserve the history of a place — or a business — if you don't know it. That's why efforts like the one in Los Angeles are important. They connect people with a community's roots.

Linda Taylor has the same aim, although she is taking quite a different approach, on Florida's West Coast.

Linda Taylor

Growing a business wisely and wonderfully

Linda Taylor
CLEARWATER, Florida

In Florida, many residents live the life of migratory birds. They head south to the Sunshine State to weather the winter months and in the summer fly north to the cities and towns they call home. Even when people move to Florida permanently, they often talk longingly about the place from which they came. It will always be "home" to them.

This lack of connection isn't just found in Florida. It's a natural byproduct of our mobility. In the United States, 20 percent of us pack up our possessions and move each year. With so much shifting from one spot to another, it becomes easy for people to lose touch with where they live.

Linda Taylor, a New Jersey native who now calls the Clearwater, Florida, area her home, has set out to reconnect people to their community through a company she founded in 1996 called It's Our Nature.

Taylor plans nature awareness activities for residents and visitors. She leads them on guided hikes and kayak paddles and describes not only the natural life of an area, but its history as well. Her activities also include elements of physical and mental wellness — tai chi, meditation, journaling, gentle kayaking.

Through her hikes, Taylor is teaching her neighbors about their own backyard, in hopes they will appreciate it and nature as a whole.

Reconnecting to place

"I want to help people feel connected to their place," she says. "Just about everybody who lives in Florida is from someplace else. A lot of them feel very disconnected to the state. You often hear people talking about their home being somewhere else; their home isn't here."

The aim of her company is to bring people in touch with themselves and where they live. At the same time, they learn to look at nature in a more appreciative way.

"I feel that my programs connect people with where they live and with each other in a way that is simple, basic and fun," she says. "I think we have lost the connection with each other in the community. A lot of people don't really care about where they live because they don't know about it. They haven't walked down a trail to a bird sanctuary and seen a dog that someone turned loose dive into a bird nest or watched as development disrupted an osprey's nest. You can't save your community until you know it.

"It is very important to be involved in your community and that is what I am trying to do. Get people involved. Sometimes it might just be joining one of my trips and walking with some like-minded people and having one of them talk about an issue that is important to them."

Taylor understands how it feels to lose touch with oneself and one's community. She grew up on the New Jersey shore, watching birds and the sea. She majored in physical education and taught it for several years, developing an intense interest in wellness. Yet, for a dozen years she had been consumed by her career as a regional sales manager for Stairmaster, the giant in step exercise equipment. By the mid-1990s, she was busy, successful, financially stable — and miserable.

"Something was happening inside my being that was telling me I needed to leave, that I needed to do something else," Taylor says. "I was beginning to lose my creative energy. I didn't have that same kind of fire that I had had for so many years. I thought the only way I could truly put my soul back into my work and have a passion for it again was to leave and do something on my own."

Following her bliss

The quest for what Joseph Campbell called our "bliss" has given Taylor a new life that is fulfilling emotional and creative needs her previous job did not satisfy. The series of successes she has tallied to date can be traced to a single, simple, but often-neglected skill — listening, a skill that Lee Iacocca once said he wished institutions would teach people.

As Ken Blanchard says in his *Mission Possible: Becoming a World-Class Organization While There's Still Time* (1997: McGraw-Hill, New York), "when we truly listen to others, it not only brings out the magnificence in them, it does the same for us." And that is what has happened for Taylor.

After she left her job, she gave herself plenty of time and plenty of opportunities to listen to her inner yearnings and those of the people who could be her clients.

She socked away living expenses for six months and spent that half year talking to others and doing market research to see if her idea — day trips that combined nature experiences with wellness and were aimed mainly at groups of women — was viable.

Taylor's research took several forms. A computer search of travel options for women revealed that no other company was offering the type of trips she proposed. She did volunteer work to contribute to the community and to continue her research. Working on a Habitat for Humanity house being built by a team of women allowed her to talk with women of varying backgrounds about her idea.

She sought the counsel of "green" business owners, such as a kayak dealer. She joined business organizations aimed at women. She became a volunteer tour guide at a local marine aquarium to test her skills as a guide.

Her ventures into the community convinced her that her proposed business had merit, and she plunged ahead. Friends and advisers eased her way. For example, when Taylor expressed concern about the financial ups and downs of a business so tied to weather conditions, a woman on one of her trips suggested a book about multiple profit centers. Taylor read it, and as a result, launched a catalog of environmentally friendly products to complement her business.

When she flung up her hands after trying to put a detailed business plan together and exclaimed to a friend, "I don't know if I can do this. I don't know if this is going to work!" the friend calmed

Taylor by advising, "Just take a baby step and lead a hike somewhere."

Taylor took her friend's advice. "I led the hike, and all of a sudden I realized 'This can work!' Sometimes you just have to dive in."

Two years into her business, the state of Florida has made Taylor the official vendor for nature walks at one of its state parks. Because of that contract, she has the potential to help improve the economic status of other businesses. A percentage of the money she makes will be paid to the park system. Her trips will rely on an independent ferryboat operator who shuttles visitors to one of the islands that is part of the park. A food concessionaire is likely to be visited by those who sign up for Taylor's hikes.

"I want to show the state and the park how what I'm doing will enhance them economically. The ferryboat operator has a strong belief that what I do will enhance his business," she says.

An atmosphere for self-expression

Some of her biggest boosts have been the comments from people who have taken her walks, particularly those who have participated in her all-women walks.

Taylor believes those activities create an atmosphere that allows women to share their experiences, shed their concerns about their physical appearance and express themselves.

"One woman said the walk fed her spiritual side and improved the quality of her family life," Taylor says. "Now she is taking her family and acting as the guide on the walks."

Another woman, an advanced kayaker, signed up for a moderately paced nature walk. "This woman told me, 'I'm doing this so I can look at what's around me and appreciate it.'

Walks can connect us.

"It's like Marjorie Kinnan Rawlings, who wrote *The Yearling* and *Cross Creek*, said: 'You cannot be in harmony with anyone else until you are in harmony with your place,'" says Taylor. "You need to find your own Cross Creek. You need to find a place that stirs your soul to go to on a regular basis. You need to identify with what moves you in nature."

She has seen women conquer fears they may have had about wandering a wilderness trail. She's seen stressed, strained faces turn soft and expressive as women learn the dance-like motion required to guide a kayak. She's heard the delighted whispers as a dolphin cavorts near the shoreline while groups do tai chi on the beach.

"The glow is amazing. A woman with a strained face suddenly looks so young, happy and beautiful," Taylor says. "Her focus is no longer 'What do I look like when I'm doing this?' as is the case with a lot of exercise, but instead 'How do I feel?' And the feeling is beautiful."

The women who participate in her trips are of all ages and often represent different cultures. "On one trip, I had four countries represented," Taylor says. "That is another important thing to me — to bring women from different backgrounds to be in the company of one another with the common thread of appreciating nature.

"I'm still working on making the whole financial picture work, but I can tell you I really believe this idea is going to work," she says. "Financially, I won't be a millionaire, but that isn't why I got into it. I really think it is going to make a difference. I feel it already has."

Lessons Linda Taylor has learned along the way:

Women often discount themselves. "We don't put a high enough dollar value on what we do. This is very common, especially for women in their own service companies. But I think, in fairness to all of us, that you have to develop a confidence in the worth of what you are doing, and that is very hard in the beginning because you are still learning."

Make it clear that your business is a business. Taylor knew she had to make it clear that her business was a serious enterprise and not just a hobby. "I had to make it a company, not just a walk. I always thought It's Our Nature would be more than guided trips — it would be a concept, a stamp of something." She developed a company name and logo that allow her company to go beyond nature walks — in fact, Taylor has already launched a related newsletter and catalog.

Find your niche. "I knew I had to find a niche to make me different." That niche, for Taylor, was adding the element of wellness to her nature experiences, whether it is moderately paced walks through the woods, kayaking on still water or tai chi on the beach. Because her business is so different, several publications have written stories about It's Our Nature, resulting in free publicity for the young company.

What looks like a mistake might not be. "I spent a lot of money developing my logo and using paper that was 100 percent post-consumer waste with soy-based ink. I did everything to make it ecologically correct. I was thinking that it was a mistake, that I put too much money into my image. But now I have people telling me they have kept my materials for a year because they held their attention. And, I think the professionalism of my materials during my presentation to the state of Florida helped me win the contract to lead tours at the state park."

Market, market, market. One of the toughest questions posed to Taylor was "Why should I pay you to take a walk in the park?" Taylor knew her walks could improve mental and emotional health as well as physical well-being. But to convince others, she first had to sell herself as the leader of these tours. Doing so made the longtime sales manager tremendously uncomfortable. "It is so hard to step out and sell myself. It was so easy when I was in sales for Stairmaster. I could stand away from the equipment, point to it and say, 'This is the greatest.'"

How do you sell yourself when you are low-key like Taylor? "I think that in some businesses, you have to market what you are, and people will see that you are authentic," Taylor says. "And I think they appreciate that."

Find inspiration in others. When Taylor faces a task that makes her heart thud and her pulse race, she remembers Eleanor Roosevelt's command: "You must do what you think you cannot do."

"You have to have the guts to step into an uncomfortable situation," Taylor says. When she wonders about the value of her business to the community as a whole, she picks up her copy of Paul Hawken's *Growing a Business*. She attended a lecture by Hawken, the founder of the Smith & Hawken garden supply catalog, and afterward asked him to sign her copy of his book. He asked her about her business. "And he really listened," she says. When she opens the cover, she sees the words he penned, his simple advice for her business: "Grow it wisely and grow it wonderfully." And again, she is inspired.

Growing where we are

Few of us live life in a single spot. We are always moving on, looking for opportunity around the next corner, over the next hill. Yet, often, the growing experiences we seek are right where we are. Staying in one place doesn't have to be limiting, as author Eudora Welty has proved. Since the 1920s, Welty has lived in the house her parents built in Jackson, Mississippi.

Welty's life was not restrained by being tied to one place. For, as she points out, most of our inspiration lies inside us.

"I am a writer who came of a sheltered life," she wrote. "A sheltered life can be a daring life as well. For all serious daring starts from within." Welty traveled far and wide, but as she said in an interview a few years ago, her love of travel was fueled in part by the knowledge that Jackson would be her final destination.

We seem to be constantly looking for something better, something brighter. Often, opportunity is right where we are, if we only look for it. It's like one planning expert said about the growth of Los Angeles: "Until the 1980s, Los Angeles continued to look outward. Well, there's no 'out' to look at anymore. We've gone as far as we can go. The next logical step is to look back at what you've created."

In simple terms, it is "brightening the corner where you are." It's exactly what Patty Erjavec has done in her hometown of Pueblo, Colorado.

Life in a sleepy little town

Patty Erjavec
PUEBLO, Colorado

Patty Erjavec and her husband both grew up in Pueblo, a city of about 100,000 that she lovingly describes as "a sleepy little town." It's the kind of place where you'd expect natives like the Erjavecs to get restless, pull up their roots and move to a place that seems bigger, better, brighter and brimming with opportunity and excitement.

But the Erjavecs didn't do that. When they graduated from college, they returned to Pueblo. Their decision probably makes them a minority among their peers. They had other options, other choices, and yet they chose to stay where they grew up, where they have family and friends, where ties bind. Staying in Pueblo meant saying good-bye to dreams of a big house and high-powered jobs. But Pueblo was where their hearts — and their families — were.

"We wanted to raise our family here," Patty Erjavec says. "We both knew we were probably sacrificing something as far as our careers were concerned, but we decided to stay. Money isn't everything.

"This is a sleepy little town where family is important. Our community has ethnic groups that have hung on to their cultures, and you don't often see that in other cities. We are big enough and close enough to Colorado Springs and Denver so that if you want to do something there, you can, and then you can always come home. I've really come to appreciate that over the years. I've traveled all over the country and to China, and it is always nice to come back to Pueblo."

As it turns out, Pueblo has doled out a fair share of challenges and opportunities — two of Erjavec's favorite terms — for a native daughter who is fast becoming a community leader. Her job as general manager of one of the city's manufacturers has taken her all over the country, demanded much of her time and led to her participation on many local boards and committees.

Would it all have been possible if she'd moved to Denver or Los Angeles or Chicago? Probably not. Even though jobs there might have offered her as many opportunities, there would have been no way the young wife and mother would have been able to take advantage of them without the support of her family. Without her mother, her late father and her in-laws, she would have been like an Indy driver without a pit crew.

Gearing up for the job

You often can't foresee where a job will take you. Erjavec certainly had no inkling, when she was hired as controller of the soon-to-open PCL Packaging in 1987, that she would be running the plant a mere five years later.

A number cruncher with scant understanding of manufacturing, she felt ill equipped for what was at best a dubious honor. The plant, which had thrived in its first two years by churning out plastic bags for major retailers like Kmart, had lost several big customers that had decided to use a type of packaging PCL did not make. Erjavec not only had to drum up new customers, she had to figure out how to run a plant with little understanding of the manufacturing process.

But Erjavec is not one to sit in a stew of silent suffering. She knew that though she was the plant's leader, she couldn't turn the company around single-handedly. There also was no one person at the plant who could teach her the intricacies of the business. What she needed was a support system, a team of people who knew the things she didn't.

"About all I knew [about the manufacturing process] at this point was that resin made film, but not much more than that," she said. "I thought, 'Oh, my gosh, how am I going to do this?' So I formed a steering committee made up of individuals with different expertise to help me run the plant. We ran the plant that way for four years. I personally couldn't have done it any other way. There was no one here to teach me, no one to allow my mind to grow. I needed those people, and they needed me."

Creating a whole from parts

Many of the employees were visibly moved when Erjavec asked them to share their knowledge by joining the steering committee. When she would query them about how a situation should be handled, they would say, "What? You're asking *me*?"

"It took awhile for people to appreciate the fact that they were being asked a question and that their input and suggestions were valued," she remembers.

The team members learned, making mistakes along the way, growing closer as they worked together.

"During that time I brought certain things to the table; they brought tons and tons to the table," Erjavec says. "I discovered that their big problem was that they didn't always know why they did what they did."

So, as employees helped Erjavec understand the equipment they operated and how it worked, she explained why they and their work were critical to the end product.

"We all became a whole, there is no doubt about it," says Erjavec.

Bringing an outsider in

But even the committee's knowledge had its limits. Erjavec realized that some problems were beyond her and her employees' capacity.

"Employees on the plant floor could only teach me so much," Erjavec says. "There was a gap. Unless I got somebody in with technical expertise beyond what we had, we would never go anywhere. It was an opportunity and a challenge for the plant."

Erjavec worried that bringing in an outsider would cause internal problems, make employees feel inadequate and destroy the teams that had been built. When she did bring in a manufacturing expert, Erjavec went on a campaign to make sure employees realized that they were still a part of the team, that their work was important, and that their help was needed to make new ideas work.

"I had to facilitate bonding, and once we saw some successes, everything fell into place. Around here, it is always 'Look what we've accomplished.' It's never, never an 'I' situation."

Today, PCL is running at full tilt. Its workforce has almost doubled to 75 people. The plant runs two shifts. No longer reliant on two to three large retailers, the company is fueled by orders from many smaller businesses. It is cutting costs, recycling a full 50 percent of its scrap instead of the 10 percent it was salvaging just a few years ago.

A valued constituency

When you talk with Erjavec, you come to the conclusion that if she wasn't in management she'd make a darn good politician. She treats her employees as a valued constituency, and while she's not out to win their vote, she is out to gain their respect and allegiance.

"You have to focus on the fact that your people are your biggest asset and if you don't have them, you really don't have anything," Erjavec says.

That's why you rarely find Erjavec sitting at her desk, tallying the numbers, as you might expect of someone with her accounting background. Instead, she's down on the plant floor, talking to employees.

She feels comfortable there; her conversations with employees arm her with ideas and insight.

Her day typically begins at 7 a.m. Unlike many early arrivers, she's not using those morning hours to shovel through stacks of yesterday's

On the line at PCL Packaging

paperwork. She comes in early to say good-bye to the night shift and hello to the day shift and to see if there are any problems that need fixing.

"The only time to get communication is between the shifts," she says. "In a manufacturing environment, your eyes and ears have to be open at all times."

It is also sometimes a matter of standing side by side with those who do the work. Erjavec has worked with her production crew, carrying ink pails and packing plastic bags, literally walking a few miles in steel-toed shoes like theirs. By doing so, "I experienced every emotion they did," she says.

She now knows exactly how it feels when the summer sun heats up the plant. Popsicles and other cool treats often appear on the production line during the warm months, courtesy of Erjavec.

Easing the monotony of manufacturing

In a way, her upbeat manner has turned Erjavec into not just the company's leader, but also its dispenser of good cheer.

She has come up with ways to beat the monotony of manufacturing — pulling employees off the line for a mini-health checkup, a drink from a juice bar, or an impromptu tug of war between work teams.

"An ongoing part of my role here is to keep people pumped up," Erjavec says. "We've had days where we'll shut the plant down in the middle of the summer and take everyone to the fair. With something like a tug of war between crews, you think 'What does that have to do with productivity?' Well, when a crew can pull that rope collectively and see the other crew fall into the mud, boy, have they accomplished something! And when they go back on that line, they're invincible."

Like most well-liked leaders, Erjavec's mood can quickly trickle down through the rest of the company.

"If I get down, everybody gets down," she says. "My mood makes a big difference. I do these things to keep me pumped up, because if I get down, everybody's down. If I've had a bad day, my personality is reflected on the floor, all the way through. I really have to watch that because we are a small company. I remember one time I was concerned about something, and I had gone downstairs on the plant floor just to walk around and apparently I had walked past a number of employees without saying hello. By the time I got back up to my desk, I heard I had walked past so and so and hadn't said hello. And what difference does it make? It makes a big difference. It's extremely important that you speak to each and every person in the same way. Have a smile on your face. And you know, I can't tell you that's the way it is for me every day, because it is not. I'm just like anybody else. I come in and I'm grouchy. I snap at somebody that I shouldn't. But there is always the element of respect. You must respect everybody."

Never sweating the small stuff

In her career, Erjavec has faced major challenges — developing an accounting system from scratch for an industry she knew nothing about, rethinking corporate strategy when major clients began to use other companies' products, and consolidating the operations of two other plants into hers.

But none of those situations can compare with her father's illness and eventual death from leukemia. Knowing that her mood often became that of the plant, she fought hard not to let her personal life affect her professional one. "You know something," she says, "it is very hard to separate your home life from your professional life. It was hard to walk in the door every day with a smile on your face and not want to bite someone's head off because your dad is dying. It took a lot for me to get through that period of time and not have it affect the quality of my performance at work."

She began to carry a little book with her, pulling from its pages the inspiration she needed to make it through difficult days. "It is *Don't Sweat the Small Stuff* by Richard Carlson," she says. "There is one sentence in it I try to always remember. It is 'Take a look at a situation and if you are going to remember it a year from now, then focus on it. But if you aren't, then let it go. Don't waste the energy on it, because you've got too many other things to worry about.' And that's pretty much the way I've tried to live."

A loyal citizen

Erjavec appreciates the opportunities her hometown has given her. She puts considerable energy back into the community through various boards and organizations as a way of saying thanks.

"I feel I owe a lot to the community as well as to PCL. Pueblo went out and got PCL and brought them here," Erjavec says. "So, I've always felt PCL should be a good corporate citizen and give back. Whenever I serve on a board, I always do it to represent PCL. I don't do it for any personal gain or fame. What I get out of it personally is growth and education."

So, in the end, staying home has been no sacrifice for Erjavec. Instead of limiting her, Pueblo has launched her.

"I guess what this proves is that you don't have to live in a major metropolitan area to stretch yourself and achieve whatever you want to achieve."

Remembering where we came from

"My dentist grew up poor, on a small farm in South Carolina. Her father was a farmer; her mother and the children worked at his side in the fields. Her parents never got much of an education; her mother was illiterate. Yet the hard-working couple made very sure that their children always got the best and most education possible.

Today, my dentist has her own thriving practice. She treats a lot of low-income families who live in the neighborhood near her office. She's been honored for her volunteer work in the community. She's sent her own children off to good colleges.

All the while, she's never forgotten those life-forming years on the farm. On the wall of her office is a framed print of a simple farmstead. It looks like springtime. And, to my dentist, it looks like home. "I can look up there, and remember where I came from," she says.

All of us have something we cherish of our past that reminds us of where we've been and helps us remember where we are supposed to be going.

Our early years are often called our formative ones; they are our molds. Eventually we break out of them and move on. But even as our shape is altered along the way, we hold to that basic form.

Our businesses are similar. They have history and heritage, the principles that were their original recipe. As the years go by, those basic recipes are experimented with and improved upon. New ingredients are added, and different mixes are discovered. We begin to accumulate a history.

Some would argue that WYNCOM, our company, is so young that it hasn't had time to develop a history. Actually, it has a very rich one. Our early years were lean ones — so bare bones that you practically remember every paper clip. Those years are indelibly etched on the brains of those of us who were here back then. And we have already begun to preserve that history.

In our offices hang portraits of several of the employees who were with us in the early years and have since retired. There's Arthur Light, the "young fellow" whose spirit was that of the rhino — he got up every morning, polished his horn and charged. Because of Arthur and his "What can I do to help?" attitude, our company sailed through some seas that would have been pretty stormy and rough otherwise. Because of him, our company mascot is the rhino. You'll find rhinos in every shape, size and form in our offices.

There's another portrait of Ina Carpenter, who shepherded our finances in the early days. Ina's main challenge was to rein me in. Her levelheadedness somewhat balanced my often out-of-budget ideas.

And there will eventually be others to hang in this WYNCOM Hall of Fame. But these people won't stare severely down at those who are new to the company, who have fresh ideas and different approaches than those before. Instead, their kind eyes and smiles will encourage and inspire.

Preserving your history is a worthy deed, as long as you don't let your company become a museum piece in the process.

It's sometimes tricky, but we must learn to cherish and remember the past without letting it limit our future. As anthropologist Catherine Bateson told journalist Bill Moyers in his *World of Ideas* (1989: Doubleday, New York): "It's a mistake to shut out the new and just keep things as they are. But it is also a mistake to address the problems of the present and the future without reference to the traditions of the past."

As leaders, we have to remember to always put our employees' work in perspective, to help them understand that they are a part of our company's story. I like the way Dr. Gary S. Hamel put it in an interview he gave with *World Executive's Digest*. Hamel said, "I believe every employee should wake up each day feeling that they are helping to build a legacy that goes beyond just themselves."

— *Larry Holman*

Businesses built to last

Many of us operate what are labeled as small businesses — companies with fewer than 500 employees. We feel mighty proud when we celebrate the fifth, 10th or 20th anniversary of the opening of our company's doors.

We may accept congratulations for our accomplishment with a weary sigh as we say, "Yes, running a small business is tough."

But do we really have it any rougher than businesses in the first half of this century, which weathered two world wars and a severe economic depression? Or how about those that survived the Civil War, the saddest and most tearing experience of our country's short history?

Now that makes our perceived difficulties look a little laughable, doesn't it? We might have trouble finding good employees, but how many of us have watched our entire workforce march off to war? We might have to make quick adjustments when the Dow dips up and down, but how many of us have seen all our assets evaporate in a stock market panic?

Yes, many of us young whippersnappers need to be reminded that some of the businesses we walk past and drive by every day weathered not just one of those trying times in our country's history, but all of them. There are hundreds of for-profit companies of all shapes and sizes that have not only survived but thrived for 100 years or more.

We need to remember, as Denis Waitley says in *Empires of the Mind*: "Cathedrals take generations to build. So do great societies, companies and families."

In the world's older nations, cathedrals and century-old businesses are commonplace. But both are still a cause for celebration in a country as young as the U.S.

If you look around your city or town, you may not find a cathedral, but you'll probably find a few century-old businesses. In Kentucky, our home state, almost 200 companies have qualified for a program created two years ago to recognize businesses that are 100 years old or even older. Most are small businesses — insurance companies, funeral homes, newspapers, banks, manufacturers, grocery stores, drugstores.

The state historical society, which created the program, knows there are even more qualified businesses out there that just haven't heard about the program or haven't taken the time to fill out the application form.

Illinois has more than 900 companies in its 15-year-old centennial business program, which has been a model for many others including Kentucky's.

While it's nice to recognize businesses for their longevity, these programs are more than a pat on the back. Their aim is to give business history the attention it deserves and to encourage business owners to preserve their company's unique story.

"We want to help make the business owners aware that they are an important part of the state's history and make the public aware that business is part of our history," says James Wallace at the Kentucky Historical Society.

Karen Everingham, at the Illinois State Historical Society, agrees. "Recognition is important because these businesses have contributed greatly to the economic stability and productivity of our state and nation. What is remarkable is that they have survived numerous periods of economic instability and depression — the scare of the 1890s, the Great Depression, two world wars, the 1970s oil crisis, downsizing during the 1980s."

The companies definitely deserve the recognition. "If you've been in business 100 years, you're doing something right," says Wallace. "If anything I had ever done had lasted 100 years, I'd be ecstatic."

Learning from our elders

All of us could probably learn a lesson or two from these elder statesmen of the business community, businesses that were built to last.

These companies do share some traits, and not surprisingly, most of them have ample amounts of the qualities that Tom Peters says make a business start-up successful — distinction, passion, culture, community, perseverance, not to mention a taste for one of Peters' favorites, reinvention.

Let's take a look at a few of Kentucky's venerable businesses and find out what has kept them successful for such a long time.

Dedication and devotion to their business.
Businesses are like a garden — they always grow
best when tended by someone who loves them, who
wants them to see them flourish. Talking to
proprietors of centennial businesses, you often
sense an abiding devotion to the company.

Running a small business is a time-consuming
task; it's nothing for a small business owner to
put in 60 to 70 hours a week. Vacations may be few
and far between. Profits will probably be plowed
back into the business instead of a new home or
car.

Yet, when you talk to many owners of businesses
that have been around a long time, they speak
with such enthusiasm and vigor you forget how
hard they toil.

When Paul Anderson, owner of the Anderson Ferry
Company, talks about the 160 trips across the
Ohio River his ferry makes seven days a week, 364
days a year, there's no grumbling, no complaint.
His business has an important purpose — it gets
people across the river faster than the highway
and saves them time, gas and money. Anderson
knows that, and he's willing to do what it takes
to make it happen.

He does wonder if his children will want to pay
the price of such devotion — little free time,
few vacations. But if the business is ever sold,
the new owner will have to demonstrate the same
dedication Anderson has shown. Anderson has said
he would consider selling his business to someone
"if I knew they had the ferry's interest at
heart."

The ability to change with the times. You don't survive 100 years — or even 10 years anymore — without being adept at adapting.

Companies that have been around a century have learned how to change not only their processes and procedures, but sometimes their product as well. Imagine where Hillerich & Bradsby, maker of the famed Louisville Slugger bat, would be if it had stuck with its original product, the butter churn, instead of switching to the wooden baseball bat? Out of business, we'd guess. And Hillerich & Bradsby has kept changing, expanding its products to golf clubs and hockey gear.

Or if Fanny Wolkow, who founded F. Wolkow and Sons of Louisville in 1893, had been averse to change? The company produced wigs for Jewish women who shaved their heads as part of an Orthodox marriage ritual. In America, that custom died. So Wolkow promptly changed her company's course and began making combs and curling irons. Today, the company sells hair products to African Americans.

In Bardstown, Tom Hurst Jr. runs Bardstown Mills, an 1820 woolen mill-turned-flourmill-turned-farm supply and feed store. Hurst keeps a careful watch on the changing agricultural scene in the rural area that is his marketplace. The large farms that were his major customers 10 to 15 years ago are disappearing, replaced by hobby farms of 10 acres or less. His store's shelves reflect the shift. He's stocking — and selling — more dog, horse, potbelly pig and rabbit food.

Response to customer needs. The passengers who board Paul Anderson's ferryboat on the Ohio River between

Cincinnati and Northern Kentucky aren't there for a scenic voyage. "Most of our customers come to get across the river," says Anderson, whose business was founded in 1817 to take farmers and their livestock from field to market. Now, most of Anderson's passengers are on their way to work or to catch a flight at the Cincinnati/Northern Kentucky International Airport. "So, you've got to keep them moving. Keep them moving and treat them right — they'll come back."

Down in Elkton, a tiny Western Kentucky hamlet, Weathers Drugs is still filling prescriptions. There are discount chain drugstores on the outskirts of town, yet the business founded by Jimmy Weathers' grandfather in 1875 continues to thrive on the courthouse square. There's good reason. When your child is sick in the middle of the night, you feel comfortable calling Mr. Weathers. Through the years, the 77-year old Weathers has often been awakened in the wee hours of the morning and asked to fill a prescription. "It was nothing unusual to get up at 2, 3 or 4 in the morning and go to the store," he says.

And while Weathers doesn't get as many of those middle-of-the-night calls now, he still gets a few on Sundays. "There is a need yet for the community pharmacy, and I think there always will be," says Weathers. "If there's a need, we'll be there."

Community involvement. In ways that are often small, but infinitely meaningful, small businesses are supporters of the community. Most small businesses can't afford those news-making million-dollar gifts to the local college or charity group. But they can give smaller amounts of money and significant amounts of their time. Small business owners double as school board members, city council members, Girl Scout leaders, soccer coaches, Junior Achievement teachers, Habitat for Humanity volunteers. They buy ads in the high school football program, help fund band trips, donate door prizes to the United Way fund-raiser. They make a big impact in many little ways.

Jimmy Weathers hopes that others don't view his business as all gain and no give. "At the store, it hasn't been all take. There's been a lot of give." Each generation of his family has handed down not only the business but also a commitment to the community. "My grandfather was mayor of Elkton; my uncle served nearly 20 years as mayor. My father was a state legislator for two terms."

Jimmy Weathers has continued the tradition. He served on the local school board almost three decades. He's been involved in his church's leadership.

"We have tried to give back to the community through our involvement," he says.

Family involvement. A number of the centennial businesses are still being run by descendants of the company founders. Jimmy Weathers' son, Harry, is following in his father's footsteps, the fourth generation to do so.

In Mize, two generations of the Oldfield family are hard at work running J.A. Oldfield and Son General Store, the community's unofficial central meeting place. Charlotte Oldfield's great-grandfather opened the store in 1876. Charlotte, her brother and their parents run the store today.

Charlotte recently returned to Mize after working for companies in other states. "When you grow up in a family business, you don't appreciate what you have until you work for other people. I am just so proud to be a part of a family that has had a business that has been around this long. You don't find that very often."

A constant construction zone

When you think about it, running a business for the long term is a lot like living your life. As Denis Waitley says in *Empires of the Mind*: "Life is not something to step back from and admire when completed. It is an ongoing process of design, laying the foundations, forming, erecting, bonding, changing, detailing, refining and renovating. We never get it quite right. It is never perfect. It is always under construction." And so is a business.

"First say to yourself
what you would be;
and then
do what you have to do. "

— Epictetus

19

Finding a Role

Each of us plays a role — or, more accurately, multiple roles — during the course of a lifetime. Employee, spouse, parent, co-worker, friend, neighbor. Some of these roles we choose, while others just sort of gravitate toward us. One of the great challenges of life is figuring out the roles we want to play, pinpointing what it is we're "about," then trying to fulfill those purposes to the best of our abilities.

Abraham Maslow wrote that "A musician must make music, an artist must paint, a poet must write, if he is to be ultimately at peace with himself. What a man can be, he must be." Stephen Covey makes a connection between this innate drive to be what we can be and the need to leave a legacy, a point addressed in our "Garden" chapter.

The "need to leave a legacy is our spiritual need to have a sense of meaning, purpose, personal congruence, and contribution," Covey writes in *First Things First: To Live, To Love, To Learn, To Leave a Legacy*. A few pages later, he offers his take on Maslow's famous hierarchy of needs: "Think of the impact on the way we spend our time and the quality of our lives when we're able to effectively meet our needs and turn them into capacities for contribution. Abraham Maslow, one of the fathers of modern psychology, developed a 'needs hierarchy' in which he identified 'self-actualization' as the highest human experience. But in his last years, he revised his earlier theory and acknowledged that this peak experience was not 'self-actualization' but 'self-transcendence,' or living for a purpose higher than self."

We all have our own names for this quest. Call it the search for meaningful work, or finding your calling, or being a part of a great team, or making a contribution, or turning your avocation into your vocation — the motivation is the same. It's about the opportunity to do whatever it is that makes us feel *alive*. If we can make a little money at it while making a contribution to our neighborhood or community, we are fortunate.

A little perspective

"I'm a basketball nut. A former jock. I came of age in locker room environments largely characterized by chauvinistic posturing and macho attitude, in the days before such behavior was so widely recognized as politically incorrect — or least before phrases such as "politically correct" and "politically incorrect" were in vogue. In those days, I had a coach who was quite convinced that he knew the precise reason for Larry Holman's existence. That reason — my *raison d'etre*, my purpose in life — was REBOUNDS. "Holman," he'd growl, "you were put here on Earth to get the ball!" Generally, he'd use a choice adjective or two to modify "ball," but since this is a family-oriented book, I'll just paraphrase.

For quite a while, I believed that coach. At 6-foot-6, I certainly had the physiology for the role. I had the mind-set as well. So I set out with a single-minded intent of grabbing that blankety-blank ball and wreaking havoc on the opposition. Throughout high school, college and a brief professional career, I plied my skills on the court, running around with a bunch of grown men in short pants, acting as if our lives depended on that bouncing sphere (which is, after all, shaped like the world).

These days, I'd like to think I have a little better perspective about what's important, at least in my own life. I still enjoy watching college and NBA basketball games, and I love healthy competition in almost any arena. But I've ditched (for the most part) the outmoded macho behavior in favor of a more sensitive and caring role: leader of a diverse and progressive company. And the teamwork exhibited by this organization rivals anything I've ever seen on a basketball court. Maybe, after all these years, I've found my true calling.

— *Larry Holman*

Finding a niche with no limits

The word "entrepreneur," which is related to the word "enterprise," has its roots in the Old French word for undertake, or, literally, "between take." As entrepreneurs, we are undertaking a challenge or enterprise — the "between" comes in as we seek to find a niche, or a special place in the world or the marketplace for what we have to offer.

In the marketing field, this is known as "positioning." Jay Conrad Levinson, in his classic book *Guerrilla Marketing: Secrets for Making Big Profits from Your Small Business* (1984: Houghton Mifflin Company, Boston), provides some insight into this process:

> The marketing plan or positioning strategy should serve as the springboard for marketing that sells. When doing your own market planning, review your offering with regard to your objectives, the strengths and weaknesses of your offering, your perceived competition, your target market, the needs of that market, and the trends apparent in the economy. This should be instrumental in your establishment of a proper position. Ask yourself basic questions: What business are you in? What is your goal? When you know the true nature of your business, your goal, your strengths and weaknesses, your competitors' strengths and weaknesses, and the needs of your target market, your positioning will be that much easier to plan...
>
> Just prior to starting on your marketing plan, you should practice thinking big. At this point, your imagination is not a limiting factor,

so let it expand to open your mind to all of the possibilities for your venture.

Tom Peters urges each of us to consider the power of branding in today's consumer-oriented world, which has made marketplace giants out of such brand names as Tommy Hilfiger, Nike, Saturn and Starbucks. Whatever your size, Peters says, there is room for brands that stand out by being special, distinct, niche-oriented and focused — brands that are, in a word, "great."

As Peters writes in *The Circle of Innovation*, "Branding means nothing more (and nothing less!) than creating a distinct personality ... and telling the world about it ... by hook or by crook." This applies just as much to the one-person, home-based business as it does to the megacorporation, he says; each of us should imagine ourselves as a brand.

Each of us has a distinct personality — our "brand."

We must feel comfortable with our roles

" If someone had told me seven years ago that I would be president of a rapidly growing company, I would have said they were crazy. At that time, I thought I had the perfect job — the opportunity to interact in the community, a challenging workload, a weekly television show and the respect of my superiors and co-workers. My husband had other ideas, however, as he began building an organization that now has about 120 dedicated employees — and continues to grow.

What would I bring to this new situation? What role could I play in a company founded by my husband? Could I have the same respect, recognition and satisfaction that I previously felt? While the answers to these — and many other questions — are still coming, I have come to the growing realization that one of the most important success factors is the degree to which we feel comfortable in the roles we play.

I am not a business woman, at least in the conventional sense. I am uncomfortable in business negotiations. I once believed that someone has to "lose" in a negotiation, and I don't want anyone to be in a "loser" position. In recent years I have come to recognize that win-win negotiations are possible, but negotiation is still not my strong suit.

Yet, while "business" can make me uncomfortable, I do have something valuable to contribute. Helping to create and foster a company culture is the role I most enjoy. The negative connotations of being a nurturer just don't make sense to me. All executive officers should encourage and listen to employees at all levels. They should be as cognizant as possible of their employees' personalities. They should serve as role models and mentors for the younger staff, offering them opportunities to learn in the company, to further their education, formally or informally. What I have found I can do — and truly enjoy doing — is helping to provide growth opportunities in an atmosphere of caring and encouragement.

Although it is important to challenge ourselves and step out of our "comfort zones" from time to time, each of us must, ultimately, feel comfortable in the roles we choose to play. No one can do or be everything. When we have fulfillment, enjoyment and enthusiasm for the many situations we find ourselves in, the level of professional and personal satisfaction is unlimited. Each of us continues to define "what we want to be when we grow up" — until they wheel us out horizontally. Being open to all options helps us to never be a "finished product." As long as I am involved in it, our company will not be restricted, nor will the people who keep it alive and changing.

— *Bunny Holman*

`Finding something new in yourself'

In her essay "My Neighborhood," Alice Steinbach, a *Baltimore Sun* journalist who won the Pulitzer Prize for feature writing in 1985, thinks fondly of the elements that make her neighborhood special — the retired couple who bring roses to her back door, the father and son who helped her get into her home when she locked herself out one night.

Steinbach doesn't buy the "Good fences make good neighbors" philosophy. "If you ask me, it's a lot simpler than that," she writes. "Good neighbors make good neighbors."

In "Second Acts," from her book *Miss Dennis School Of Writing* (1996: The Bancroft Press, Baltimore), Steinbach points out the difficulty of choosing a career. Most people, she says, decide on a career at an age when they don't have a clue about themselves and their potential. And, once a choice is made, people often feel they can't turn back.

"To which I reply: there is no right path and the sooner we all learn this, the better off we'll be," Steinbach writes. "There are many different paths by which we may arrive at our desired destination — and while a straight line may be the fastest route, who's to say it's the most interesting or productive one?"

Examples she gives of second acts include writer Tom Clancy, who gave up a successful insurance career, and actress Ruth Gordon, who won a best supporting actress Oscar at age 72 for *Rosemary's Baby*.

"Second acts are not about going back: They're about going forward," Steinbach writes. "They're about finding something new in yourself as you grow older."

'Have a little fun, make a little money'

Though I say "Have a little fun, make a little money" with tongue at least partly in cheek, it has become something of an unofficial slogan for WYNCOM employees. One employee, known for her outspoken irreverence, modified it to "Have a hell of a lot of fun, make a hell of a lot of money." That would be nice, too! Obviously, she was just following my exhortations to "make no little plans."

I wholeheartedly believe that we should have fun with our jobs. They have to be more than just a paycheck if we are to put our hearts and souls into them. In fact, "job" is probably the wrong word to use, since it has somehow acquired a negative connotation over the years.

Having a healthy sense of humor is part of the equation. So is a childlike sense of adventure. And being excited, enthusiastic and passionate about our life's work, whatever that work might be. When we approach our work with that kind of attitude — whether that work be building bridges, teaching children, getting rebounds, sweeping streets or figuring actuarial tables — I feel we can truly redefine what work, and by extension the workplace, can be.

— *Larry Holman*

Greetings from the family

Judi Jacobsen
SEATTLE, Washington

Entrepreneurial success for Judi Jacobsen was in the cards ... greeting cards, that is.

More than two decades after her artistic talents and the advice of friends led her to design cards featuring her original artwork, Jacobsen is CEO of a company that handles 8,000 accounts nationwide and also sells its products throughout the world.

Madison Park Greetings is a company whose message is reflected equally in its products and in its mode of operation. Themes of family, caring, commitment, integrity, trust and mutual respect are omnipresent. This is a company that knows its purpose, having asked and answered such defining questions as: What is it we do? Why do we do it? What do we stand for? What is our essence? What, and who, is truly important to us?

One result of answering these questions is a mission statement that leaves no doubt as to the company's intent:

"The mission of Madison Park Greetings is to glorify God by impacting the world in a positive way. We intend to promote the art of communication, provide meaningful employment, produce purposeful products, and maintain the highest ethical business standards. Madison Park Greetings is committed to our customers. We intend to provide extraordinary customer service and to consistently produce the finest quality products."

Jacobsen hopes people don't take too narrow a view of her company's offerings, based on the mission statement's reference to God. The ever-increasing repertoire of greetings includes designs and messages for almost everybody — though those who favor the negative approach to birthdays and other occasions will have to look elsewhere.

"Some people ask, 'Are you a Christian greeting card company?' What is that?" Jacobsen says. "The best way to describe our product line is to say what it isn't. It's nothing off-color or mean-spirited. We have humorous cards, but they're in good taste — nothing that would offend anybody or put anybody down."

The company's approach to business has drawn its share of positive recognition. In 1993, Jacobsen received a Louie Award, the greeting card industry's equivalent of an Oscar. The next year, she was named Washington State's Small Business Person of the Year, and got to fly with her husband, Conrad, to Washington, D.C., to meet President Clinton. That same year, she and the company received the Mayor's Small Business Award, Nellie Cashman Woman Entrepreneur of the Year and Washington State Minority Small Business Advocate of the Year Award. And in 1996, Jacobsen was a finalist for the 1996 Northwest Entrepreneur of the Year Award.

A 'cottage industry' ... and beyond

The company now known as Madison Park Greetings was conceived in 1977, when Judi Jacobsen, who had just given birth to her fourth child, began selling her paintings at Seattle-area arts and crafts fairs. Soon she began holding an annual "Christmas House" in her home and selling paintings there. As the holiday event expanded each year, other artists got involved. Friends suggested, convincingly, that her original art would look great on greeting cards. So she and another local artist, Lucy Rigg, joined forces and with a small investment formed a company called Lucy and Me.

The partners started with eight Christmas card designs and eight everyday cards, with a signature look best described as "country." Local stores began carrying the cards, which quickly attracted a following. The timing was right, as Jacobsen recalls: "The vast majority of 'alternative' greeting card companies were just coming into being."

The successful partnership continued until 1984, when Jacobsen and Rigg decided to divide the company. Jacobsen then started a new company, Me Two, with the help of her daughter, Laurie. Two years later, her oldest son, Mark, joined them, professing a desire to take the company beyond its identity as a homespun "cottage industry." The company began hiring select artists and pursuing a wider variety of looks and directions. In 1989, Jacobsen's second son, Brian, signed up, further reinforcing Me Two's family focus. In subsequent years, that feeling has steadily grown, with the addition of employees' mothers, mothers-in-law, fathers-in-law, friends and neighbors.

The company underwent its third — and FINAL, Jacobsen insists — name change in 1994, in conjunction with a relocation of its offices to a site big enough to accommodate the growing enterprise.

Although initial discussions had envisioned a pastoral country setting, perhaps an old farmhouse, the family decided to stay in the city, "not only to have economic impact, but also to develop a program to work with our city's youth."

But the search for a building was frustrating, as nothing available seemed to have enough warehouse space for the company's burgeoning inventory of cards. After more than a year of searching, brothers Mark and Brian Jacobsen, while driving randomly around town, came across a dilapidated old bakery on the corner of 11th and Union in downtown Seattle.

The Jacobsens saw promise in the run-down property and worked with an architect and a construction company to turn it into a showplace for not only Madison Park Greetings — which by that time had incorporated city park themes into its cards and overall image — but also for tenant companies. The development known as Madison Park, which also includes an adjacent building, is now home to a number of businesses offering upholstery, martial arts instruction, coffee and more.

The first tenant was Hamilton Custom Press, located directly beneath Madison Park Greetings. Hamilton, which prints greeting cards, is also a loyal partner, and the two companies have grown increasingly successful together. Jacobsen says, "Their great service and location have made them our main supplier in a mutually beneficial business relationship."

Madison Park now employs between 30 and 40 people, depending on the time of year, since the greeting card business is a seasonal one. (It is worth noting that business has its own schedule; for example, the Christmas rush comes in the spring.) Of those employees, Jacobsen says, "Almost everyone has been a friend or family member, somebody whom somebody knows. This has helped create an atmosphere of one large family, where every employee feels a part of the company."

Caring for employees, customers, community

The family emphasis is reflected in the company's caring attitude, which includes regular communication meetings as well as morning prayer sessions — "a few minutes for any concerns people have" — for those who wish to participate.

Jacobsen, a lifelong Seattle resident, grew up in a family-owned business, Pacific Trail Sportswear. This exposure provided her with much insight into the inner workings of a family business — the most important lesson of which was "really caring about people," she says. "My father felt that one of the best things you could do was give people meaningful employment. When he died, a trade magazine featured an article on him, and it ended by saying, 'He was a man of integrity, and his word was beyond reproach.'"

In addition to her father's influence, she is grateful for the influence of her mother and her grandmother, "who was deaf and came all the way from Sweden and made a life of her own here without knowing anybody after her mother died." In terms of contemporary women in business, however, she claims no real role models "because I didn't really plan this; it just kind of evolved."

The dual themes of family and home have permeated her entire existence. Graduation from the University of Washington with a degree in home economics. Marriage during her junior year of college to her high school sweetheart. Four children, three of whom are involved with Madison Park Greetings or its spin-off company Madison Design, and 12 grandchildren.

The company's caring attitude extends to its philosophy of customer service. "Having integrity means treating people before profit in many ways, though you need to have them hand in hand," Jacobsen says. "People know we're dependable. When we say we'll have our product out, we have it, and it's good quality. We don't sell every store down the street the same thing, so they can have some individuality in what they offer. When a customer has a complaint or concern, we'll get right back to them and handle the problem. We'll replace anything that doesn't make them happy."

Social involvement is also an important part of the equation. Madison Park Greetings employees have been heavily involved in work with inner-city children and other projects. Lately, the primary emphasis has been on Seattle's deaf community. With one exception, everybody in the company's production department is deaf. All the employees have learned sign language.

In addition, the company participates in a mentoring program with local business, two universities — Seattle Pacific and the University of Washington — and the Seattle Art Institute.

Jacobsen's ability to build a close-knit, family-oriented company that treats its employees, customers and community well is clearly a result of her belief that "People are more important than anything else." For more proof, of course, you could always look in the cards.

Doing good ... without knowing it

In one of his essays in *All I Really Need To Know I Learned In Kindergarten*, Robert Fulghum discusses his barber of 16 years, who has left the business to go into building maintenance:

> I never saw him outside the barber shop, never met his wife or children, never sat in his home or ate a meal with him. Yet he became a terribly important fixture in my life. Perhaps a lot more important than if we had been next-door neighbors. The quality of our relationship was partly created by a peculiar distance. There's a real sense of loss in his leaving. ...
>
> Without realizing it, we fill important places in each other's lives. It's that way with a minister and congregation. Or with the guy at the corner grocery, the mechanic at the local garage, the family doctor, teachers, neighbors, co-workers. Good people, who are always "there," who can be relied upon in small, important ways. People who teach us, bless us, encourage us, support us, uplift us in the dailiness of life. We never tell them. I don't know why, but we don't.
>
> And, of course, we fill that role ourselves. There are those who depend on us, watch us, learn from us, take from us. And we never know. Don't sell yourself short. You may never have proof of your importance, but you are more important than you think.

It reminds me of an old Sufi story of a good man who was granted one wish by God. The man said he would like to go about doing good without knowing about it. God granted his wish. And then God decided that it was such a good idea, he would grant that wish to all human beings. And so it has been to this day.

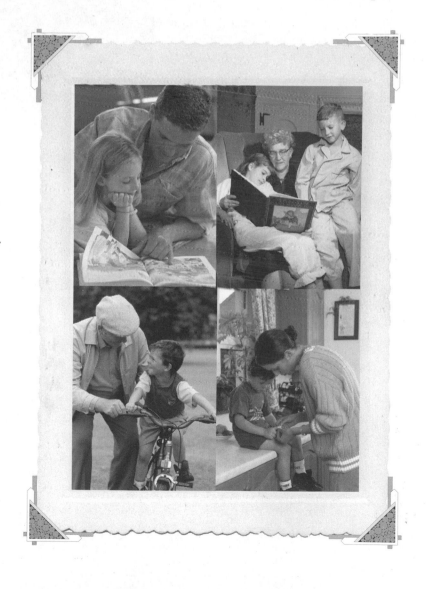

'This is what I want to do with the rest of my life'

Linda Franta
KANSAS CITY, Missouri

"Music has charms to soothe a savage breast," wrote the English playwright William Congreve in 1697 (in an often-misquoted phrase). Now, more than 300 years later, Linda Franta is experiencing firsthand the curative powers of song. When she dispenses her soothing musical charms, people respond to her in ways that most performers can probably only imagine.

Linda Franta is a music therapist in training, and she speaks with the calm assurance of someone who has found her calling. "This is what I want to do with the rest of my life," she says from her office in the University of Missouri-Kansas City's Henry W. Bloch School of Business and Public Administration, where she has held a job for the last six years while simultaneously working on her second degree.

Music therapists don't play sold-out shows at Carnegie Hall ... or shoot videos for MTV ... or have albums or singles in the Billboard Top 100. What they do, however, might well be considered "magic," were it not for its firm basis in scientific fact. Through personalized, intimate, heartfelt performances, music therapists have the power to make a real difference in the lives of people who need it. In Franta's case, these people include physically handicapped, mentally retarded and autistic children, as well as terminally ill hospice patients.

Extensive research has demonstrated that music can create a variety of responses in the people for whom it's played. Physiologically, the two main areas it affects are blood pressure and heart rate. Therefore, for a hospice patient, a soothing song can bring lowered blood pressure and heart rate, a calmness in one's final days. Because music also can help release a body's endorphins — "your own natural morphine" — it also can reduce a patient's required dose of morphine or other painkillers.

Franta recalls one patient, terminal and fading, who "couldn't get settled down." She played a recording of mellow pianist Richard Clayderman, and not long afterward, the patient's nurse "looked up and said, 'Gosh, his blood pressure's down.'" The music had indeed reduced the man's blood pressure, prompting his wife to say it had been the best day he'd had all year.

"That's what we're trained to do," says Franta, who is accomplished at piano, accordion and guitar. "I've had all the anatomy and physiology classes. We learn that music will do that. Of course, it can also do the opposite. When we hear a stirring Sousa march, for example, that can rouse us, raising our blood pressure and heart rate."

For other hospice patients, the music's effects are perhaps more emotional than physiological.

Some patients long for the opportunity to revisit past days, to take a final stock of their lives, to make amends, to purge long-dormant hostilities or frustrations, to forgive. Getting to that point, accessing those buried emotions, can be difficult. But, through the power of music, it is possible to transport them back to where they need to go. In the words of the Trisha Yearwood hit (written by Hugh Prestwood), "the song remembers when."

"We have to be able to ask somebody, 'What's a song you remember from your childhood?' and then be able to play it. Then we ask why they remember it, and that just opens the door," Franta says. "Hospice gives them a chance to talk about their childhood or whatever, and the music gets them there faster. They can go to a psychiatrist for YEARS, and all you have to do is play a song that meant something to them, and they're ready to talk."

Autistic children, while seemingly withdrawn into their own world, are not beyond the reach of music's charm. Franta speaks with pride of the girl from an autistic class who, touched by the music from the therapist's accordion, ventured forward, forgetting her shyness, to feel the instrument's keys, its buttons, its bellows.

Music therapy can also provide a salve to the physically and mentally healthy. Franta forged a connection with the 10-year-old son of one hospice patient. She had already brought some musical relief to the woman, in one instance lowering her heart rate from 145 to 120 within an hour. Now young Scott, losing his mother, needed some comfort of his own. It came in the form of "My Heart Will Go On," the love theme from the movie *Titanic*, a song with a message that had struck a deep chord with Scott. "I took my accordion and played the melody for him in the original key. After he heard the way the song sounds on the accordion," Franta recalls, "I said to him, 'If I redo it in the key of C, you can play it on the keyboard without using the black keys. Do you think you can do that?'

"It's really a simple song, just the melody. So I asked him how he could read the music, then rewrote it for him in the different key and made up these sheets for him. I wrote the words to the first verse with the music, and on the last page I wrote all the words for him and called it 'Scott's Song.'"

His mother died, but Scott was left with a personally meaningful memorial — as well as the lasting comfort offered by a sympathetic friend during a difficult time. Franta, meanwhile, was left with yet another affirmation of her career choice.

'A perfect match'

Franta serves as coordinator of the Bloch School's executive master's (EMBA) program. Previously, she had worked as coordinator of special events. She's quite fond of her current job, though she will be leaving it soon.

"This is a good place to work," she says. "It's a really exclusive program, and I've been here since we started building it. I think the world of Bill Eddy, the dean of the school. And I absolutely love the people in this program; I call them my kids." On the other hand, she has heard her calling, and it means change.

She recalls a conversation with her friend and colleague Rick Stillwell, director of executive education: "Rick says, 'Linda, it's the difference between having a job and having a career.' He's right. Here, I nurture students and I'm their 'mom,' but there ... I've been going to school a long time to have this opportunity. I'm a perfect match for it."

It has taken remarkable dedication to get to this point. By the time she earns her second B.A., a complete degree in music and psychology, she will have put in a total of 170 class hours at the university's music conservatory, plus several hours of "juries," a series of demanding performances in which degree candidates demonstrate their mastery of technique before a panel of judges. Even after seven years of piano instruction, the juries can be grueling. In addition, there are the semester-long "clinicals," similar to internships (at the time of this writing, Franta is doing her fifth and final clinical at St. Luke's Hospice).

The music therapy program requires the learning of a portable instrument because a piano may not be available everywhere a music therapist's services are required. So she also learned to play the accordion and the guitar. Because the accordion uses keys like those on a piano, that often-maligned (but in fact extremely versatile) instrument is an ideal substitute for keyboardists. The University of Missouri–Kansas City even has an accordion orchestra — the only one in the United States.

"You learn to differentiate — to see the music, the melody, in your mind," she says. "Then you learn to play chords with it. Playing the piano was a real benefit to me in learning to play the accordion. You have to learn at a higher level in order to be able to do this."

Although music therapy has been around since the 1950s, and was used with soldiers during the Korean War, awareness of its capabilities is still growing comparatively slowly. Franta became interested in the field in about 1988, becoming increasingly excited about how she could harness her knowledge and experience in music, psychology and physiology to positive use.

Her employer has been understanding of her long-range goal, facilitating her pursuit of that goal in more than one way. First, as an employee of the university, she gets a fee remission, a major financial break for Franta, who had two children in college when she began working on her music therapy degree. Bill Eddy helped her even more a few years ago, surprising her by having a piano brought into the building, downstairs from her office, so she could get in some practice during the workday.

"He's such a nice guy," Franta says of Eddy, who also plays piano and whose wife, a clinical psychologist with a Ph.D., has two degrees in music. As the EMBA program grew, so did Franta's workload, and she eventually became so busy that she sent the piano back over to the conservatory on campus. Still, as she prepares for her ultimate career, she will never forget the dean's gesture.

After completing her degree, she hopes to work through a hospital, continuing to go into hospices as well as people's homes, sharing her talent and compassion. The life of a music therapist can at times be an emotionally draining one — "I lost five patients this semester," she says, before adding, "but I can do it." She takes solace in the fact that, one person at a time, she is doing something to make people's lives better.

Already, she has accumulated many memories of those she has helped — and there will undoubtedly be many more in the years to come. Dying hospice patients whose pain she will ease. Patients whose forgotten memories she will help uncover. Mentally and emotionally damaged children who, their barriers penetrated by the power of music, will open up to her. People who will find, in the simple strains of a song, a source of comfort during a time of great loss.

"To know that you count, at the end of the day ..." Franta says, pausing as she considers the possibilities of the career she has chosen. Her mind goes to young Scott, and his *Titanic* theme. "This child ... what did I do? I gave him three sheets of paper in a fancy envelope, and he has something to forever remember his mother by.

"This is what I want to do with the rest of my life."

20

Epilogue: See Ya 'Round

"We cannot live only for ourselves. A thousand
fibers connect us with our fellow-men."

—Herman Melville

The sun is setting over the rooftops, and it's
time to go home. We're glad you were able to join
us for our little jaunt around the neighborhood.
We just hope you've enjoyed it as much as we have.
After all, it's given us the opportunity to get
acquainted with some of our neighbors, see what
they're up to and, perhaps, glean a few lessons
from them. It's amazing, really, how we can learn
from people who, at least on the surface, might
seem to have little in common with us.

You've probably noticed many of the same themes
repeating themselves from chapter to chapter,
reinforcing the undeniable interrelatedness of
this small, yet vast, worldwide neighborhood we
live in. Small because of the magic of technology
that shrinks geographic boundaries — and also
because of the increasingly complex networks of
connections and relationships we have formed —
the neighborhood remains simultaneously vast in
the unlimited opportunities it offers.

The themes? Under the broad umbrella of "leadership," we quickly rattled off (in no particular order) such elements as: service, communication, humanity, empathy, harmony, interconnectedness, relationships, diversity, personal and professional growth, organizational development, setting and achieving goals, adaptability to change, willingness to *initiate* change, innovation, adventure, courage, perseverance, teamwork, education and lifelong learning ... we could go on and on.

Each of these concepts relates to the ideas contained in the subtitle of this book: *Making connections, building relationships, energizing communities ... where you work and live.*

Wherever you go ... there you are

From our home base of Lexington, Kentucky, to our American neighbors in places like California, Texas, Florida, Colorado, Alabama, Wisconsin, Virginia, Massachusetts, Tennessee, Missouri, Alaska, Washington State and Washington, D.C. ... and overseas to such exotic locales as Japan, Ghana and the Marshall Islands, we continually find a thread of humanity linking common dreams, goals and challenges. In our diversity lies incredible similarity.

Someone named A.G. Sertillanges once wrote something that seems quite appropriate here:

> *It is futile to linger endlessly over differences; the fruitful research is to look for points of contact.*

The fact that we have no idea who Sertillanges is, or was, only serves to strengthen our point that everyone has something to teach us.

A question of balance

So many of the decisions we must make today and tomorrow come down, ultimately, to issues of balance. Can we find the common ground among approaches so diverse as to appear entirely contradictory? What do we choose when it's mind versus heart, reason versus emotion? Do we honor structure or flexibility? Progress or preservation? Technology or simplicity? Profit or humanity? Mandate or consensus? Agreement or debate? Individualism or interdependence? Adventure or caution? Long-term or short-term? Career or family?

The obvious, but all too often overlooked, answer to these questions is, in fact, another question: "Is it REALLY an either/or proposition?"

By this point, we're sure you'll agree that the answers to our sustained success lie not in dogged adherence to one viewpoint or another, but in the ability to see both sides, to find and assemble what Dr. William J. Carroll, earlier in this book, calls "pieces of the truth."

'I don't have a budget; I have a dream'

In the early days of WYNCOM — actually, before the company was even known by that name — we had a controller named Ina Carpenter. Ina retired several years ago, but she remains a dear personal friend and also a friend of the company. She's something of a legend, in fact, and after her retirement we had a portrait of her commissioned to hang in the boardroom (where it was recently joined by a painting of Arthur Light, our retired vice president).

Ina was my polar opposite in terms of how our brains operated, particularly when it came to money. In those days, we literally had just a handful of employees, plus a subcontractor or two. Everything was run very informally. If a subcontractor came in and asked for an advance payment on a project, I'd walk over to Ina's office and have her write a check.

Fiscally, Ina was very conservative, and I certainly needed that at the time. As WYNCOM has grown, we've had to adopt some of the corporate structure that goes with a larger organization, so I have other checks and balances to keep me in line.

Back then, however, there was only Ina, who became very fond of saying, "We can't do that, Larry — we can't afford it!" And often I would respond, "But I don't have a budget, Ina — I have a dream!" So it became something of a joke, even though I was serious about it in a way.

This philosophy goes hand in hand, I think, with the "make no little plans" quotation I'm so fond of repeating. There are times when we just have to bite the bullet and commit our resources to something, even if there's an element of risk involved. At these times, we don't let the "hows" distract us from our goals. Instead, we go ahead and set the goals *before* we get bogged down in the details of how we will achieve them.

I'm not advocating sticking our heads in the sand and being totally unrealistic. In the words of Casey Kasem (of "American Top 40" fame), "Keep your feet on the ground and keep reaching for the stars." Ina Carpenter kept me grounded, as does Bunny. But I still have my dream, and I'm going to keep reaching for it!

— *Larry Holman*

A great adventure

In summary, we'd just like to say that writing this book has been nothing less than a great adventure for us. We started off with a general theme in mind, but no idea of our ultimate destination — or what we would learn from the many neighbors who shared their stories with us. We ended up in some places that we hadn't expected, but we're glad we made the connections.

Thanks again for coming along with us. We'll see you around the neighborhood.

About the Authors

Bunny and Larry Holman are partners in life and in business. In 1992, the wife/husband team founded WYNCOM, Inc., a Lexington, Kentucky, company aimed at pumping the heart and soul back into the worldwide workforce through innovative lectures by the keenest minds in business.

Their company teams with selected colleges and universities to bring noted experts in business management such as Ken Blanchard, Stephen Covey and Tom Peters to communities around the world. In these highly successful partnerships, WYNCOM stays behind the scenes, putting the emphasis on its valued school partners.

The Holmans have developed a company that practices what its speakers preach. By involving the employees in every level of the business and letting them make decisions based on their own knowledge and experiences, WYNCOM tries to become a model for these practices. Early on, the Holmans realized that the company needed management views that went beyond theirs. This led to an infusion of new ideas and opinions, such as sharing detailed information about the business with the employees through open-book management.

In its relatively short life, WYNCOM has received numerous accolades. In 1996, 1997 and 1998, the company was included in the Inc. 500, a prestigious listing by the business magazine of the fastest-growing, privately held companies in the United States. In May 1998, the Holmans were included in *Success* magazine's list of the 100 Richest Entrepreneurs in America. In his 1997 book, *The Circle of Innovation*, Tom Peters gave WYNCOM the ultimate compliment, explaining that because of his confidence in the company, he decided to have it handle all of his public lectures, breaking his own "don't put all your eggs in one basket" rule.

Before WYNCOM, the Holmans worked in higher education. As director of a diversified community education program at Transylvania University, a small liberal arts college in Lexington, Bunny had a role that ranged from creating an innovative cultural education program for Japanese newcomers to interviewing university administrators, professors and local celebrities on a cable television show. Before he got the entrepreneurial bug and started his own marketing and training company, Larry was executive director of a highly successful management development center in the business college at the University of Kentucky.

The Holmans are proof that opposites attract. He's tall; she's not. She's focused; he has 55 thoughts every 30 seconds. She thinks about today; he looks ahead to tomorrow. He is her biggest fan; she credits him with being her mentor. Their blended traits and talents have given their company a foundation that is firm yet malleable.

As their business travels have taken them far beyond Kentucky, they've come to realize that their global neighborhood has limitless lessons to teach about success in life and in business. This book, their first written together, recounts many of those lessons from their neighborhood — and YOURS!